T3-BOJ-631

THE CODE

OF MAN

ALSO BY WALLER R. NEWELL

What Is a Man?

Ruling Passion: The Erotics of Statecraft in
Platonic Political Philosophy

Bankrupt Education:
The Decline of Liberal Education in Canada
(with Peter C. Emberley)

THE CODE

LOVE   COURAGE   PRIDE   FAMILY   COUNTRY

OF MAN

WALLER R. NEWELL

ReganBooks
An Imprint of HarperCollins*Publishers*
www.reganbooks.com

WHITE PLAINS PUBLIC LIBRARY
WHITE PLAINS, NEW YORK 10601

Pages 259–260 constitute an extension of this copyright page.

THE CODE OF MAN. Copyright © 2003 by Waller R. Newell. All rights reserved. Printed in the United States of America. No part of this book may be used or reproduced in any manner whatsoever without written permission except in the case of brief quotations embodied in critical articles and reviews. For information address HarperCollins Publishers Inc., 10 East 53rd Street, New York, NY 10022.

HarperCollins books may be purchased for educational, business, or sales promotional use. For information please write: Special Markets Department, HarperCollins Publishers Inc., 10 East 53rd Street, New York, NY 10022.

FIRST EDITION

Designed by Yee Design

Printed on acid-free paper

Library of Congress Cataloging-in-Publication Data
Newell, Waller Randy.
    The code of man : love courage pride family country / Waller R. Newell.—
1st ed.
        p. cm.
    ISBN 0-06-008751-X (acid-free paper)
    1. Masculinity. I. Title.
HQ1090.N49 2003
305.31—dc21

                                                            2003046644

03 04 05 06 07 BVG/RRD 10 9 8 7 6 5 4 3 2 1

It is character that counts in a nation as in a man. It is a good thing to have a keen, fine intellectual development in a nation, to produce orators, artists, successful business men; but it is an infinitely greater thing to have those solid qualities which we group together under the name of character—sobriety, steadfastness, the sense of obligation toward one's neighbor and one's God, hard common sense, and, combined with it, the lift of generous enthusiasm toward whatever is right. These are the qualities which go to make up true national greatness.

—THEODORE ROOSEVELT

Contents

ACKNOWLEDGMENTS

Once again it is my pleasure to thank Judith Regan for her continuing strong support for this book and her keen interest in the debates and issues that inform it. I am also grateful to my editor, Cal Morgan, for his usual impeccable edit and sound instincts about the shape of the manuscript.

Special thanks are due to the Earhart Foundation for its generous support during the period in which I researched and wrote this book. I should also mention that an earlier version of the introduction was delivered as a public lecture for the John M. Olin Programme on Politics, Morality, and Citizenship at the Institute of United States Studies, the University of London. I would like to thank the Institute and its director, Gary McDowell, for the invitation to speak and for their hospitality during my stay in London.

As usual, many friends and colleagues have rendered good advice, useful tips, and practical assistance. Thanks are due in particular to my agent, Chris Calhoun, of Sterling Lord Literistic. My student research assistants, Geoffrey Kellow, Matthew Post, and Stephen Turpin, also provided some very useful help.

In this as in all things, my wife, Jacqueline Etherington Newell, was my chief partner, providing generous amounts of insight, needed criticism, and inspiration.

I would like to dedicate this book to the memory of my brother, Richard Newell, and my uncle George Newell, both of whom passed away while I was writing it.

Introduction

This is a book about how to be a man. I ask the reader to join me on a search for the manly heart. There are five stages on that journey, corresponding to the five main ingredients of a satisfying life—love, courage, pride, family, and country. The correct balance of these five virtues, I will try to show, is the secret of happiness for a man—a life that is emotionally, erotically, and spiritually satisfying.

But do we really need to be reminded of how to be a man? After all, the heroic response to the attacks on the World Trade Center and the Pentagon on September 11, 2001, proved that manliness still exists in abundant supply. Americans may not talk much about manliness, but they know how to show it. At the same time, however, the recovery of manliness in response to the calamity may have been a close call. In the aftermath, many wondered: Were we somehow vulnerable to the attack? By this they meant not merely vulnerable in terms of military might or security measures, all of which were speedily addressed, but a more troubling possibility: Were we *spiritually* vulnerable? Had the world grown to believe that Americans were corrupt, lazy, self-indulgent, and hedonistic, lacking conviction in our way of life and unwilling to defend it? This dialogue will go on for a long time, and the meaning of manly virtue is central to it.

Many said that 9/11 had brought the "Age of Irony" to an end. No more frivolity, easygoing relativism, or flippant disdain for the old-fashioned virtues. In many ways, 9/11 was a moral wake-up call, reminding us that, after thirty years of debunking the traditional virtues, we are as much in need of them as ever, and perhaps did not do enough to convince the enemies of democracy that we still know what those virtues are and how to act on them. War is never desirable, and there is no silver lining to the slaughter of innocents. Still, the history of all civilizations and countries shows that war can spark a period of soul-searching, stocktaking, and moral regeneration, spanning all subcultures and reminding us of our shared responsibilities as citizens. President Bush has wondered aloud whether Americans spend a little bit too much time playing video games and enjoying their other toys, and not quite enough time giving of themselves for others. These reflections are common to all shades of the political spectrum, and they in no way amount to blaming the victim. It is a natural response to human suffering to wonder if we can avoid calamities of the same kind in the future by heeding the call to improve ourselves, individually and as a nation. If we don't ask ourselves such painful questions, then the innocent victims will have died in vain. If something good can come of the tragedy, helping us avoid a repetition of it, then their deaths will be more greatly hallowed than if we had simply returned to our usual routines.

This has happened many times before, and it will doubtless happen again. In his novel *Nana,* Emile Zola chronicled the moral disintegration of Paris into an endless playhouse of jaded pleasure seeking. The book portends the devastating defeat of France in 1871 by the armies of Bismarck's Prussia, to be delivered like the judgment of God on Sodom and Gomorrah. Closer to our own era, the movie *Casablanca* summed up the feeling produced in many by the rise of Nazi Germany—that it was time to put aside the nightclub-hopping cynicism of the Lost Generation and join the battle for good against evil. The further we go back in time, the more often we encounter such reflections on the value of war as a moral wake-up call. One of the original versions is St. Augustine's *City of God.* He used the sack of Rome by Alaric the Goth in A.D. 410 to raise the same questions: Did the Roman Empire invite aggression because its ancient civic and military virtues were played out as a result of an underlying spiritual exhaustion?

The response of Americans to 9/11 was a triumph. But, far from proving that we don't need to reflect on the meaning of manliness, it only shows how urgently this debate must be carried on and deepened. The Age of Irony did not happen overnight, and however sobered we may

have been by the terrorists' devastating attack, its effects won't disappear
overnight. They are still with us. The events of 9/11 can be a blessing in
disguise if the valor they brought forth inspires us to recover the wellsprings of manly virtue, not only in the heat of action but through longer-
lasting reflection. It's the greatest conceivable testament to America
that, when faced with an unspeakable cataclysm, it can reach deep down
into the moral fiber built up through centuries of challenge. But during
the intervals of peace, when we have time to reflect, we need to nourish
that moral fiber with patient and thoughtful self-examination. Americans
proved their manliness on 9/11 with deeds. Now we need to recover the
words, because in the long run of a nation's life, it is the words that inspire and shape the deeds.

There is a beautiful image, originating in Hindu thought and repeated
by the ancient philosopher Plato, that compares the human soul to a celestial chariot riding through the heavens. For me, this image best sums
up the five paths to manliness I mentioned at the beginning—love,
courage, pride, family, and country—and how they relate to one another
in an integrated and satisfying life. According to this ancient image, the
charioteer stands for the human mind. The horses stand for the two most
powerful of human passions, love and valor. The proper ordering of a
man's soul requires that the passions of love and valor always be guided
by the dictates of reason. If the horses are not sufficiently reined in by
the charioteer, if they are allowed their own way, these powerful steeds
will pull the celestial chariot out of its heavenly arc, plunging it into a
lower world of chaotic lust and violence. If, however, the charioteer is
firmly in control of his steeds, the chariot of the soul will continue to soar
upward to the celestial heights of eternal happiness, fulfillment, and
honor.

But—and this is crucial to the secret of manliness—it's not just a matter of controlling the horses. It's not just a matter of repressing the passions by the dry dictates of reason. On the contrary: the charioteer can't
make his chariot go anywhere unless the ascent to happiness is fueled by
the energy of those powerful horses. If that energy weren't there, the
chariot would just as surely crash as when the horses are out of control.

So it is in the soul of a man. The mind cannot achieve happiness unless it is fueled by the passionate energies of love and daring. The point is not prudishly to suppress these passions but to direct them away from bad goals, like coarse pleasure seeking and brutal aggression, and toward constructive goals—the cultivation of those moral and intellectual virtues that enable us to be good family men, friends, and citizens. The image of the chariot evokes the proper balance of love and courage in the heart of a man. A man needs to know who—and what—is truly deserving of his love. Only then will he know when—and why—he may need to fight to defend them. The proper balance of love and daring on behalf of his family, friends, and country entitles a man to feel proud of himself, and deservedly so.

During the last thirty years or so, we have sometimes come close to losing sight of that balance. The harmony of the five paths has often been disrupted by a war between love and daring in the heart of American man. So this book is not only a journey in search of the manly heart, traveling the five paths to their common destination, but a recollection of how we have sometimes lost our way during the last three decades. Before we can recover the key to the manly virtues, we have to remember exactly when and how we lost it. Moreover, the search for the manly heart must never be confused with mere traditionalism, a snobbish and sterile veneration of the old way simply because it is old. In order for the traditional teaching to be a living one, we have to show how our need for the five virtues emerges from our *present* confusions and dilemmas. It's not enough to mourn the passing of the good old days. We have to start with our current longings and reflect on how our lack of an adequate moral and erotic vocabulary gives us a road map for the journey back to the manly heart—which is, of course, also a journey forward to the happiness for which we all long. Often the key to the treasure box is a lot closer than we imagine, right under our noses.

That's why readers of this book will find some surprising leaps and comparisons—Plato emerging alongside movies and sitcoms, eros leading us to Mozart and Eminem. I explore popular culture, movies, television, video games, rock music, and fashion not because I necessarily endorse their content, much less because I think they are adequate for an understanding of the times they reflect. But I will argue that pop culture can provide important clues to our repressed longings. Through pop culture, we often experience the guilty pleasure of vicariously enjoying ways of life that are forbidden to us by our prevailing social orthodoxies. These longings may begin as frivolous or trivial, but they can, surprisingly, furnish a more direct path back to the profound teachings of the Western tradition than what sometimes passes for scholarship in our centers of learning.

In this respect, my book is very much in the spirit of Camille Paglia's *Sexual Personae* or Allan Bloom's *Closing of the American Mind,* although I'm fairly certain Professor Paglia would not share my views, while my old friend and teacher Bloom would have found them congenial. But the point is that the creative interpretation of popular culture is not a recent fad. When conventional academics turn their noses up at the dread concept of "popularization," they may believe that they are defending traditional academic values against shallow faddishness, but the opposite is true. The disdain of academics for writing about popular culture is itself a very recent development in Western culture. It is largely a product of the high modernism of the 1950s, when the social sciences and humanities turned to a sterile obsession with methodology in the belief that the rigor of logical positivism and mathematical modeling would enable them to distinguish themselves from the tweedy, pipe-smoking dons of the Victorian era. This transition required writing articles that only other methodologists could read (along with composing atonal music that only musicologists could appreciate, and writing novels about professors writing novels). What was all too often forsaken was the robust connection between the art of thinking in the academy and the moral concerns of the educated public. Until the 1950s, the greatest scholars often as not had broad appeal outside of the academy, if indeed they held academic positions at all. That tradition has been reviving, and we need more of it.

We are certainly aware today, at the start of the new millennium, that there is a crisis of manliness in America. A spate of best-selling books testifies to the range and seriousness of the debate. Important as it is to expose destructive trends in the contemporary understanding of boys and men, however, at the end of the day we also need a positive account of the manly virtues as the surest basis for educating young men to respect others and channel their spirited impulses into the duties of family life, friendship, and a vigorous moral citizenship. After we have exhausted the polemics, we need to find inspiration from sources that transcend the divisions between liberal and conservative or Left and Right. We need to recover the positive tradition of manliness.

That is the purpose of this book. In its pages, we'll discover a lost history of astonishing depth, complexity, and brilliance. From Homer through the ancient Greeks and Romans, the Bible and the Stoics, tales of medieval chivalry, the code of the Renaissance gentleman, the stormy temperament of the Romantic man of feeling, down to the fragmentation of manhood in the protests of the Beats, rock, and rap—in all of these rich sources I explore what I call the search for the manly heart.

As one would expect, there have been enormous shifts and variations in how the manly virtues have been understood and practiced throughout three thousand years of historical and cultural change. Faith-based understandings of manly behavior, for instance, have always differed profoundly from a purely secular understanding of human nature and worldly honor and prestige. In addition, the American understanding of manliness, while in some ways transplanting older European concepts to the soil of the New World, developed a unique hybrid in which the ancient virtues were given new meaning through the opening of the frontier and America's troubled but awe-inspiring quest to live up to its own ideals of justice and freedom for all.

For all of these changes, however, there is a fundamental consistency to how our ancestors understood manly honor and pride, a consistency that is more important than the differences. When we read Winston Churchill's description of Lawrence of Arabia as "a soldier as well as a savant," a man who combined the virtues of battlefield prowess with the sagacity of the statesman and, most impressively, the depth of a scholar, we hear a language that stretches in an unbroken pedigree back to Aristotle and Cicero. This combination of active and contemplative virtues is one of the most enduring themes in three thousand years of experience of what it means to be a man.

More broadly, what unites these past ages is a treasure trove of wisdom and observation as men have discovered their distinctive virtues and vices through grappling with the perennial dilemmas and demands of love, courage, pride, family, and country—the five paths whose proper ordering gives us the key to the secret of happiness for a man. When Teddy Roosevelt admonishes the graduating class of Groton in 1912 that a real man combines courage with tenderness and a contempt for bullies and oppressors, he is speaking the essential vocabulary of Plutarch or the Bible. The major break in the understanding of manliness is not between, say, the nineteenth century and any particular preceding era but between my generation of Baby Boomers and the entire preceding complex of teachings.

In some ways, TR and Churchill have more in common with Homer and Shakespeare than they do with us. During the last thirty years, we turned our backs—disastrously and inexplicably—on this incredibly resilient heritage. Thirty years of stereotyping taught us to equate manliness with macho, piggish, violent behavior. But according to the entire preceding tradition of the West (and, for that matter, the non-Western world), macho behavior was considered *un*manly, the very *opposite* of manliness. And that error, I will argue, is the source of the current crisis of manliness. Understanding where we have gone wrong is the first step in finding a map back to the treasure trove.

Describing the history of manliness as "lost" implies that it was lost at a specific point in time, and also that it can be found again. How did this collective amnesia overcome us? After all, it is hardly the case that during the last thirty years America sank into a morass of despair or lack of resolve. On the contrary: that period witnessed the inexorable triumph of liberal democracy over the last great totalitarian tyranny of the modern era, the evil empire of the Soviet Union and its satellites. This was a bipartisan triumph of statesmanship, nerve, and on occasion military might worthy of the greatest struggles for freedom of the past, an epic worthy of Thucydides or Gibbon. And yet, during that same period of freedom's ascent and moral triumph over its last and most intransigent global foe, a dark passage opened up for young men at home.

Indeed, something very strange happened on the way to the victory party. After winning the Cold War and defeating the evil empire, American men began to wage a war against themselves. The opening salvo was the Oklahoma City bombing, followed by the rampage killings of Jonesboro, Columbine, and elsewhere, all carried out by alienated and underparented young white males. What were the underlying causes of this campaign to destroy the manly heart just as the greatest external threat to the flourishing of the American dream had been neutralized?

In the lengthy national debate that followed these tragedies, many explanations were suggested. According to most observers, Oklahoma City was in a category different from the high school shootings. The former, we were told, was mainly a matter of the ideology of the lunatic Right—the murky world of self-described militias and their belief in the illegitimacy of the American government. In the case of the high school shootings, different sorts of explanations were invoked, mainly sociological rather than ideological. The damaging effect of violent video games and splatter films, the easy access to unsecured guns in the parents' homes, the connection between Goth fashion and Satanism, the impact of divorce on teenage dysfunction, the cruelty of student cliques—all were advanced in an effort to come to terms with the horrible events.

All of these explanations are valid to a point, and I will explore them in the pages to come. But I believe that the underlying causes of these episodes had more in common than is usually assumed, and that we have to part with our accustomed categories in making moral sense of them. Just as Oklahoma City was not an ideological act in the traditional sense of a coherent revolutionary political program, but shared in the same anomie and alienation that characterized the shooters at Columbine, the high school killings were not mere instances of personal alienation, however profound and troubling; they were connected, I believe, to a deeply distorted view of America.

What are the underlying causes? They are rooted in the troubled relationship between love and honor in the soul of the American man. One cause is the stigmatization of moral history in our schools and universities, including the positive contribution of martial honor to the struggle for justice and the cultivation of a virtuous character. The other cause is the appalling degeneration, since the 1960s, of our cultural standards for manly love and erotic passion into coarse sexual aggression and misogyny. Both causes stem from the parody of manliness as macho belligerence that has dominated our public discourse for the last three decades. Let us look at the two causes and their common root.

An important clue comes from the remark by one of the Columbine killers that his group thought Hitler was "cool"—just another character from a splatter film. Like many teenagers, he had little sense of the moral and historical context of Nazism and totalitarianism. Schools and universities generally no longer teach history as a moral narrative with heroes and villains and the struggle to help good triumph over evil. Increasingly, we have lost the sense that war can be ennobling when it is fought to defeat tyranny and rescue the oppressed. Whereas our victory over Hitler in World War II produced a long celebration and reflection on the evils of Nazism, our victory over the equally evil Soviet regime produced no comparable national dialogue or sense of collective patriotic triumph. At times, it seemed as if we were embarrassed to say we had been right—as if rejoicing in our triumph over an evil tyranny was somehow backward or boorish behavior.

In many universities today, a student can major in international relations without reading the memoirs of Metternich, Lloyd George, Churchill, Acheson, or Kissinger. War is generally treated as an aberration driven by a selfish power agenda, regardless of the regime that undertakes it and the purposes it embodies. Military prowess is rarely treated as intrinsically honorable or dishonorable depending on the cause for which it is employed. Even World War II can be interpreted retroactively as yet another lamentable expression of a universal patriarchal impulse toward hegemony, rather than as something caused by the unjust ambitions of Germany and Japan.

As a consequence of this stigmatization of history as a moral narrative and of the place of military honor within it, the male taste for a just contest has been deflected to trivia such as computer games, with their endless landscapes of purposeless carnage, or more lethally, a series of private and nihilistic miniwars waged against classmates, the federal government, or any other random target for revenge or the satisfaction of a longing for status. (The Columbine killers also reportedly fantasized about a "movie deal" resulting from their planned rampage.) If the nation had been able to celebrate properly its victory in the Cold War, a just war of diplomacy and counterforce against the worst surviving totalitarian system since the Third Reich, perhaps some of the aggressive energies wasted so tragically in high school shootings could have been sublimated and uplifted by being directed toward a common patriotic pride. Before we can discourage violence, we have to recognize the meaning of courage on behalf of a just cause, and explore the details of its psychology, so that we are equipped to distinguish legitimate moral force from mere rashness or fanaticism.

Any parent or teacher knows how fascinated boys and young men are by war. Instead of trying to suppress or extirpate this boyish pleasure in the glories of combat, we should recognize it for the precious resource that it is. This energy can be directed toward the study and admiration of just struggles against oppression both at home and abroad, whether it be our own injustices or those of a foreign tyrant. In combination with an exposure to the other virtues, teaching about courage can lead young men to rise above the mindlessness of their boyish attraction to Rambo-style carnage and identify with the stirring exploits of battlefield heroes like Douglas MacArthur and civic heroes like Martin Luther King, Jr. A boyish taste for martial courage in a good cause can fuel a later appreciation in a young man for the more subtle qualities of civic courage. But before that can happen, we have to recover from the cultural amnesia of the last three decades and rediscover the traditional sources of instruction and reflection on the cardinal virtues of courage, moderation, justice, and wisdom as they apply to the character development of young men.

At this point, we have to note an important complication in the discussion of the manly virtues. There is a dark side to masculine psychology. Feminists have half a point when they argue that boys and young men are more rambunctious, competitive, and hierarchical than women, who are often portrayed by contrast as more nurturing, consensual, and intuitive. The question is: What is the best way of dealing with this impetuosity and competitiveness? The answer is not to try to get rid of such energies but to sublimate and rechannel them toward the service of some constructive moral purpose, both in civic life and in family relationships.

The Civil War and Abraham Lincoln's abolition of slavery, the Allies' defeat of Nazism—these struggles on behalf of justice would not have taken place had they not provided positive outlets for manly pride and righteous zeal. The solution to the darker side of male psychology is not to reengineer mens' souls so as to crush their ambitious impulses, as is attempted with Alex, the latter-day Alcibiades of Anthony Burgess's *Clockwork Orange*. His warlike energies have no constructive outlet in the materialistic and bureaucratized Orwellian state into which he is born, and therefore he can only turn to criminality. Thirty years of attempting to change the nature of men have only demonstrated how utopian such a project is, doomed to failure by human nature and undesirable in any event. Instead, we need to direct manly honor and pride away from the nihilistic violence of the rampage killings and the fantasies of aggression fed by splatter films, video games, and rap, and redirect them toward a sound set of ethical aspirations.

As we read in Plato's *Republic*, when ambition is properly subordinated to the guidance of reason and conscience, it can play a healthy role in a man's psychological makeup by providing the emotional energy for his attempts to be virtuous and to master his ignoble impulses. But before we can try to redirect these darker passions, we have to admit they exist and recover that psychology in its troubling as well as its encouraging dimensions. For these reasons, the exploration of *manly* virtue is different from the exploration of virtue in general, and more problematic. As this book will show at length, manliness has both positive and negative traits. The same boldness that can invigorate public service and courage on behalf of a just cause—one's community, friends, and family—can also, if not properly channeled, lead to imperialism, tyranny, and crimes of passion.

Indeed, as we know only too well from the century just past, the attraction of young men to struggle and glory has been perverted to serve some of the worst tyrannies known to human history. Nazism and Bolshevism both appealed strongly to young men, and encouraged a perverse "idealism" through which these young men could convince themselves that wars of aggression and mass murder would bring about a golden age for all mankind. Young men are attracted to revolution because it can appear to justify heroism, valor, and self-sacrifice, which have fewer permissible outlets in modern democratic society than in the martial and aristocratic societies of the past.

Modern theories of motivation from Hobbes to contemporary social science are unequipped to account for and make sense of this depraved version of the warrior spirit, because those theories reduce human behavior to banal material self-interest, dismissing all forms of glory seeking and honor as uniformly irrational and undeserving of any more discriminating examination. The horrors of twentieth-century totalitarianism, and of terrorism as we enter the twenty-first century, have forced us to abandon this pedestrian theory of human motivation, which ignores the capacity for honor and self-sacrifice whether well or badly employed, and return to the full-blooded evocations of tyranny and ambition found in Plato and Aristotle. Before we can educate and moderate these darker masculine passions, we have to accept that they exist. Otherwise, we will suffer the same fate as the foolish sheep in Aesop's fable who agree to accept an offer of peace from the wolves.

To take a famous example, Shakespeare's *Romeo and Juliet* shows how hard it is to contain the spontaneous energies of young men. The youths in the play are obsessed with pointless duels, vendettas, and feuds among their families, while Romeo's and Juliet's love for each other is seen as violating their loyalty to their own flesh and blood. The play is awash with outrage, violence, and illicit passion. According to the classical tradition and its Renaissance inheritors, the way to deal with the negative side of manliness is to rechannel its energies into the service of the cardinal virtues: justice, moderation, courage, and wisdom.

These virtues are obviously not restricted to men. They are common to men and women. Owing to the distinct features of male psychology, however, these virtues have to be cultivated in boys and men in different ways than in girls and women, and they manifest themselves differently. So, in embarking on a search for the manly virtues, we must familiarize ourselves not only with the final destination of the virtues themselves but with the passions that fuel the journey—the distinct features of male psychology, including those aberrant and dangerous tendencies that pose a threat to virtue and at the same time provide the energies and zeal that can be directed toward its pursuit.

We must not turn away from the darker side of manly behavior if we are to make the aim of a moral education stand out more clearly by contrast. Readers of *The Code of Man* can therefore expect to encounter a number of rather vivid villains, sinners, scoundrels, poltroons, mountebanks, cheats, and liars, in addition to heroes, soldiers, citizens, saints, statesmen, knights, and gentlemen. As Shakespeare's splendid young Prince Hal, the future hero-king Henry the Fifth, confides to the audience, the sunlight of virtue that he aspires to cultivate will shine more brightly by contrast with the sordid vices of his misspent youth.

These complex issues of character development bring me to the second cause of the war against the manly heart: the degeneration of manly love into sexual coarseness and misogyny. One of the most popular recording artists in America during the last few years is the white rapper Eminem, whose semiliterate lyrics detail his desire to rape his mother, murder his girlfriend, and beat gay men to a pulp, corollaries of his overall teaching that "we're all animals." The shrewdly crafted video for his alter ego Slim Shady shows a mob of indistinguishable Eminem look-alikes rolling off an assembly line with dyed blond hair and boxer shorts high above the crotches of their baggy jeans. The point is that Eminem is at one with his fans, a mirror image of their own descent to the lowest common denominator of vulgarity. Like his predecessors the Rolling Stones and Madonna, the boy from the trailer park has discovered the secret of superstardom in our era: Say the unthinkable. The more you are criticized, the greater will be your profits. Eminem's sales soared after he was excoriated by George W. Bush, Al Gore, Joe Lieberman, John McCain, and Lynne Cheney.

An earlier observation bears repeating in this connection. Thirty years of stereotyping have equated manliness with macho, piggish, violent behavior. But according to three thousand years of tradition, from Homer through the Renaissance and down to modern heroes like Theodore Roosevelt and Winston Churchill, macho behavior was considered *unmanly*. If you teach boys and young men that their gender is collectively disposed to be aggressive, mindless, and exploitive toward women, that's exactly how they will behave. It will become a self-fulfilling prophecy.

That's what we've seen increasingly in recent years. The infamous "wilding" incident in Central Park in the summer of 2001 was a direct result of a culture that had reduced manliness to a vicious parody: stupid, brutal, and infantile. As Richard Price put it in his novel *Blood Brothers*, today's young male in his twenties and thirties isn't a boy and he isn't a man—he's a "guy." And, with testosterone gel hitting the market, we'll see the pathetic spectacle of men in their forties, fifties, and sixties trying desperately to remain "guys." This obsession with sexual potency is the clearest sign today of the infantilization of masculinity, like middle-aged rockers strutting arthritically around a stage in torn jeans and studs. Sex is fine at any age, but a man is supposed to evolve, mature, and become more reflective and thoughtful as he grows older. A man who wants the same sex drive at fifty that he had at twenty is a man who hasn't grown up.

The coarsening of eros has reached epidemic proportions in contemporary youth culture, and it's often spread by the communications technology we regard as the hallmark of our economic supremacy. The mounting violence of video games has contributed to the depersonalization of human relations and the treatment of women as objects for sexual exploitation. Look at some recent examples as described by the manufacturers' promotional materials: *Fallout 2* features the chance to "fall in love, get married, and pimp your spouse for a little extra chump change. Hey, it's a dark and dangerous world." Another new game, *Thrill Kill*, matches players against a "femme fatale" clearly modeled on Madonna—Belladonna Maria Cocherto. Clad in latex and carrying a cattle prod, Belladonna "serves no one. To even get close to her is to tempt death." Her hobbies are "reading, baking, spankings."

Any child doing research on the Internet can find what purports to be free information on sex education and safe sex, in which sexual activity is depicted in terms synonymous with pornography. One free Web site, the Coalition for Positive Sexuality, features a *Just Say Yes* glossary aimed explicitly at teens and preteens. The glossary includes graphic descriptions of bondage and discipline, dominance and submission, sadism and masochism, clits, cumming, masturbation, oral sex, and anal intercourse (defined as "when something [a dick, finger, dildo, cucumber, whatever] penetrates your butt"). I stumbled upon this Web site while trying some keywords concerned with contemporary debates about male psychology. My computer skills lag far behind those of my teenage nephew. If I could chance upon this revolting stuff so easily, so could any boy. What an introduction to the world of love and sexual intimacy.

We're always told that, as long as "no one is harmed" and everyone gives their consent, it is perfectly permissible to treat others as objects for one's own isolated pleasures. All forms of sexual contact, including sadomasochism, are treated as equally desirable, since their only purpose is the physical satisfaction of the individual, isolated practitioners. Acts of sexual intimacy are stripped of their tenderness and converted into heartless techniques for self-gratification with accompanying hygienic safeguards. No reference whatever is made to human relationships as complicated wholes of delicate feeling, love, and hope, in which sexual pleasure takes its place as an expression of affection and optimism about the future, rather than as the sole aim for which all human relations are organized. This is what Plato meant by *eros* (the ancient Greek word for love), and when I discuss erotic satisfaction in this book, I mean it in this sense. According to the traditional teaching of the West originating in Plato, eros is the longing for moral and emotional fulfillment through union with another human being. But increasingly in recent decades, this vision of love as an organic complex between lover and beloved, in which passion is sublimated and refined by esteem and honor, has been reduced to a legal transaction among individuals who demand that their rights be spelled out and adjudicated.

When the complexity and delicacy of eros are driven underground by this realm of heartless sexual technology, passion inevitably seeks a new outlet, returning among young people as ever more wanton sexual experimentation. Young people are divided between a daytime world of deeroticized work and a nighttime world of booze cans, raves, and party drugs. Banished from the daytime world and severed from its properly subordinate role in any mature and rich conception of love, the body breaks free from this antiseptic realm in its nighttime domain, and seeps back into the daylight realm through advertising and pop culture. What begins as a hidden subculture of dangerous experimentation returns to the daylight in the form of Calvin Klein underwear ads that flirt with pederasty. The brutalization of relations between men and women is retailed to the middle classes by the creators of Eminem and other such acts, until rape and murder become routine features of the most banal television entertainment.

We can crystallize the confusion over the balance of love and honor in the heart of contemporary man by thinking about movies, one of the few original art forms added to the history of culture by modern democratic civilization and often an important mirror of the Zeitgeist. As a measure of how much we have lost in the last thirty years, let's compare Humphrey Bogart's character in *Casablanca* with Ralph Fiennes's character in *The English Patient*. In the forties classic, Rick overcomes his isolationist cynicism to serve a noble calling, the fight against Nazi tyranny. He must sacrifice love for honor, but this sacrifice intensifies his love for Ingrid Bergman's character and charges it erotically. Ingrid Bergman's character makes the same sacrifice and undergoes the same transformation. They have different emotions, characters, and contributions to make as a man and a woman, yet both are equally strong, morally impressive, and erotically attractive. Later in this book, I will devote some time to the classical models that Bogart's and Bergman's characters recall, Odysseus and Penelope in Homer's *Odyssey*. As a man and woman they are different but in every way equal—they balance each other, each is incredibly strong-minded and strong-willed, and both can rule, albeit in different spheres. They are the only ones formidable enough for each other's love.

    Casablanca offers a striking contrast with *The English Patient*, a film that was ballyhooed endlessly as a work of high art and yet was, in my view, so expressive of how literary, moral, and cinematic standards have declined together. *The English Patient* offers a whining, affected yuppie of our own era ludicrously transplanted to the era of World War II. He believes that the war's frustration of his love life removes any moral difference between the Nazis and the Allies. The film's drearily predictable lesson, straight out of Deepak Chopra and Sally Jessy, is: I need to take more time for me! The Me Decade is imported surreptitiously into the era of *Casablanca*, so that a strictly private passion is more important than anything else on earth, including the struggle against tyranny. The heartfelt and intelligent dialogue of the earlier film, the erotically charged tension between love and duty experienced by Bogart's and Bergman's characters, is replaced by sad-sack maundering about the meaninglessness of life and a weary indifference to the distinction between tyranny and democracy when it interferes with one's personal satisfaction. The film's inner emptiness is padded out by beautiful cinematography and a travelogue of Italy heavy on food, fashion, and furniture, including the oh-so-chic Todi. The silly accents and not-quite-right "upper-class" dialogue remind one of Baby Boomers playing dress-up in one of those mystery games set in the 1930s that you stage in your living room.

Fortunately, there have been some rays of hope in recent years to counteract this bauble of Boomer snobbery and to remind us of the complexities of mature love. I think of A. S. Byatt's marvelous novel *Possession*. Her novel shows that Victorian restraint and delicacy—the adulterous love between a great male and female poet and his ultimate inability to desert his wife—are not only morally more admirable but erotically richer, deeper, and more magnetic than many relationships between men and women today, precisely because strong feelings are sublimated by a higher duty and refinement of expression. The Victorian love story, Byatt's novel within a novel, is much more appealing than the affectless trysts and careerism of the contemporary scholars in the framing story who are tracking it down. Byatt's novel proves that it is still possible to write great literature on an old-fashioned theme: how a man's love for a woman can act as a vehicle for his own self-perfection, if he is willing to sacrifice his immediate gratification for the sake of honoring his obligations.

I believe that the young men of today are every bit as open to this delicacy of sentiment, this refinement of the heart's passion, as the young men of earlier generations. I see it in my students every day—tender youths who, despite a superficial veneer of hip cynicism, are capable of great love and long for a partner with whom to share their lives. But they have been robbed of the moral and erotic vocabulary that past generations received as a cultural inheritance, and with whose aid they could express and articulate those feelings. We urgently need to restore that gift to them. In the chapters to come, I will discuss such classics of romantic love as Rousseau's *Emile,* one of the best treatments of how a young man's erotic passions can be converted into a motive for self-improvement and the development of a sound character. Rousseau's young hero, named for a fabled Roman general, finds his surest motive for joining civil society and fulfilling his duties as a citizen in his passionate attachment to a young woman, Sophy. It is because he wants to be worthy of Sophy, in whom he sees all the goodness, gentleness, and decency that he would like to possess himself, that Emile overcomes his passions and makes himself grow up. The greatest lesson of the traditional teachings about erotic matters is this: Love perfects.

To sum up: The confusion over love and honor in the manly heart stems from our self-induced amnesia about the true meaning of manhood, turning our backs on three millennia of accumulated wisdom and experience to embrace a silly and vicious parody of manhood that has become a self-fulfilling prophecy. What do I mean, then, by the positive tradition of manliness? I have already suggested some of its themes. The rest of this book will explore the question in sources as diverse and compelling as Homer, Aristotle, St. Augustine, Mozart, Jane Austen, Tolstoy, the Romantic poets, the American Founders, down to the contemporary perplexities about manhood that we encounter in rock, rap, and other countercultural visions of our own era.

But a useful guide should provide a road map, so here at the outset I will suggest two enduring features of the search for the manly heart. The first is a code of honor and a capacity to feel shame at failing to live up to that code. The second is a balance of active and contemplative virtues. With a pedigree at least as old as Plato, these two traits interweave like Ariadne's golden thread of memory throughout the three millennia explored in this book. As I suggested at the beginning of this introduction, as recently as Winston Churchill's praise of Lawrence of Arabia, with its echoes of Cicero's praise of Scipio Africanus the Younger, one finds this pedigree preserved intact well into the twentieth century (and, indeed, even closer to the present in a work like John F. Kennedy's *Profiles in Courage*). It is admirable for a soldier to show courage in battle, but it is even more admirable when he develops the higher qualities of informed citizenship, culture, and intellect.

A worthy man is compassionate, decent, and gentlemanly toward others out of a sense of pride. He will not stoop to behave viciously, and he will not demean himself by acting cruelly toward women or anyone else. One of the major costs of turning our backs on the positive tradition of manliness is that we have all but lost the capacity to use this full-blooded language of old-fashioned moral exhortation. When someone misbehaves, we use bloodless code words like "that's inappropriate." Using the wrong salad fork is "inappropriate." When someone exhibits bullying, cruel, or violent behavior, it's not "inappropriate," it's *wrong*. Such a person deserves the opprobrium of being called a shameless villain and scoundrel. The men in the Central Park "wilding" weren't behaving "inappropriately." They were behaving like swine.

A man does not seek out a fight, but he will fight to protect himself, his family, and his country. A gentleman is silent unless he has something worthwhile to say. He is reserved, dignified, and mannerly. When he does speak, he pays you the compliment of being candid. Recent examples? We will all have our own candidates, including such giants as Aleksandr Solzhenitsyn and Nelson Mandela. I would also suggest John McCain. Whether you agree with his policies or not, he has that traditional balance of active and contemplative virtues going back to Plato and the Renaissance: he is both a man of unquestioned valor in battle and a thoughtful statesman. His sense of irony about politics and himself, that wry smile and teasing humor, are appealing because they speak of large reserves of inner confidence and a sense of the occasional absurdities of running for elected office. We haven't seen that since JFK. Too many of our politicians are oleaginous and mock-earnest, like prissy parsons or an overly solicitous maître d', lips permanently pursed in "concern."

But all is not lost. Things have been improving at the level of the Zeitgeist. The genderless, pouch-toting "caring male," the Alan Alda type of the 1970s, proved to have little lasting appeal for either women or men. As often happens, popular tastes have been ahead of the elites in recovering the positive tradition of manliness. In this respect, the movies

Fight Club and *Gladiator* are bookends. In *Fight Club,* a representative young man of today splits into two equally unappetizing extremes. Ed Norton's character is the wimpy, nerdy "caring male," pathetically attempting to meet women by cruising an endless round of sensitivity, self-help, and encounter groups. He creates Brad Pitt as a kind of blond beast alter ego—a swaggering, sexy S.O.B. who treats women like dirt and has them flocking around him, and whose violence is completely nihilistic and purposeless, a revolutionary without a cause except the empty posture of action for the sake of action. That's what the macho stereotype left us with: men can either be wimps or pigs. You can be "sensitive" at the sacrifice of all dignity and inner strength, or you can be a "real man" pursuing mindless violence and sex. The middle ground, where pride and compassion moderate each other, is difficult to find.

Gladiator, in refreshing contrast, gave us a glimpse of that missing middle ground. Strong, quiet, and dignified, Maximus is a man who remains steadfastly loyal to his wife and family, turning down offers of sex and advancement from an emperor's daughter. He fights for his country bravely but without relishing violence. He is relentless in avenging himself against a brutal and immature tyrant, but he is generous in victory. No wonder women loved this movie—and men, too. An earlier generation of men had to deflect their yearnings for heroism and war on behalf of a just cause to the futuristic fantasies of *Star Wars* and *Star Trek.* With *Gladiator, The Patriot,* and *Black Hawk Down,* popular culture has started to reclaim the missing history of manliness, along with the moral narrative of history that has been disappearing from schools and universities.

We can't return to the past. Recovering the positive tradition of manliness is not a recipe or a blueprint. It's the start of a process of reflection, of an inner transformation of the manly heart. With all due respect to Susan Faludi, those brawny steelworkers whose disappearance she laments in *Stiffed* aren't coming back. And modern men can't expect, or even wish, to become Caesars and Napoleons. But if war and statesmanship changed considerably in the twentieth century, one part of human nature has remained the same: the complexities of love. Love is still the inner voice of the manly heart. Our love for another is what makes us want to become better men—mature, reliable, decent, and honest. Shakespeare, Jane Austen, Wordsworth, George Eliot, Emerson, Edith Wharton—all the great writers of the past speak to us directly about love, as if they were alive today. If we want to be honorable men, we have to work to make ourselves worthy of love and respect. And *that's* encouraging!

The agony, nihilism, and confusion revealed by those desperate acts in Oklahoma City and at Columbine High School point to a wide-ranging moral and social crisis surrounding the proper role for manliness in the new millennium. After the moral wake-up call of 9/11, American society is committed as never before to taking a long, hard look at the crisis of manliness in its troubled boys and young men, and to devoting serious energies to its alleviation. Sensible people increasingly realize that it takes nothing away from our continuing support of equal opportunity for women to devote special attention to the long-neglected plight of boys. If "family values" is to mean anything more than a pleasing slogan, we must draw upon the wellsprings of the deepest ethical and religious traditions of American and Western civilization, both to hone our diagnosis of the current agony of manliness and, more important, to provide the healing balm of insight, compassion, rectitude, and guidance. In many ways, young men today are in deep spiritual trouble. But they are also yearning for a way back to the noblest ideals of American manhood. This book is intended to be an aid in that effort, a broad and open-minded, but at the same time morally rigorous, exploration of the manly virtues drawn from the speculative, historical, and literary treasures of the West.

The answer is to return neither to a primordial Mother Goddess nor to primeval fantasies of male shamanism and campfire dances. Responsible and satisfying friendships between men and women can only be lost in the pursuit of a sectarian and rejectionist "gender identity." Instead, we need to aim for the highest fulfillment of which all people are capable—moral and intellectual virtues that are the same for men and women at their peaks—while recognizing the diverse qualities that men and women contribute to this common human endeavor for excellence. We need a sympathetic reengagement with traditional teachings that stress that while men and women share a capacity for the highest virtues, their passions, temperaments, and sentiments can differ, resulting in different paths to those common pinnacles.

In *The Code of Man*, I will ask readers to join me on a detective hunt for residual signs of manliness and to identify signs of a reemergence of the love of heroism in contemporary youth culture. From there we will begin the journey along the five paths: love, courage, pride, family, and country. The reader will be invited to reflect on a positive account of manly pride and honor, drawn from some of the greatest works of the Western tradition, as the only sure basis for educating young men to treat others—and themselves—with respect.

At bottom, searching for the positive tradition of manliness is one of our most promising and inviting contemporary avenues back to the Great Books. In my experience as an educator, I find that young people are still inclined by nature to fall in love with this journey to the stars and back. For me, the purpose of teaching the Great Books is to give my students a passport to this odyssey of the mind and heart. Moreover, as a number of best-selling books illustrate, Americans of all ages are having a love affair with the Western canon. Precisely as schools and universities, bewitched by an already outmoded cant of political correctness, turn their backs on these treasures in favor of the abysmal litany of victimology, the broader reading public seeks them out like thirsty travelers longing for an oasis of spiritual and intellectual refreshment. The Great Books are the most reliable compass for our recovery of the true meaning of manhood. As the new millennium begins its uncertain voyage into an uncertain future, we need that ancient compass more than ever.

Many of the Great Books contain allegories for the journey of the soul from one's particular time, place, and attachments to a transcendental perspective where the mysteries of human existence, love, faith, and longing are illuminated. After this journey to the heights of insight, we return to our own time and place better able to appreciate both its shortcomings and its virtues. One such epic is Homer's *Odyssey*. Behind its tales of magic and daring is the story of a father and a son who have lost each other and are searching for a way back home. As Odysseus makes his way back home from Troy, he is deepened by the many perils he faces. His son, Telemachus, embarked simultaneously on a search for his father, matures into a man by trying to live up to his absent father's expectations. Spiritually enriched by their wanderings, father and son reunite, their life back home permanently transformed by their exposure to the wider world. A similar cycle of transcendence and return is sketched by Plato in his famous Image of the Cave in the *Republic*. Our pursuit of the truth helps us to shed the chains of the prejudices that shackle us to an unreflecting attachment to the status quo. We journey upward from the dark cave of ignorance toward the beautiful sunlight of the truth. Having glimpsed it, we can reconcile ourselves to the here and now because we know there is something more noble—the virtues that make us better men and women.

I.

LOVE

A RECENT STUDY OF BOYS IN JUNIOR HIGH SCHOOL SHOWED THAT, the day after watching professional wrestling on television, they called girls "hos" and "bitches" much more frequently than on other days of the week. It's one more item in the avalanche of evidence of the coarsening of eros and the decline of a vocabulary of refinement between men and women—and how it begins at a depressingly early age. Throughout the cultures of mass entertainment, popular music, and fashion, the expression of delicate sentiments, courtesy, or heartfelt feeling between men and women is frequently derided as embarrassing and uncool, to the point where it has almost vanished. Open the pages of *Vanity Fair* or *Details,* and you see sleek, glossy young people who look like celebrities, draped in Calvin or Tommy or Mondavi, but always sullen and unsmiling as they glare at you through their sunglasses from the Hamptons or the Upper East Side. The message is: You too can be a celebrity, as long as you know the hip things to buy and always have a snarl at the ready. The approved cultural style is one of detachment, narcissism, and casual, unfeeling sex. As the poet Phyllis Gotlieb puts it in a way that sums up this culture of disaffection, "I'd rather heave a brick than say I love you."

There are many causes for this coarsening of eros. But the main one, in my view, is the caricature of manliness as macho, brutish, and aggressive behavior. Dinned into boys and young men for several decades now, it has become a self-fulfilling prophecy. David Foster Wallace, by some accounts the most popular of American writers on college campuses, has chronicled this effect in his *Brief Interviews with Hideous Men*. Here's his version of how men talk about women among themselves:

K: What does today's woman want? Whether it sounds Neanderthal or not, I'm still going to argue it's the big one . . .

E: Like take your classic Madonna-versus-whore contradiction. Good girl versus slut. The girl you respect and take home to meet your Mom versus the girl you just fuck.

K: Yet let's not forget that overlaid atop this is the new feminist-slash-postfeminist expectation that women are sexual agents too, just as men are . . . that for today's woman, it's almost mandatory to fuck around. . . . What today's woman wants, in short, is a male with both the passionate sensitivity and the logical firepower to discern that all her pronouncements about autonomy are actually desperate cries in the wilderness. . . . They want you on one level wholeheartedly to agree and respect what they're saying and on another, deeper level to recognize that it's all complete horseshit and to gallop in on your white charger and overwhelm them with passion.

So much for the project of changing male attitudes. Having been a college professor for some twenty years, I can confirm that David Foster Wallace's depictions of how young males discuss women are utterly convincing in their accuracy. They provide evidence for wondering whether one of feminism's main accomplishments has been to give men an excuse to act on their own basest impulses. Women say they're sexual agents, too, so why not give them what they want? After thirty years of relentless behavior modification, the grand result is that young men in college—the future meritocratic elite of America—feel justified in shamelessly proclaiming: Women want "the big one." This view of women is directly opposed to the goal toward which feminists have always claimed to be working. But when you tell women they should lose their old-fashioned hang-ups about femininity and assert their right to behave as coarsely and immodestly as men, and at the same time tell men that they are collectively prone to exploit women, what else should you expect?

This self-fulfilling prophecy is reinforced by the general trend in entertainment culture that encourages self-indulgence and hedonism. What began in the 1960s as relatively innocent and tentative extramarital experimentation and wife swapping (highlighted in movies like *Bob &*

Carol & Ted & Alice) rapidly gave way to the heartless sexual acrobatics of *Last Tango in Paris* and the Dionysian sex and violence orgies of the Manson Family and Altamont. Today, these once shocking images have become routine, millions of them flickering across our eyeballs as we munch our Doritos, so that a Madonna video with S & M overtones becomes one small brick in an electronically simulated world of virtual normality.

And yet, every so often the baffled longing for love breaks through. You can cut human nature off from its sources of guidance, but you can't get rid of it. As long as human beings exist, they will long for love, and love is a structured longing with its own peculiar logic, language, and psychology. Young people feel pressured to conform to the glossy images of snarly narcissism and hip indifference to others, but in their hearts they want to recover their voice and find another person to love. In this chapter, we will explore a proposition so deeply rooted in three thousand years of the Western tradition that to recover it today would amount almost to a moral revolution, since so little attention has been paid to it in the last thirty years. This is the proposition that erotic passion and intimacy are fully satisfying *only* when men and women strive to exercise their capacities for moral and intellectual virtue.

But before turning to that hopeful message from the great thinkers and artists of the past, let's continue our rather dismal tour of the erotic wasteland of recent years. Another contributing factor to the coarsening of eros is the project of creating a genderless personality. The prevailing orthodoxy in our leading universities is that sexual roles are "constructed" out of nothing, and that we must "deconstruct" them in order to liberate ourselves from their restrictions on our spontaneous impulses. The belief that there are natural and intrinsic differences between men and women is held to be a root cause of war, violence, and injustice, because it reinforces the iron grip of patriarchy and conservatism. The need to "deconstruct" traditional differences between men and women leads to a fascination with androgyny, transvestism, bisexuality, sadomasochism, and other contrarian lifestyles. Precisely because they are so atypical, and for most people so unusual, they allegedly demonstrate that all gender distinctions are potentially plastic and open to breaking down and radical reshaping, if only we could part with our old-fashioned conservative belief in a permanent human nature with an innate capacity for virtue and vice. Here is how the *Yale Alumni Magazine* describes Yale's program in gender studies:

> In exploring how and why we assign particular roles to men and women, scholars in gender studies are naturally drawn to the exception to norms—what Joshua Gamson calls "category disruptions." "One way to see how gender is socially constructed is by looking at transgendered people, those who change their gender identification through their dress or by having their bodies surgically altered," says Gamson. . . . "It's an opportunity to think about the notion that gender could be organized differently. The same is true with bisexuality, which can make trouble for the idea that all we've got are 'gay' and 'straight.' "

In other words, there are *no* natural, intrinsic differences between men and women. Since "we" constructed them in one way—as men and women—"we" can reconstruct them in any way we please by dissolving them in the soup of polymorphous sexuality and then remolding their parts. That means we have to define the norm in terms of the extreme. Young people have to be taught that there's no such thing as male or female behavior by nature, and this can be done by exposing them to the more idiosyncratic excesses of the sexual contrarian. Sexual plasticity is taken to imply freedom from other bourgeois hang-ups, like property rights and political authority, so that the sexually "marginalized" become romanticized in the same way the proletariat once was—what the leading postmodernist thinker Jacques Derrida has called the "new international" of the culturally dispossessed. Whereas the old international had been made up of the economically oppressed, the new international will be a grab bag of the culturally alienated, all uniting to combat American patriarchy and hegemony.

What begins as an academic doctrine in the leading universities filters into society at large through graduates who go on to become teachers, social workers, and journalists. As we saw in the discussion of the *Just Say Yes* Web site, graduates of these programs may believe they have an ethical mission to make young kids learn about such contrarian lifestyles as bondage, whipping, and anal intercourse before they're barely aware of their own sexuality, to impart the lesson in their most formative years that there's no such thing as human nature and no intrinsic distinction between coarseness and delicacy. We are infinitely malleable and, once we liberate ourselves from the shackles of middle-class morality, free from any sexual restraints.

What begins as a well-intentioned and even high-minded attempt in the universities to free students from stereotypes and intolerance toward minority groups often translates in the wider culture into a voyeuristic taste for "kink" and "transgression." Novels like Bret Easton Ellis's *Less Than Zero* or those of David Foster Wallace depict casual experimentation with gay sex by straights as a way of showing that you are hip and nonbourgeois because you attach no lasting feelings to sexual encounters of any variety. My straight male students sometimes casually describe another male as "cute" or go to gay bars. They're not "conflicted" about their own sexuality, as the social workers' bromide would have it. They're playing the postmodernist glass bead game of trying on a kaleidoscope of sexual masks and personae. It's cool, a way of distancing yourself from the specific vocabulary of love between men and women and treating all erotic contact as reducible to wordless physical hedonism.

As for gay people themselves, they are among the major victims of this entertainment culture of kink. Since brainless sexual frenzy, pedophilia, S & M and other contrarian practices are no more typical of gay people than of straights, I can't believe gay people are well-served by the success of a television series such as *Queer as Folk*. Already a big hit in Britain, the American version is one of the most popular series on the Showtime Network. Ratings like those suggest that its audience is not restricted to gays, and I wouldn't be surprised if only a minority of gay people even watch it. Its sole accomplishment is to transfer to gays a series of the stupidest and most vulgar stereotypes previously reserved for the majority sexual preference. At its best, it resembles a same-sex *Melrose Place* or *Beach Blanket Bingo*. There's even a kooky "den mother" like the kind hilariously parodied in John Waters's *Cry-Baby*, the whacked-out older couple who run the club where the young people hang out and who "don't knock the rock." At its worst, the show is pure porn.

As a mass-retailed image of gay culture, it shows a thoroughly unappealing crew of hardened narcissists who spend every day in an incredibly monotonous cycle of casual sex, drugs, and disco hopping. The main character, Brian, a twenty-nine-year-old man, seduces Justin, a seventeen-year-old boy; at one point he orders him to show up so he can try out a new dildo on the teenager as a warm-up for anal intercourse. ("I'm going to fuck you till your eyes pop out," he says over the phone to the boy, who's in his bedroom at his parents' house when he receives this summons.) The episode passes without the script expressing the slightest moral disavowal. Its sole purpose is to expose how uptight the boy's father is about his son's older lover, with the heavy implication that he should lighten up and voluntarily deliver his underage son over to the jaded Brian. Large audiences of straight people are presumably getting a vicarious kick out of this predator. Because the series depicts the gay community as a world of wild abandon in order to satisfy the voyeurism of the mass market, gays are forced to play the role of the noble savage in Gauguin's paintings. We attribute to them a licentiousness and abandon that we secretly crave for ourselves. I suspect people watch *Queer as Folk* in the same way that affluent whites used to go slumming at the Cotton Club.

Just as the real-world consequence of the caricature of manliness as macho actually increases male aggressiveness, the deconstruction of sexual identity encourages a culture of immaturity and childishness, of men who remain boys in order to avoid the responsibility of a mature long-term relationship or prove themselves worthy of love by aspiring to decent and thoughtful conduct. This infantilization of men is noticeable in ways large and small. As George Will has observed, authority patterns in American business are no longer marked by grown-up clothing. Executives and dot-com billionaires work in black T-shirts and chinos like the kids outside on their skateboards. Go to any shopping mall, and you'll see men and boys wearing the same outfits of T-shirts and shorts, and a lot of the men lined up with their kids at the grocery checkout will have ear studs or tattoos.

Is it a big deal? Not terribly. But it is a sign of the times pointing to more worrisome trends. The neighborhood I live in, full of civil servants, lawyers, and academics with combined six-figure incomes, is also full of adolescent hip-hop boys "jailing" with their baggy jeans sagging at the crotch to expose their boxers. Like their idol Eminem, they make that peculiar downward jabbing gesture with their fingers in a hook shape, always reminding me incongruously of Mussolini haranguing the crowd from his balcony. It's an aggressive gesture that says: "Don't expect me to make an argument. This is how it is." When you pass them on the way to the 7-Eleven to pick up milk, they shoot you that squinting, sideways look that Tom Wolfe calls "the felon's stare," a gesture which, he says, seems to occur spontaneously to every well-heeled American teenage boy. And yet, as my wife once observed, by letting their jeans sag around the hips, they make themselves helpless. The jeans restrict their walking like a hoop skirt, while the four inches of exposed boxers make them look like babies whose diapers are bulging out of their rompers. It's a combination of defiance and self-infantilization, a wish to experience helplessness behind the defiant finger-jabbing facade, an unconscious cry for parenting and discipline. The same goes for the shaved heads and the studs. The punk aesthetic is an unwitting return to traditional gestures of penance and self-mortification, a subconscious desire to reexperience moral constraint through a crude physical simulacrum for the ethical and religious teachings often not available from school and family.

Lest my prognoses seem too bleak, let me add at this point that a countermovement has been under way for some years now to rethink the thirty-year project to stigmatize manliness. It is part of a larger concern with what many Americans perceive as the country's moral drift. Many opinion polls show that a majority of Americans are worried about the growth of immorality and the decline of trust, and their concerns have been explored by the new communitarians, including Jean Bethke Elshtain and Amitai Etzioni. The new communitarians form a school of thought whose members believe that narcissistic self-indulgence has gone too far in American culture, and that we need more emphasis on our duties to the common good as opposed to our right to live exactly as we please. At the same time, authors and public policy advocates like David Blankenhorn and Barbara Dafoe Whitehead have drawn attention to the devastating effects of the divorce culture and the weakening of family ties, especially on boys. These concerns are not restricted to conventional distinctions between liberal and conservative, Left and Right, or religious and secular. A writer in her twenties, Wendy Shalit, has called for a reconsideration by women of the value of modesty. And

Tom Wolfe has enjoyed the greatest success and critical acclaim of his career with *A Man in Full*. The book is fearlessly old-fashioned in ignoring the tired, self-referential modernism of academic writers, whose novels are about professors writing about professors; instead, it plunges into the fabulous maelstrom of everyday American work, a world in which grit, pluck, ambition, and bravery are still admired, in all classes and by all ethnic groups, and both sexes.

The countermovement against the stigmatization of manly virtue is also reflected in movies of the last decade or so. From *Fatal Attraction* to *American Beauty*, we've seen a return to the "bourgeois" values of assuming responsibility for your actions, keeping the family together, not acting on your impulses, and growing up. As reviewers have noted, these movies have a more than slightly antifeminist tone—Glenn Close's character in *Fatal Attraction* and the wife played by Annette Bening in *American Beauty* are career-driven viragoes. And that's the problem. These films may perform a healthy function by venting the frustrations of men over the thirty-year project, and with what they rightly perceive to be the prevailing orthodoxy that depicts men as collectively worthless. But it's no great improvement to replace the caricature of American man as a sexist pig with the caricature of American woman as a kind of Cruella De Vil in the executive suite.

We need more than the caveman reaction of *Fatal Attraction*'s blood-soaked climax, or of the scene (admittedly hilarious and cathartic) of Kevin Spacey smashing the dishes at dinner in *American Beauty*. Satisfying as it may be to see Glenn Close splattered against the wall by the protecting caveman Michael Douglas, this is a crude and self-defeating way of trying to restore a more balanced perspective on the complicated and often troubled efforts of men and women to be friends as well as lovers. To identify manliness with this brutal spasm of reactive violence, even when the motive is understandable, is ultimately just to reinforce the darker currents in our culture and contribute to the victory of the parody of manliness as macho. The ex-wife or sexually predatory career woman who tries to break up your marriage, gain single custody of your kids, throw you in jail for failing to make alimony even though she makes more money than you do—in these mass entertainment vehicles, she's just another "ho." And if, as the fantasy of *Fatal Attraction* implies, it's okay to kill a "ho" to defend your family, then why not kill agents of the FBI, or bite an opponent's ear off in a boxing match? Morally and psychologically, it's not that far from the fantasy of a man's justified revenge on a predatory woman in *Fatal Attraction* to the debased misogynistic fantasy of rape, sexual torture, and murder offered in the book and movie *American Psycho,* which were treated as works of serious art.

In all of these cases, what starts as an intelligible frustration by men about their lot in the contemporary world is used as an excuse to indulge in deeply objectionable and murderous feelings that end up justifying the most extreme version of the feminist caricature itself. What begins as a protest against the caricature ends up as its justification. Physical strength is not what's needed to make men feel like men again; what's needed is strength of character.

We need to find our way back to what the film critic Michael Medved calls "mature romance"—that is, love as a character-building experience. And I believe that, despite the bleak evidence sketched in this chapter so far, the best hope for reclaiming the positive meaning of manliness still lies in the sphere of romantic relationships. The validity of the traditional teachings about manly virtue is somewhat less clear in other spheres of contemporary living. One could argue, for instance, that nobility in war is no longer possible because advanced military technology (including nuclear weapons) has both made the consequences of war unthinkable and rendered battlefield courage irrelevant. Similarly, in the age of egalitarian mass society, one could argue that statesmanship may no longer call for the pride of a Caesar or even a Churchill. As I will make plain in later chapters, I believe these arguments against courage and pride are grossly exaggerated, if not completely false. But they have a surface plausibility. This is not so in the case of romance and the love between men and women. Here we have a direct connection to the past, and it is more immediately and self-evidently clear in the erotic sphere than in the other spheres of moral experience that human nature has not changed. Sexual life, marriage, and the search for a partner present us with the same dilemmas and quandaries, the same temptations to vice and opportunities for virtue, as they have for millennia. Men need to listen to the inner voice that says: I want to love and be loved. And then they need a guiding framework and a guiding narrative for articulating their love. To that we now turn.

EROS AND SELF-PERFECTION

The wisdom of the West about erotic relations between men and women can be summed up in a single maxim: Love perfects. It is a common theme throughout three thousand years of reflections on the meaning of manliness, from Plato's *Symposium* to Castiglione's *Book of the Courtier,* from Shakespeare's *Romeo and Juliet* to Mozart's *Marriage of Figaro.* A man's love for a woman can give him the strongest possible motive to overcome his own vices in order to prove himself worthy of her. His erotic longing provides him with a mirror in which he can view himself through his beloved's eyes, seeing his own shortcomings clearly for the first time and, in so doing, find an erotic motive to develop his own best qualities.

This maxim runs counter to one of the most widespread and fallacious assumptions of our age—that pleasure and duty necessarily contradict each other. The jargon of authenticity is dinned into us from a million pounding signals in the entertainment culture, telling us that we need to satisfy ourselves first and foremost and set aside the artificial constraints of morality or faith.

But according to millennia of reflection, a man can experience mature and satisfying passion *only* through the cultivation of those moral and intellectual virtues that make others admire us.

The classic work here is Plato's marvelous dialogue the *Symposium.* According to this work, the philosopher Socrates was initiated as a young man into the mysteries of love by a wise and majestic woman, the prophetess Diotima. She reproached him for being too obsessed with the abstract rigor of astronomy and math and blind to the complexities of human need. As he recalled with gratitude many years later, Diotima taught him that when our erotic attachment to another is guided properly, it provides us with the emotional energies we need to develop the virtues that make us worthy of love. Diotima's Ladder of Love is a progressive ascent from bodily desire to the higher levels of family life, citizenship, and culture, until having reached the highest rungs, we have absorbed all those qualities of mind, heart, and soul that make a man complex, reflective, and interesting to himself and others. At every stage of this ascent, we become more virtuous and more satisfied emotionally. A man is attracted to a woman because he sees beyond her physical beauty to those qualities of character that he longs to possess in himself. By uniting with her, he hopes to gain some of her gentle calm and goodness, and some relief from his own darker impulses of lust and aggression. But in order to prove worthy of her and to make himself appealing to her, the man must demonstrate that he already has some of these same moderate qualities himself, or at least is willing to strive for them. It's a chicken-and-egg argument through which most of us have lived.

Diotima's Ladder presents a logic of love. Eros is an orderly longing that benefits both partners by holding each to the highest standards and creating a miniature "common good" between them. In this sense, it has little in common with the more flamboyant versions of romantic passion, a more modern kind of outlook originating in the eighteenth and nineteenth centuries (although, as we'll see in a moment, it has some roots in the medieval conception of chivalry). In contrast with the Platonic logic of love sketched by Diotima's Ladder, romantic passion often evokes the wild abandon, frenzy, and volcanic emotions of a Lord Byron, or the characters in the novels of Balzac and Dostoevsky, where men destroy themselves to pursue a satisfaction that is doomed from the beginning, and whose more recent progeny are the Dionysian death gods of contemporary pop culture, from James Dean to Kurt Cobain.

To be sure, romantic passion of the obsessive Byronic kind was not unknown among the ancients. The fable of Orpheus and Eurydice evokes a love between man and woman so strong that it lasts beyond the grave. In Virgil's *Aeneid,* the exiled Trojan hero Aeneas must renounce his passion for Dido, Queen of Carthage, in order to fulfill his destiny as the founder of Rome. She mounts her own funeral pyre and stabs herself as Aeneas watches the rising flames from his departing ship. Both stories, so emotionally and visually sweeping, inspired seventeenth- and eighteenth-century operas, the archetypal musical expression of a life-transforming love.

In the ancient world, female deities were often depicted as sources of wisdom for men about the mysteries of nature and how they might round out their own excessively masculine characters with the more feminine characteristics of subtlety, intuition, empathy, and maternal benevolence. Apollo, the most beautiful and artistic of the Greek gods, the patron of the muses, shares his chief cult site at Delphi with its earlier inhabitant, the Earth Goddess Gaia. Her influence endures through Apollo's priestess the Pythia, named for the serpent that guarded the Earth Goddess by her sacred spring, slain by Apollo when he took over the site. Although Apollo displaces Gaia, he does not drive out her influence. On the contrary: Apollo, who was originally a harsh warrior god from the barbaric lands to the north, is softened and beautified by the intertwining of his identity with the female goddess of fertility, fecundity, and desire. He does not so much conquer the Goddess as merge with her. His priestess, the Pythia (literally, the "Pythoness" or python-woman), is clearly a holdover from the earlier reign of the Earth Goddess and her serpent, now enshrined as the male god's chief partner. It's only by the sublimation of his own excessively masculine traits through his partnership with Gaia that Apollo evolves from a mere warrior into the beautiful, ever youthful, and gracious god of art and music.

The sublimation of excessively masculine traits (think of the club-wielding plunderer Hercules, roaming around stealing cattle and seducing farmers' daughters) by the principle of the feminine embodied in a goddess is a continuing theme in ancient literature. It's reflected in Odysseus's special partnership with Athena, the Goddess of Wisdom, who teaches him that victories over the trials and dangers of a mortal's life are won more often through clever reasoning, patience, and intuition than by physical force. As we have already seen, Socrates claims that a mysterious prophetess taught him about the importance of love. Indeed, the majestic, wry, and commanding Diotima reminds me a lot of Homer's depiction of Athena, suggesting a partnership between the philosopher and the feminine principle similar to the one between the hero and the goddess extolled by Homer. Finally, and not surprisingly, sites in the ancient world later associated with the Virgin Mary—for instance, Ephesus in Turkey, where she is said to have lived out her final days—were often previously major cult centers of powerful goddesses like Gaia and Artemis.

But the very fact that these formidable female presences were goddesses and not flesh-and-blood women (the Virgin Mary is a different case, to which I'll turn in a moment) generally prevented ancient literature from exploring a purely human obsession between a man and a woman as a theme for serious moral or psychological reflection. That, as I say, is a more modern, Romantic kind of love. As we'll see at greater length in Chapter 4, detailed relations between real men and women were generally treated from ancient times down to the Renaissance in the context of the family and the household. Aristotle, to cite one of the major authorities for that entire period, encourages husbands and wives to view each other as friends. But for the philosopher, the highest friendship a man can have is the love of another person who is devoted to pursuing the same moral and intellectual virtues he is, and that other person is more likely to be a man than a woman. In Aristotle's conception, marriage is a stable, rational, and orderly kind of partnership, much more like the world of Jane Austen than that of Byron or Dostoevsky, and with no unseemly displays of overwhelming passion or emotional extravagance.

The comic poet Aristophanes has a more lighthearted and sentimental view, and doesn't demand the same rigorous standards from men and women as the philosopher. Included by Plato as one of the characters who discusses love with Socrates in the *Symposium,* he touchingly portrays the motive for love as a man and a woman searching to reunite their "splits." Back at the beginning of time, he says, men and women were single beings, rolling around like wagon wheels or calamari, perfectly happy in their unified bliss and unaware of alienation or frustrated yearnings. But because we became arrogant, building a tower (rather like the Tower of Babel in the Bible) in order to climb to the heavens and kick out the gods, Zeus punished us by splitting us into male and female halves. Today, when a man and a woman fall in love, each is yearning for that missing half. The same is true for gay people—they are men and women looking to rejoin their same-sex splits. Aristophanes' lesson behind the humor (in some ways he was the Mel Brooks of classical Athens, including the flatulence jokes) is that eros is the longing for completion through the love of another human being.

In general, though, among the ancients who write about high themes such as the soul and the virtues, we don't find much intoxication, fascination, or sexual obsession with the beloved as the key to understanding human psychology. Strictly personal love affairs and wooing went against the grain of mainstream classical taste. This was not because the Greeks and Romans were prudes. Far from it. If you tip the guide at Pompeii, he'll show you rooms not usually included in the tour that depict an astonishing range of imaginative sexual diversions and positions unlikely to occur to an Episcopalian such as myself. The Pompeians, it appears, were robustly interested in having a good romp. But the idea that a serious man would lose himself emotionally in a love affair, thereby neglecting his more important political ambitions, business interests, and drive to advance the fortunes and status of his family and clan, was considered a form of "madness," as the Stoic moralists put it when discussing excessive eros. That went for the women as well. The heroic queens, wives, and mothers held up as prodigies of virtue by the great tragedies of Aeschylus and Sophocles display the same admirable character traits as their male counterparts—strength of will, self-control, bravery in the face of danger, dignity in defeat, occasional fury in protecting their families and kingdoms. They endure their fate with fortitude when sold into slavery, never losing their queenly bearing and contempt for their oppressors. Cross them or try to steal their royal husbands, and they're likely to slit your throat. Only in comedy do we meet ordinary, everyday folks—working stiffs, housewives, merchants, and floozies—as opposed to the great aristocrats who are always bearing up under adversity in the tragedies. But while there's lots of sex, adultery, and bedroom farce in authors like Petronius and Ovid, who are bent more on amusement than on edification, there's not much resembling what we mean by "romance"—no idealistic fervor about serving a lady and improving one's own character by proving one's devotion to her. When Ovid writes about adultery, it sounds like something from the swinging suburbs of Cheever or Updike. As the narrator in his poem *On Adultery* puts it: "So, that husband of yours is going to be at the party. Well, I hope he chokes; let him drop dead, who cares?"

Fervent devotion and self-sacrifice on behalf of a lady first appears with the Middle Ages and the cult of the Virgin. She is the embodiment of divine compassion and love; in serving a lady who possesses a share of those same gentle and chaste qualities, a knight is serving the Mother of

God as she is embodied in his beloved. Of course, we must be careful to distinguish knightly chivalry from the purely this-worldly eros that Socrates praises as the route to cultivating one's highest moral and intellectual faculties. Christian theologians like St. Augustine were scandalized by what they regarded as the folly of the pagans in believing that human beings had the capacity to achieve perfection in their own natures, in an entirely worldly manner, and without acknowledging their complete dependence on God and salvation.

In *The City of God,* one of the foundational texts of Christianity, St. Augustine in effect breaks Diotima's Ladder into two pieces—a lower half of fleshly corruption and sin, and a higher half, which points to the eternal life that awaits us in Heaven. Whereas Socrates had seen a direct progression from ordinary sexual desire to the higher forms of erotic fulfillment—an ascent through family and civic virtue toward the divine pleasures of contemplation—for St. Augustine it is an intolerable mark of human pride, arrogance, and folly to believe that human nature is capable of such an ascent to transcendence on its own. No perfection is possible for man within this mortal realm, according to the saint. Solely by repressing our natural passions, by treating our bodies as fleshly prisons from which only God and Christ can release us after death, can we avoid falling even further into sin.

Because there can be no higher vision of natural love within this fallen, secular realm, eros is reduced to a purely fleshly drive. Love degenerates into the madness of endless lust, a sick compulsion by which Satan lures us to give up our chance for salvation and join him in Hell. In the paintings of Sassetta, that most Augustinian of artists, the wise and majestic goddesses like Aphrodite and Athena so admired by the ancients are reduced to the image of a temptress—a slut, a she-devil, luring the saint with her corrupt wiles, lurking naked in a thicket by the roadside, beckoning him to depart from the straight and narrow path and join her in her shady bower of vile and delicious concupiscence. The Earth Goddess Gaia and her python, symbolic of how the feminine links the masculine to the wisdom of nature, is transformed by Christianity into Eve and her partner the snake, symbolic of how the feminine corrupts the masculine through the sin and sensuality of natural life. Whereas Apollo becomes a fuller man through his symbiotic partnership with the

Earth Goddess and her serpent, in the Christian view of nature, man loses his direct connection with God through the wiles of a woman and her serpent, and so is expelled from the Garden of Eden.

For the pagans, as we've observed, women were either being paragons of queenly suffering and fortitude of the kind extolled in the tragedies or having their share of fun with their husbands and lovers in the comedies. Sexuality was something to laugh off and enjoy, a roll in the hay. It was not a serious theme like war, peace, statesmanship, and tyranny. In his *Confessions,* by contrast, St. Augustine makes sexual passion a serious theme. Because it's a sin, he can't laugh it off. And for the same reason—that carnal desire endangers his salvation—he must explore it in a kind of serious and humorless detail that struck pagans as being in extremely vulgar taste. The pagan motto was, as Aristotle puts it, "Everything in moderation." That means you shouldn't have sex all the time, but by the same token you can still have a fair amount of it. There's nothing wrong with sex in itself. It's only a drawback when it distracts you from the more serious pursuits of a gentleman's life, such as public honor, family reputation, and the life of the mind. For St. Augustine, by contrast, chastity is the only solution. Carnal pleasures are thoroughly despicable and lead only to perdition. But, as a fallen mortal tainted by the original sin of Eve, St. Augustine not only can't achieve chastity but worries that even aiming for it might in itself be a dangerous sign of pride, the arrogant assumption that he can master his lusts on his own. So he careens back and forth between sexual escapades that disgust him like a revolting illness and the deepest depths of cheek-burning shame and mortification. "God grant me chastity," he begs, "but not yet." Pagan audiences would have had a chuckle over that, but for the saint it's not a witticism: It's the confession of an agonizing struggle between divided selves.

Because Christianity breaks the Ladder of Love into two disconnected pieces, the Christian civilization of the Middle Ages tended to view erotic matters as a series of sharply contrasting extremes—Heaven versus Hell, the otherworldly versus the fleshly, chastity versus lust, purity versus sin. For the Christian, virtue is not (as it was for the ancients) the flowering of our natures but a constant spiritual struggle against natures that are hopelessly tainted with sin. Only in a devotion to Mary is there any relaxation of these drastic extremes, any respite from the fires of Hell raging in us through our loins and lusts. Although the saints drive eros out the front door, the cult of Mary returns it through the back door in a chastened but peculiarly sweet, sublime, and touching form. In his classic study *Mont-Saint-Michel and Chartres*, Henry Adams argues that the cult of the Virgin was at the heart of medieval Christendom, supplying the dimensions of tenderness, compassion, and emotionalism less characteristic of the three male branches of the Trinity. The Virgin, he writes, "showed a marked weakness for chivalry." Not only did the Queen of Heaven lead her knightly armies into battle but she embodied the perfection they sought in the damsels they loved. Some knights even forsook earthly love to serve as the Virgin's own champions, with a devotion free from fleshly desire.

Mary will forgive you for your failure to be chaste, just like a mother will forgive a son for behaving badly. As long as you try to be good, she will understand your failings. Mary is neither a goddess who completely transcends human life nor a mortal woman tainted with the sin of Eve. She is a woman linked to the divine, and hence free of sin. In worshiping her, however, you're worshiping not a distant and majestic goddess like Athena but a real flesh-and-blood mother. Michelangelo's amazing statue group in the Vatican, the *Pietà*, depicts the ideal woman in Marian terms, and is therefore like nothing found in ancient sculpture. She is not a goddess but a real mother, cradling her son's broken body after it's been taken down from the cross. Overcome with grief and pity, she holds him in her lap like a baby, and at that moment becomes every mother who has grieved for a suffering child.

Mary as the God-woman is the model for the medieval damsel and the code of knightly chivalry. Mirroring the extremes of Christian theology—the wide gap between the City of Man and the City of God, between the sinful drives of the flesh and the innocence of spiritual purity—tales of chivalry often feature a conflict between adulterous love and one's higher duties to king and Church, ending in the downfall of the sinners. Lancelot and Guinevere's illicit passion is perhaps the best-known example; it leads both to betray their duty to the faultless monarch Arthur. The high ideals are always present, as a standard by which to assign the appropriate condemnation of sinners like Lancelot

and the praise of truly good and chaste knights like Sir Gawain. The ideal
of knighthood is perhaps best summed up by Chaucer:

> *A knight there was, and he a worthy man,*
> *Who, from the moment that he first began*
> *To ride about the world, loved chivalry,*
> *Truth, honor, freedom and all courtesy.*
> *Full worthy was he in his liege-lord's war,*
> *And therein had he ridden (none more far)*
> *As well in Christendom as heathenesse,*
> *And honored everywhere for worthiness.*
> *And always won he sovereign fame for prize.*
> *Though so illustrious, he was very wise*
> *And bore himself as meekly as a maid.*
> *He never yet had any vileness said,*
> *In all his life, to whatsoever wight.*
> *He was truly perfect, gentle knight.*

The code of medieval chivalry is explored at length in the legends of
King Arthur and his knights. The perfect knight was expected to be
brave but also refined, and to treat women at all times with respect. He
was also expected to be pious, setting an example for those below him in
the social order through his devotion to God and the teachings of the
Church. As a Christian soldier, he was never to use his skill in fighting to
afflict the innocent. He should draw his sword only to serve justice and
out of compassion for those who suffered undeservedly. In matters of
the heart, the perfect knight acted with restraint and modesty as he
wooed his fair damsel. As a chivalrous man, he wanted his lady to love
him for his worthy character. A man's love for his damsel gave him the
strongest motive to overcome his vices, in order to make himself admirable and worthy of her affection. This is the happy paradox of the
chivalric ideal: Once the knight's erotic passion has been properly reha-
bilitated by being focused on the ideal of womanhood—his damsel's reflection of the supreme goodness of the Virgin—it can furnish the surest
inducement to moral decency.

During the High Middle Ages people began to write more openly

about the purely sensual aspects of love, and to relax the Augustinian extremes of lust and chastity. *The Art of Courtly Love,* by Andreas
Capellanus, is a classic from the High Age of Chivalry. Written in the
twelfth century, it diagnoses all the sweet suffering of love:

> Love is a certain inborn suffering derived from the sight of and excessive
> meditation upon the beauty of the opposite sex, which causes each one
> to wish above all things the embraces of the other and by common desire
> to carry out all of love's precepts in the other's embrace.

Eight centuries after these maxims were written, a reader has no difficulty grasping their meaning:

> Nothing is worse than when the one you love doesn't love you back:

> That love is suffering is easy to see, for before the love becomes equally
> balanced on both sides there is no torment greater, since the lover is al-
> ways in fear that his love may not gain its desire and that he is wasting his
> efforts.

A man's love for a woman makes him acutely aware of his own imperfections and gives him the strongest possible motive to overcome them.
When the woman returns his love, a man's imperfections seem to vanish,
reemerging as virtues:

> Love causes a rough and uncouth man to be distinguished for his hand-
> someness; it can endow a man even of the humblest birth with nobility
> of character; it blesses the proud with humility; and the man in love be-
> comes accustomed to performing many services gracefully for everyone.
> O what a wonderful thing is love, which makes a man shine with so many
> virtues and teaches everyone, no matter who he is, so many good traits of
> character!

A man who indulges in excessive carnal pleasures will never know
what it means to love, because he lacks the capacity for loyalty to a single
beloved:

> An excess of passion is a bar to love, because there are men who are
> slaves to such passionate desire that they cannot be held in the bonds of
> love—men who, after they have thought long about some woman

straightway desire her embraces, and they forget about the services they
have received from their first love and they feel no gratitude for them.
Men of this kind lust after every woman they see; their love is like that of
a shameless dog. They should rather, I believe, be compared to asses, for
they are moved only by that low nature which shows that men are on the
level of the other animals rather than by that true nature which sets us
apart from all the other animals by the difference of reason.

The Art of Courtly Love provides us with thirty-one simple rules for
sublime longing and torment. Here are a few of their highlights:

Marriage is no real excuse for not loving.

Every lover regularly turns pale in the presence of his beloved.

When a lover suddenly catches sight of his beloved his heart palpitates.

He whom the thought of love vexes, eats and sleeps very little.

A lover can never have enough of the solaces of his beloved.

Nothing forbids one woman being loved by two men or one man by two
women.

As the Middle Ages gave way to the Renaissance, knightly chivalry
gave way to the peacetime refinement, luxury, and etiquette of court life.
Ladies were won now not so much by fighting in battle or winning a
jousting match but by an elaborate courtship involving exquisite manners, wit, and conversation. Even so, love was not reduced to carnal self-
indulgence of the bawdy kind that we find in Ovid, Petronius, and the
other comic poets of the pagan era. The longing for an unattainable love
was still thought to stimulate finer and nobler passions than an easy tum-
ble in the hay. A man's fidelity to a lady with whom he was truly in love
was a better way of life than giving in to every passing carnal whim—although one could have more than one such romance!

With the rise of the Renaissance and, later, the Enlightenment,
chivalry was gradually transformed into the more secular conception of
the "gentleman." The ideal of the gentleman no longer rested primarily
on the bedrock of faith but returned to the worldly cultivation of man's

natural tastes, mental powers, and feelings explored in ancient Greek and Roman literature. The ancient writings on love that had scandalized the early Christians now started to make a comeback. So it is that Diotima's Ladder of Love passed down to Castiglione's influential Renaissance dialogue on manly refinement, *The Book of the Courtier*.

As Castiglione portrays the perfect gentleman, he must possess all the virtues praised by the ancients—prudence, justice, liberality, magnificence, honor, gentleness, pleasantness, and affability. According to one of the characters in the dialogue, Ottaviano, temperance is the basis for them all. But by temperance Ottaviano has in mind something very different from the grim Augustinian struggle to crush the desires. In order to experience the satisfaction of moderating our passions, he argues, we have to taste the passions in the first place. Being a prude isn't a sign of virtue, just of a dishrag with no strong emotions or longings to master.

> Therefore it is not well to extirpate the passions altogether in order to get rid of disturbances; for this would be like issuing an edict that no one must drink wine, in order to suppress drunkenness, or like forbidding everyone to run because in running we sometimes fall.

In other words, there's more to admire in a man who drinks moderately than in a teetotaler. The first man is tasting a pleasure in moderation, balancing his enjoyment of the senses with a devotion to the higher requirements of duty and intellect. He enjoys a fine wine. But he won't get so drunk that he's too hungover to work efficiently the next day. The teetotaler, by contrast, can't claim any kind of victory over unruly passions, because he's too lame to have any in the first place. When the passions are guided properly, they provide us with the energy we need for the virtues themselves. It's wrong to get angry for no good reason. But being incapable of anger is just as bad, because then you lack the guts and pluck to fight against bullies and evildoers. Reason must govern the passions like a rider who makes his horse obey. But a rider without a horse isn't going anywhere, just as reason without passions to furnish the energy to carry out its commands is weak and ineffectual:

> Note that those who tame horses do not prevent them from running and jumping, but have them do so at the right time and in obedience to the

rider. Hence, the passions, when moderated by temperance, are an aid to virtue, just as wrath aids fortitude, and as hatred of evildoers aids justice, and likewise the other virtues too are aided by the passions; which, if they were wholly taken away, would leave the reason weak and languid, so that it could effect little, like the master of a vessel abandoned by the winds and in a great calm.

With the spread of ideas like those found in *The Book of the Courtier*, women could be loved for their own sake, not necessarily as embodiments of the Virgin Mary. The ideal of knightly chivalry was gradually supplanted by the Renaissance ideal of courtliness. A man did not need to see his public role restricted to the grim contest of war and the strict code of honor attending it. Instead, a full man, a gentleman, was as much at home in the polished world of the court as on the battlefield, and could alternate with ease between martial valor and the gracious manners, style, wit, and flair of a cultivated man of leisure. He could lead an army one day, collect statuary the next, and then compose a sonata or translate an ancient poem into his own language.

The meaning of love underwent an equally profound transformation. Reaching back into Greek and Roman works like Plato's *Symposium* and Ovid's love poems, men came to see love in more purely human terms. A man could admire, revere, and long for a woman as a human being like himself, not as a symbol for the Virgin or an intermediary for his spiritual love of God. Authors like Castiglione open up a topic severely restricted in the Middle Ages: How might a man's love for a woman act as a purely sensual, this-worldly motive for him to perfect his own natural abilities so as to make himself worthy of her? The standard for manly self-perfection is as high as before. But the reward can be enjoyed in the here and now, not postponed to the afterlife. Ultimately, a man should love a woman for her virtues of mind and character, using them as a standard for measuring his own. He should not remain on the vulgar level of attraction to her physical beauty and to sexual pleasure alone. But, in contrast with the demands of chivalry and its ideal of chastity for both men and women, there's nothing wrong with enjoying those sensual delights to the fullest *before* one ascends the Ladder of Love to more worthy objects of desire. You can take some time hanging out on the lower rung. There's nothing sinful about bodily pleasures in themselves as long as you keep them in their proper place, subordinated to a man's more serious aspirations for honorable achievement and cultivation.

Let's look a little more closely at *The Book of the Courtier,* Castiglione's Renaissance version of the Platonic Ladder of Love. Another of the central characters in the dialogue, Cesare, speaks eloquently of how a man's erotic passion for a worthy lady gives him the strongest motive to aim for goodness. Without the softening influence of a woman, a man's life would be barbaric, and without her levelheaded and calming power, a man is prone to anger and melancholy:

> Who does not know that without women we can feel no contentment or satisfaction throughout this life of ours, which but for them would be rude and devoid of all sweetness and more savage than that of wild beasts? Who does not know that women alone banish from our hearts all vile and base thoughts, vexations, miseries, and those turbid melancholies that so often are their fellows?

Far from distracting a man from the great affairs of business and state, his love makes him better at achieving his ambitions, because he wants to shine in his lady's eyes:

> And, if you will consider well the truth, we shall also see that in our understanding of great matters women do not hamper our wits but rather quicken them, and in war make men fearless and brave beyond measure.

In fact, Cesare continues, *only* a lover has a serious crack at becoming a good man:

> And certainly it is impossible for vileness ever again to rule in a man's heart where once the flame of love has entered; for whoever loves desires always to make himself as lovable as he can, and always fears lest some disgrace befall him that may make him be esteemed lightly with her by whom he desires to be esteemed highly.

We've come a long way from St. Augustine!

Cesare's next point will please many readers of my generation and give them some verbal ammunition for the ever-increasing number of horny young whippersnappers who surround us, roaring past us in clouds of dust on the highway and plundering all the smaller sizes in clothing stores. Because a man's self-esteem depends upon his lady's admiration, older men make better lovers than younger men because they are more mature. Young men are understandably drawn to physical beauty alone. There's nothing wrong with that, Cesare says. Although such drives must be restrained, it's perfectly normal for a young man to feel them. But every sensible man is grateful for getting past the phase of raging hormones so that he can love a woman more for the beauties of her soul than for her body. That's the only way love can endure. Bodily beauty fades in both men and women. But when a man and a woman also love each other for the good qualities they bring to the partnership, their youthful passion will blossom into a lifelong friendship. That's why, when we have a proper understanding of erotic matters, maturity is more satisfying than sexual frenzy. As another of Castiglione's characters, Pietro, sums it up:

> It nearly always happens that young men are wrapped up in this love which is sensual and wholly rebellious to reason, and thus they become unworthy to enjoy the graces and benefits which love bestows upon its true subjects; nor do they feel any pleasures in love beyond those which the unreasoning animals feel, but anguish far more grievous.

By contrast, older men are better lovers because, in addition to remaining appreciative of a woman's bodily beauty, they long even more intensely for the beauty of her mind and character:

> Therefore their possession of it always brings them good, because beauty is good, and hence true love of beauty is most good and holy, and always works for good in the mind of those who restrain the perversity of sense with the bridle of reason; which the old can do much more easily than the young.

So throw away that Viagra and read a book!

The Romantic Lover

Finally, we come to Romanticism, the great modern watershed of eros. Beginning in the eighteenth century with Jean-Jacques Rousseau, the Romantic writers try to find a modern replacement for the almost vanished traditions of chivalry. Rousseau is looking for a way of returning to the austere dictates of Roman manliness and medieval knighthood on the basis of the modern secular individualism established by the Enlightenment. He believes that the Enlightenment has too narrow a conception of manly fulfillment, and that its emphasis on bourgeois economic competition and prosperity stultifies the human spirit.

Voltaire had famously argued that men should give up their old-fashioned duels and vendettas and their obsession with courage on the battlefield and turn to more peaceful economic pursuits. As he put it in *Candide,* "Cultivate your garden." But for Rousseau, the modern era's emphasis on individual self-advancement and the enjoyment of material goods had the effect of robbing other spheres of life of their sublimity, nobility, and self-sacrifice. If becoming prosperous and gratifying one's appetites is the order of the day, why not apply the same narrow hedonistic calculus to matters of the heart? Forget all that old-fashioned claptrap about serving your lady; just go out and get laid. "We scoff at the knights of old," he bitterly observes. "They knew the meaning of love. We know nothing but debauchery."

Rousseau believed that the Enlightenment had irrevocably stripped human nature of its religious beliefs and its unquestioning loyalty to the blood and soil of the fatherland. But given that there is no returning to the inspiring but vanished feudal and religious bonds of the past, he asks: Can human nature on its own become the basis for the spiritual richness and depth of passion that former ages derived from faith?

It is interesting that Rousseau concedes the authority of modern scientific and empirical rationality. Whereas the classical, medieval, and Renaissance teachings we considered earlier argued that the character-building powers of love were the reflection of a higher divine harmony in the universe, Rousseau grants that modern physics and materialism have established that those sublime conceptions of love are illusions that cannot be empirically verified. But given the choice between a rational truth that drains life of meaning and an illusion that enables us to live more nobly, he argues, we must choose illusion over truth. This is the essence of the Romantic credo.

> There is no real love without enthusiasm, and no enthusiasm without an object of perfection real or supposed, but always present in the imagination. What is there to kindle the hearts of lovers for whom this perfection is nothing, for whom the loved one is merely the means to sensual pleasure? Nay, not thus is the heart kindled, not thus does it abandon itself to those sublime transports which form the rapture of lovers and the charm of love.

In the earlier teachings, the Ladder of Love was taken to be an objectively real account, not only of human nature but of the universe at large. From Plato's original version of the erotic ascent down to the works of Renaissance admirers like Castiglione, the proper objects of erotic longing—family life, civic virtue, and divine transcendence—were considered to be not mere poetic enthusiasms or bursts of literary creativity but truths about the world, possessing as much objective validity as astronomy or mathematics. For Rousseau, by contrast, the objects that love longs to possess are illusions—and what's more, we Romantics *know* that they're illusions even as we pursue them! After the triumph of modern science, no one can believe that the universe is governed by divine reason. But it doesn't matter that the objects of erotic longing are mere figments of the artistic imagination. What matters is that these illusions of our own creation stir in us the deepest fervor of passion, tenderness, and devotion:

> Love is an illusion, I grant you, but its reality consists in the feelings it awakes, in the love of true beauty which it inspires. That beauty is not to be found in the object of our affections, it is the creation of our illusions. What matter! Do we not still sacrifice all those baser feelings to the imaginary model? And we still feed our hearts on the virtues we attribute to the beloved, we still withdraw ourselves from the baseness of human nature. What lover is there who would not give his life for his mistress? What gross and sensual passion is there in a man who is willing to die?

Rousseau and his followers sought to restore the chivalric and Renaissance credo of the man who perfects himself in order to prove worthy of a lady's love. At the same time, they realized that a man's idealization of a woman might be mainly the product of his own imagination, more a projection of himself on an imaginary ideal than a real woman. But that didn't matter. The Romantics say: If the illusion makes you a better, deeper, and more feeling man, choose illusion over truth. They wanted to recapture the mystery and transformative powers of love in order to compensate for what they saw as an increasingly materialistic, self-interested modern age. This is Rousseau's great project in the *Emile,* as much a novel as a philosophical work, and one of the first manifestos of Romanticism.

In the *Emile,* a young man perfects his own character through his devotion to a young woman he admires from afar. Rousseau appears in the novel as one of his own characters, and undertakes to raise the boy from earliest youth to manhood strictly on the basis of nature. Jean-Jacques, as the boy familiarly comes to know his tutor, takes Emile from his biological parents when he is a toddler and assumes a role in the boy's life akin to that of a benevolent deity with absolute control over his actions and environment. Emile is educated as a natural man, free from the corrupting pleasures of bourgeois materialism and the artificiality of Parisian and court society. His natural goodness and simplicity are fortified by an education in the great Greek and Roman classics, stressing manly valor, purity, moderation, simplicity, and modesty. One of the models Jean-Jacques provides for him is Telemachus, son of Odysseus and the hero in his own right of the *Telemacheiad,* the first five books of Homer's *Odyssey.*

The capstone of Emile's education is his passion for his future wife, Sophy. In Sophy he sees the virtues that he wants to cultivate in himself, and his longing to be worthy of her gives him the impetus to strive harder to perfect himself. She becomes his ideal. Serving and protecting Sophy and their future children will provide Emile with a passionate, sentimental motive for assuming his public role as a good bourgeois citizen. To a large extent, Rousseau concedes, Emile is idealizing a girl he barely knows. Nevertheless, she does possess spontaneous virtues of compassion and charity, rather like a secularized version of the Virgin

Mary. Her kind deeds among the local poor touch Emile deeply and so-
lidify his love for her.

Emile is attracted to Sophy because she is chaste and unattainable,
and also because she rounds out his own nature with qualities of composure, sensitivity, and modesty, which the naturally rambunctious young
man lacks but to which he is attracted precisely because they are different from his own qualities of soul. Emile's longing for Sophy turns him
overnight from a robust, rosy-cheeked boy completely satisfied with a
life of science experiments, carpentry lessons, and romping through the
woods into a budding Byron, full of moony sighs and transports:

> At the name of Sophy, you would have seen Emile give a start. His at-
> tention is arrested by her dear name, and he awakes all at once and looks
> eagerly at one who dares to bear it. "Sophy! Are you the Sophy whom my
> heart is seeking? Is it you that I love?"

Before falling in love with Sophy, Emile had a very practical bent. He
was good with tools and enjoyed learning math and science. But he was
completely unsentimental and, like many little boys, utterly uninterested
in sunsets, art, or the other beauties of nature and civilization pointlessly
urged upon them by adults. But now his passion for Sophy makes his
feelings and his imagination blossom:

> Behold him in the intoxication of a growing passion; his heart opens to
> the first beams of love; its pleasant fancies reveal to him a whole world of
> new delights and enjoyments; he loves a sweet woman, whose character
> is even more delightful than her person; he hopes, he expects the reward
> which he deserves.

Because Emile and Sophy learn to love and to honor each other before they even spend much time together at close range, before any
thought of physical passion enters their still-innocent minds, they are
friends before they become lovers. Consequently, once they are permitted to marry, they can abandon themselves to their sexual passion with
no feelings of shame or confusion. Sexual pleasure does not have to substitute for friendship, because their friendship was already in place.
Because their honor for each other is firmly in place before their love be-

comes physical, that mutual respect will remain as the fires of youthful passion give way to the steadier partnership of married life:

> Their first attachment took its rise in mutual affection, in community of honorable feelings; therefore this affection is lasting. It abandons itself, with confidence, with reason, to the most delightful madness, without fear, regret, remorse, or any other disturbing thought, but that which is inseparable from all happiness.

Emile finds in Sophy an ideal of repose, tranquillity, and sweetness that answers to his own erotic longing for completion. As a man and a woman, they are different but complementary, and equal in their essential human dignity and rights. Striving to win Sophy's love, to become lovable in her eyes, gives Emile the motive to make himself into a decent fellow, to work hard at his studies, and to reflect on the duties of citizens toward other citizens, since he longs to marry her and have their family take its place in the wider society. People need a motive to be good citizens—the private satisfactions of family life.

For her part, Sophy has always hoped to meet a young man like Telemachus, the stouthearted and steadfast son of Odysseus in Homer's epic poem the *Odyssey*. The flat-souled young men of the bourgeois era don't interest her:

> Sophy was in love with Telemachus, and loved him with a passion which nothing could cure. When her father and mother became aware of her infatuation, they laughed at it and tried to cure her by reasoning with her. They were mistaken, reason was not altogether on their side; Sophy had her own reason and knew how to use it. Many a time did she reduce [her parents] to silence by turning their own arguments against them, by showing them that it was all their own fault for not having trained her to suit the men of that century; that she would be compelled to adopt her husband's way of thinking or he must adopt hers, that they had made the former course impossible by the way she had been brought up, and that the latter was just what she wanted. "Give me," said she, "a man who holds the same opinions as I do, or one who will be willing to learn them from me, and I will marry him; but until then, why do you scold me? Pity

me; I am miserable, but not mad. Is the heart controlled by the will? Did
my father not ask that very question?"

Trying to sound reasonable to her parents, she assures them she
knows there is no real Telemachus in present-day France. She'll settle
for someone who comes close:

> Is it my fault if I love what has no existence? I am no visionary; I desire
> no prince, I seek no Telemachus, I know he is only an imaginary person;
> I seek someone like him. And why should there be no such person, since
> there is such a person as I, I who feel that my heart is like his? No, let us
> not wrong humanity so greatly, let us not think that an amiable and vir-
> tuous man is a figment of the imagination. He exists, he lives.

Jean-Jacques, who will soon educate Emile in Fénelon's retelling of
the story of Telemachus from the *Odyssey*, believes he has a suitable
candidate for Sophy. She is looking for a young hero, and once she meets
Emile, she believes she may have found him.

Rousseau brings us full circle because he attempts a return to the
Ladder of Love on the basis of modern egalitarianism. Not everyone approved of the attempt. The conservative thinker and statesman Edmund
Burke dismissed the *Emile* as a mixture of "lewdness and pedantry," and
sober rationalist that he was, generally deplored Rousseau's efforts to (as
we might now put it) remythologize the world. As Burke saw it,
Rousseau foolishly rejects the modern era's solid gains in liberty and enlightened self-interest in favor of a nostalgic journey back to ancient
dreamscapes of Spartan valor, misty forests, damsels in distress, and
knightly quests. Admittedly, there is something disconcerting in the
Emile about how a philosophical argument merges without warning into
a bucolic myth, with Rousseau inserting himself into his own narrative as
the character Jean-Jacques. One pictures him lurking in the shadows or
behind the hedgerow as he contrives to bring his blushing young ward
Emile together with the chaste and pure-minded Sophy. At times,
there's a bit of a voyeuristic undertone. When my wife and I studied the
Emile in a seminar with Allan Bloom, she and her girlfriends could
barely stifle their laughter at Rousseau's weird praise of Sophy's "little
feet—her precious little feet."

Still, if one can overlook the purple prose and somewhat overstrained literary effects, there's a very important point to it all. Sophy may have been dreaming of a young hero from the pages of Homer, but in Emile she gets a boy who is very much a product of the modern age. Before introducing Emile to his future bride, Jean-Jacques has brought him up as little more than a healthy animal, a country boy who can fend for himself. He has a good dose of math and science, and the first stirrings of an interest in Plutarch and the heroes of antiquity. But he also practices a trade, and Jean-Jacques has taught him to be frugal. He will not lead the life of a swashbuckler, a brilliant commander, or an exquisite gentleman of the court—he's a humble carpenter. He is named for a famous Roman general, Aemilius Paulus, who was praised in antiquity for the same balance of virtues that Cicero praised in Scipio Africanus the Younger and that Churchill was later to praise in Lawrence of Arabia. But young Emile is a rustic, and Sophy will learn to be content with the humbler, less spectacular virtues to which we more ordinary modern men and women can aspire.

On the basis of those more modest expectations, however, Rousseau is the first modern thinker to restore in its full pedagogical sweep the traditional maxim with which I began this discussion of the Western tradition of erotic longing: Love perfects. It is because Emile wants to be worthy of Sophy, in whom he sees all goodness, gentleness, and decency, that he overcomes his passions and is able to grow up. In her, he sees the virtues that he aspires to cultivate in himself, and his longing to be esteemed by Sophy gives him the impetus to strive harder to perfect himself. Above all, Rousseau argues, Emile will find his surest motive for joining civil society and fulfilling his duties as a citizen, husband, and father through his romantic passion for Sophy. The material rewards of modern individualism are not enough, either for a satisfying personal life or for a healthy democratic culture. Love is the link between the individual and the common good, and the family is the chief ennobler of modern liberty, preventing it from degenerating into mere profit seeking and materialistic self-indulgence.

In the wake of Rousseau, Romantic love is marked by two main themes. The first is what the filmmaker Luis Buñuel calls "the obscure object of desire." Romantic literature explores the ambivalent character of the beloved. How much of her is real? How much of her qualities am I projecting upon her? There is no simple answer. The other main theme is the conflict between the promptings of our natures—most fully revealed by erotic longing—and the demands of civilization and duty. For the earlier tradition, from Plato to Castiglione, no such conflict can or should exist. By ascending the Ladder of Love, we purify our own passions and invest them in the higher and more lasting pleasures of the soul; and by improving our own characters in order to prove worthy of the beloved, we also cultivate precisely those virtues required of us as decent citizens and loyal members of society. For the Romantics, by contrast, there is always an agonizing contradiction between the lusts and longings that rage in us and the sobriety and restraint we need to be dutiful citizens and husbands.

This tension between nature and duty is beautifully evoked in some of Mozart's operas. *The Magic Flute,* for instance, offers us two paths to love. On the one hand, the simple rustic bird-catcher Papageno is like Rousseau's version of man as he is in the state of nature, free from the burdens of civilization, refinement, and ambition. Although Papageno has no great virtues, he has no wish to harm others. He spends his time chasing girls and trying to stay out of trouble. His master, by contrast, the heroic young Tamino, is an ideal knight-errant who displays his courage and devotion by rescuing Pamina, a damsel in distress, from her evil abductor, the ogre Monostatos. In order to prove worthy of her, Tamino must undergo a variety of physical and spiritual trials, including a long ritual of purification during which only noble thoughts can prevent him from being devoured by the flames. And yet, in the end, Mozart offers no firm judgment as to which path to happiness is better—the innocent frolics of the horny bird-catcher or the ardent self-sacrifice of the brave young knight. This ambivalence would have been unthinkable for the chivalric tradition, which would have relegated the sidekick Papageno to a worthy but lowly role in comparison with the higher perfection of the knight. For Mozart, however, nature and duty take us along different paths. By playing the magic flute, an old symbol of the rites of Dionysus, the ardent young knight is able to unlock his own emotional life and, by rounding out his character, prove himself worthy of Pamina's love. But when Tamino, upon learning that his damsel in distress Pamina is still alive, plays the magic flute in joy, Papageno echoes the melody on his own more rustic pan pipe. He spontaneously enjoys the satisfaction his master must strive to achieve through disciplined self-overcoming.

Another version of the erotic tensions between nature and civilization comes to us in Mozart's *Marriage of Figaro.* This opera is a kind of harbinger of the coming reign of Romanticism and its displacement of the Enlightenment's code of gentlemanly polish and worldliness. Most of the opera is a bedroom farce in which Count Almaviva tries to seduce the young women who serve in his household, particularly Susanna, the fiancée of his valet, Figaro. As older men, both the Count and his servant detest the beautiful young Cherubino, a boy who looks like an angel but who is horny as hell, and who is doted on and petted by the ladies of the household, amused at the ease with which they can tease and tickle him into a frenzy of adolescent lust. The tone is lighthearted and a little jaded, expressive of the Enlightenment's tolerance and sophistication in matters of adultery and illicit passion, reaching back into the amorous verse of Petronius and Ovid. And yet, at the very end, there is a stunning shift of musical and moral tone. Trapped into a confession of his infidelities, Count Almaviva realizes that he does not want to lose the love of his wife. The jaded and witty amorality of the opera shatters as the Count sincerely begs forgiveness from his long-suffering spouse, who throughout the opera has been hiding her heartache and humiliation under the requisite Enlightenment facade of amusement and good manners. The deliciously shimmering tone of the music changes in the last few minutes, swelling into the ethereal sound of the Mass as the Countess utters her immortal and sublimely compassionate lines: "I forgive you. I am kinder than you." She is a secular version of the Virgin, the embodiment of suffering and redemption through forgiveness. In this stunning reversal, we see the beginning of the Romantics' creed: Modernity has made love too jaded by sacrificing depth of feeling, self-restraint, and delicacy.

The tension between love and duty remains a staple of Romantic literature. Perhaps its most mature and satisfying exploration comes in the novels of Tolstoy. Although some of the Romantics appear to revel in a passion that completely alienates a man from society, Tolstoy offers a more balanced appraisal of the gains and losses of illicit love. In *Anna Karenina,* he gives us the story of a woman who is dissatisfied with her marriage and a man who, as a professional soldier in a time of peace, has no outlet for his energies. She is tired of keeping up appearances, and he is tired of cardplaying and boozing in the officers' club. Anna's husband, Prince Karenin, is a high-ranking civil servant gravely devoted to his duties. But while he is reserved to a fault, he's not a monster. Tolstoy will not give us the easy way out of contrasting an oppressed wife with a monstrous husband. In leaving the marriage, she knowingly deserts her child and a husband who, although not exciting or emotionally forthcoming, treats her with respect and gives her wide leeway to live her own life. Her lover, Vronsky, must abandon his career in order to live with her abroad. Both end up bored and empty. An overwhelming passion, Tolstoy implies, does not always make up for the fulfillment that comes from family, career, and civic duty. Sometimes compromise with a less than perfect marriage will bring a man and a woman more contentment and peace of mind over the long run than throwing it all away for a brief interlude of spontaneous and unlimited passion—a fire that, because it burns so intensely, is doomed to burn out quickly.

PASSION RESTRAINED: JANE AUSTEN'S DISSENT

Our final exploration of love takes us to the novels of Jane Austen and reminds us that women are sometimes the best authorities on the meaning of manliness. Austen casts a cool eye on the Romantic world of gloomy heaths, moonlit graveyards, deserted abbeys, and Byronic torment. With her, we enter the clear sunlight and pale blue skies of the English home counties, with their green, ordered meadows, refined manners, and financial solvency. In this world, love between a man and a woman is certainly something to be desired—but not at the sacrifice of all sense of proportion and one's obligations to family and rank. In *Sense and Sensibility* she offers a discriminating assessment of two sisters, the levelheaded and responsible Elinor, and Marianne with her swirling scarves and tempests of Romantic feeling. Of the two sisters, who personify sense and sensibility respectively, Austen clearly prefers Elinor and sense. *Sensibility,* after all, is the term Rousseau had used to encourage us to trust our feelings even when they contradict the evidence of reason—in the *Emile,* specifically, to prefer the romantic illusion of an all-consuming passion to the quotidian reality of mature and rational affection.

For Austen, Rousseau and the Romantics pose a false choice between unreflecting passion and coldhearted reason. *Pride and Prejudice* is, among other things, a decisive riposte to Romantic accounts of love originating with the *Emile.* When Mr. Darcy first proposes marriage to Elizabeth Bennet, she is angered by his conspicuous lack of gallantry. As she sees it, Darcy is acting as if he would be doing her a favor to marry her, since his wealth and lineage so greatly exceed her own. Her revulsion is increased by what she takes to be Darcy's obstruction of her sister Jane's relationship with his friend Mr. Bingley, and his apparent injustice to the dashing young soldier Wickham. Every nuance of reasoning and feeling is precisely expressed.

Mr. Darcy begins:

"In vain have I struggled. It will not do. My feelings will not be repressed. You must allow me to tell you how ardently I admire and love you."

Elizabeth's astonishment was beyond expression. She stared, colored, doubted, and was silent. This he considered sufficient encouragement, and the avowal of all that he felt and had long felt for her, immediately followed. He spoke well, but there were feelings besides those of the heart to be detailed, and he was not more eloquent on the subject of tenderness than of pride. His sense of her inferiority—of its being a degradation—of the family obstacles which judgment had always opposed to inclination, were dwelt on with a warmth which seemed due to the consequence he was wounding, but was very unlikely to recommend his suit.

When he ceased, the color rose into her cheeks, and she said . . . , "If I could *feel* gratitude, I would now thank you. But I cannot—I have never desired your good opinion, and you have certainly bestowed it most unwillingly. I am sorry to have occasioned pain to any one. It has been most unconsciously done, however, and I hope will be of short duration. The feelings which, you tell me, have long prevented the acknowledgment of your regard, can have little difficulty in overcoming it after this explanation."

Extremely wealthy and from an old and distinguished family, Mr. Darcy is one of the most eligible bachelors in England. He believes he has behaved nobly by overcoming his perfectly intelligible objections to marrying so far beneath him, ready to sacrifice every advantage of rank in order to act purely out of love, as a gentleman should do. He expects not only that Elizabeth will agree to marry him but that she will admire him for being so selfless. In Elizabeth's eyes, however, Mr. Darcy seems to view his capacity to love her as an act of condescension to an inferior, and a source of self-congratulation. He is profoundly shocked by her refusal of his proposal.

> Darcy, who was leaning against the mantel-piece with his eyes fixed on her face, seemed to catch her words with no less resentment than surprise. His complexion became pale with anger, and the disturbance of his mind was visible in every feature. He was struggling for the appearance of composure, and would not open his lips, till he believed himself to have attained it. The pause was to Elizabeth's feelings dreadful. At length, in a voice of forced calmness, he said, "And this is all the reply which I am to have the honor of expecting! I might, perhaps, wish to be informed why, with so little *endeavor* at civility, I am thus rejected. But it is of small importance."

> "I might as well enquire," replied she, "why with so evident a design of offending and insulting me, you chose to tell me that you liked me against your will, against your reason, and even against your character?"

When Darcy proposes for a second time, both he and Elizabeth acknowledge the faults they displayed during his first proposal. Each has shown a measure of pride and prejudice toward the other. Darcy redeems himself by proving correct in his low opinion of the cad Wickham (who elopes with Elizabeth's foolish sister, the boy-crazy Lydia) and by his generosity in helping the Bennets deal with the subsequent scandal. For her part, Elizabeth is forced to the mortifying reflection that Mr.

Darcy was partly justified in his criticisms of her mother's vulgarity and her father's neglect of his daughters' upbringing. She tries to apologize for misjudging him:

> "Mr. Darcy, I am a very selfish creature; and, for the sake of giving relief to my own feelings, care not how much I may be wounding yours. I can no longer help thanking you for your unexampled kindness to my poor sister. Ever since I have known it, I have been most anxious to acknowledge to you how gratefully I feel it. Were it known to the rest of my family, I should not have merely my own gratitude to express."

> "If you *will* thank me," he replied, "let it be for yourself alone. That the wish of giving happiness to you, might add force to the other inducements which led me on, I shall not attempt to deny. But your *family* owe me nothing. Much as I respect them, I believe, I thought only of *you*."

He will not allow her to apologize; the fault was all his for his earlier inept proposal:

> "What did you say of me, that I did not deserve? For, though your accusations were ill-founded, formed on mistaken premises, my behavior to you at the time, had merited the severest reproof. It was unpardonable. I cannot think of it without abhorrence."

> "We will not quarrel for the greater share of blame annexed to that evening," said Elizabeth. "The conduct of neither, if strictly examined, will be irreproachable; but since then, we have both, I hope, improved in civility."

The young lady and gentleman, certain now that their future happiness as husband and wife is secure, have the sweet experience—known only to lovers—of competing with each other to ask forgiveness. It's one of the few situations in life where confessing your own failings is both enjoyable and profitable, since in owning up to your faults, you prove to your beloved that you are trying to be a good person, someone worthy of his or her love, and because the willingness to forgive your failings proves how desirable you are to your beloved in other respects. When we love a person, we overlook faults that would make us dismiss anybody

else, because that person's lovable attributes make the vices worth over-
looking—as long, of course, as the person really *does* try to reform.
Darcy continues gallantly to castigate himself:

> "I cannot be so easily reconciled to myself. The recollection of what I
> then said, of my conduct, my manners, my expressions during the whole
> of it, is now, and has been many months, inexpressibly painful to me.
> Your reproof, so well applied, I shall never forget: 'had you behaved in a
> more gentleman-like manner.' These were your words. You know not,
> you can scarcely conceive, how they have tortured me; though it was
> some time, I confess, before I was reasonable enough to allow their
> justice."

Elizabeth now regrets that her earlier words were so stinging:

> "I was certainly very far from expecting them to make so strong an im-
> pression. I had not the smallest idea of their being ever felt in such a
> way."

But Darcy doesn't want her to retract her earlier rebuke. He believes
he fully deserved it:

> "I can easily believe it. You thought me then devoid of every proper feel-
> ing, I am sure you did. The turn of your countenance I shall never for-
> get, as you said that I could not have addressed you in any possible way,
> that would induce you to accept me."

> "Oh! Do not repeat what I then said" [she replied]. "These recollections
> will not do at all. I assure you, that I have long been most heartily
> ashamed of it."

The genius of this book is that it shows the importance of men and
women *talking* to each other about themselves. In contrast with the
wordless swooning of Emile, Austen's characters are constantly discussing the events of their lives. This kind of dialogue is very different
from our recent trendy fixation on "communicating" with each other and
"being real." What this generally means is that I say what's bothering me
and what I want, and then you do the same. Austen reminds us that, on

the contrary, genuine communication between a man and a woman must be a dialogue unfolding over months and years, governed by patience and a willingness to bite your tongue if too much candor will hurt your partner and bring the exchange to a premature end. Learning about each other takes time and a measure of discretion. By learning to be friends before they marry, Elizabeth and Darcy form a realistic expectation of their future lives together—tender but not sentimental, willing to give and take without expecting perpetual bliss.

I find that my male students, who range in age from eighteen to about thirty, respond differently to these sorts of books as they grow older. The youngest undergraduates are likely to prefer something like Homer's *Iliad,* with its tales of war and pride. Those who are a little older like the *Emile,* partly because the speechless obsession of Emile's love for Sophy is akin to their own experience, and partly because Rousseau himself was such a wild man (a street kid who ended up a celebrity pursued by a succession of wealthy aristocratic ladies). The most mature students eventually discover Jane Austen, having previously dismissed her as a "women's writer." Not coincidentally, this often happens as they are settling into long-term relationships and thinking about marriage, the major theme of every one of Austen's books. Having mistakenly imagined a woman writing page after page about tea parties and cucumber sandwiches, many students are surprised by how wickedly funny she is, and how deeply insightful into the characters of both men and women.

Nothing can match Austen's combination of dry-as-tinder exactitude as she pitilessly exposes the foibles of her fellow humans with her large-hearted sympathy for the quandaries young people face when they embark on the odyssey of a life together. Austen has a rare ability to let her characters make asses of themselves without any interference on her part, as in the lugubrious Mr. Elton's ill-fated proposal to Emma Woodhouse and her scrambling effort—while trapped with him in a carriage—to find just the right words to crush his ludicrous impulse beyond any hope of renewal in a way that does not exceed the bounds of good manners. What my male students discover to be most charming is how silly Austen's female characters sometimes find men, with their strutting bids for attention. They begin to realize that their own girlfriends and wives have sometimes been indulging the same kind of silliness in them. For a man to see himself through a woman's eyes, and to imagine how he might appall or amuse her, is the real beginning of growing up.

Readers may object that I have posed a false extreme between the kinds of love endorsed by Rousseau and Austen, as if we must choose between irrational passion and a perhaps too mild and bloodless affection. So let me add that the delicacy of courtly love can still surface in the more pragmatic world of modernity. Edith Wharton's novel *The Age of Innocence* is an unforgettable story of a respectable young man's unfulfilled passion for a not quite respectable European lady of American origins, Countess Olenska. It offers a compromise between Rousseau and Austen. Can a man be in the grip of a passion for a woman that does not completely overwhelm him but affects him deeply enough that he does not act with complete rationality or express himself with the precision of a Mr. Darcy? In Newland Archer, Wharton offers us just such a balance of outward conformity to duty and inward pangs of regret over what might have been; such feelings deepen and enrich his inner life even as he finds a kind of happiness in devotion to his wife and family. He is like a Vronsky who is tempted by Anna Karenina but, in the end, walks away; like a Mr. Darcy who marries Elizabeth but harbors a tinge of regret forever after over not taking a more daring course with his life.

Years after Newland flirts with the idea of an affair with the Countess, having succumbed to the expectations of his family and class and made a good marriage, he goes to Paris with his son and considers visiting the Countess. He makes it to her building in the handsome quarter near the Invalides, but he cannot bring himself to go up. After years of wondering whether he made the right decision by sacrificing an illicit passion to the responsibilities of family and social standing, he realizes that the memory of what *might* have been between the Countess and him is more beautiful than the reality of such an affair could ever have been. He has done the right thing by marrying sensibly and within his class, as Austen would recommend. But he still feels a Romantic remorse for the illicit passion he might have enjoyed. In the end, his chief consolation is savoring the memory of this never-realized erotic temptation. He did not destroy himself and his family; his pang for the temptation avoided is a keener sensation after all these years than the actual pleasure could possibly have remained, had it been consummated. He did not actually taste the overpowering carnal delights enjoyed by Count Vronsky and Anna Karenina when they abandoned every tie to family and society as they acted on their illicit longing. But Newland Archer did not suffer the brutal sense of emptiness and disappointment experienced by Tolstoy's lovers when the fires of passion died down and they realized they had burned every bridge back to the more enduring if calmer satisfactions of marriage, family, career, and a place in society.

The final lines of *The Age of Innocence* are among the most moving evocations of the balanced rewards and sacrifices of manly duty in American (or any) literature:

> Archer sat down on the bench and continued to gaze at the awninged balcony. . . . Then he tried to see the persons already in the room—for probably at that sociable hour there would be more than one—and among them a dark lady, pale and dark, who would look up quickly, half rise, and hold out a long thin hand with three rings on it. . . . He thought she would be sitting in a sofa-corner near the fire, with azaleas banked behind her on a table.
>
> "It's more real to me here than if I went up," he suddenly heard himself say; and the fear lest that last shadow of reality should lose its edge kept him rooted to his seat as the minutes succeeded each other.
>
> He sat for a long time on the bench in the thickening dusk, his eyes never turning from the balcony. At length a light shone through the windows, and a moment later a man-servant came out on the balcony, drew up the awnings, and closed the shutters.
>
> At that, as if it had been the signal he waited for, Newland Archer got up slowly and walked back alone to his hotel.

CONCLUSION: LOVE OR JUSTICE?

These journeys into the complexities of eros and how the elixir of love can improve the soul all lead to one compelling conclusion—that it is precisely in these traditional understandings of manly passion and the refinement of erotic longing that we will find the surest means for encouraging respect between men and women. All the sources we have explored in this chapter see love as a partnership. Men and women contribute different virtues to the common whole that makes up their life together. This approach is far likelier to succeed in promoting friendship among young people today than focusing exclusively on the legally enforceable rights of the individual. It goes without saying that women and men should have equal rights as individuals to excel and earn the rewards of talent and hard work. In instances of oppression, unequal pay, or domestic violence, everyone must have recourse to the full protection and enforcement of those rights in law. But there is more to love and friendship than rights. Loving and respectful human ties include the rights of the individual. Unlike other spheres of life, however—business transactions, crime prevention, or the protection of our basic civil liberties—love and friendship cannot rely exclusively on legal rights. They must ultimately be based on virtues of mutual trust and gratitude between the partners, and the harmony of the differing but complementary qualities they bring to the couple, family, or friendship.

Our contemporary confusion over these matters is perhaps best summed up by the use of the term "relationship." A relationship can be about anything—real estate transactions, investing in the stock market, bringing a civil suit, buying a car. But love is not a subset of all relationships. It is unique. To treat love as a subset of all relationships is to imply that its problems can be approached in the same way as a dispute over a real estate deal or the violation of due process. However, when love becomes synonymous with the assertion of a right, the affection disappears. Marriage becomes interchangeable with a business transaction. The difficulty with this approach is that, in families, people treat one another well, including respecting their rights, as a *consequence* of their affection for one another and out of a sense of duty. As soon as you *demand* that a spouse, friend, or partner love you, the love vanishes (it's exactly the same principle with gratitude—if you have to extract it, it's gone). I can readily recognize and even act to protect the rights of other people. But that does not imply that I love them. Indeed, as a matter of taste and preference, I would prefer to have no intimate contact at all with most of them. When I treat loved ones well, by contrast, it is because I love them, not primarily or exclusively because I respect their rights, although my love *includes* respecting their rights just as thoroughly as I respect the rights of my fellow citizens in my more distant ties to the society around me. The observance of rights can be enforced and compelled. But love is never coerced.

II.

COURAGE

HAVE YOU EVER MET A BOYOSAURUS? THAT IS THE TERM COINED BY the Canadian journalist Joseph Brean to describe something that everyone has observed about boys:

> Film makers and paleontologists have long known this simple fact to be true: Boys love dinosaurs. Boys are suckers for loud roars and inaccurate computer-generated terror. They shudder in their seats. They have the nightmares. They buy the toys.

The love of young boys for maximum dinosaur violence is recognized by the film industry. According to the anthropologist Douglass Drozdow–St. Christian, "The first *Jurassic Park* was a girl's movie, because it had a strong environmentalist theme." The third installment of the series, by contrast, was marketed exclusively to boys, because "this one is about fear and conquering monsters."

Girls and boys relate to their dinosaurs in very different ways. Girls want to nurture them. Boys want to become their comrades. According to Joseph Brean, when boys visit museums, "they expect the dinosaurs to be large and vicious. . . . Girls, on the other hand, like to imagine taking the vegetarian hadrosaur home as a pet." Gayle Gibson, who spent eleven years leading the dinosaur tours at the Royal Ontario Museum in Toronto, sums up her experience of thousands of kids' visits: "For the girls, a dinosaur is kind of a secret friend, but for the boys it's a secret protector."

I can confirm these stories with my own tour of that same dinosaur skeleton collection with my ten-year-old nephew. Nothing in the museum interested him more than the dinosaurs, and he asked the guide dozens of questions. By contrast, when it came time to look at the rock collections, he literally fell prone to the floor with boredom. Only the Egyptian mummies interested him half as much, and then it was mainly the mummy of a small boy that caught his eye. He asked me if we could do that to his younger brother. (I said no.)

As I read these reports about boys and dinosaurs, one phrase jumped out at me: that boys liked *Jurassic Park III* because it was about "fear and conquering monsters." As we'll see in this chapter, that in a nutshell sums up many discussions of courage in the Western tradition. Courage is a virtue we summon out of ourselves when confronted with someone or something terrifying.

But is courage a trait we should really be encouraging in boys? Is it, in fact, a virtue, as the traditional view from Homer, Aristotle, and the Bible to Theodore Roosevelt and JFK has consistently maintained? Or does any praise for the use of force merely serve to exacerbate what is already a strong built-in tendency in boys to be violent? Instead of praising some kinds of aggression as virtuous, should we perhaps be working harder to get rid of it altogether?

As numerous studies demonstrate, boys are certainly more prone than girls to spontaneous aggressiveness and combativeness. This trait can have its lighter side, as seen in the boyosaurus. But it's not always a laughing matter. Sometimes little boys who are fascinated with the power of a *Tyrannosaurus rex* grow into older boys who actually want to destroy people they perceive to be their foes. Many times throughout the 1990s, the same ghastly scenario unfolded—an underfathered young man suddenly and without any previous signs of violence sprays his classmates and teachers with bullets.

The most notorious case involved Timothy McVeigh, the product of a broken home, who looked for something to blame for his terminal drift and rootlessness, and decided his own government was the oppressor. The result was a libertarian Jihad fed by the fantasies of the lunatic Right that the American government is in fact the "Zionist occupying authority," suppressing individual liberties on behalf of the world Jewish conspiracy. But often there's no ideological or political motivation. The killers at Columbine and other high schools were usually just kids who felt excluded from the In Crowd of the beautiful and the athletic—Tom

Sawyer in fatigues, hefting an assault rifle in place of the more innocent slingshot.

Parents, educators, and political leaders have all agonized over these developments as signs that the culture is in crisis. Some have made the case that virtual violence in video games and action movies has become a model for real life. Young men who, in a previous era, would have picked a fistfight, or confined their anger to their private feelings, now find it all too easy to make a direct transition from the violence that washes over them from TV, movies, and video games into their own situations, and to apply the methods of a Rambo in their own suburban enclaves.

To me, there is little doubt that this entertainment culture of virtual violence contributes to an atmosphere that prompts real-life rampage killings. There may not be a direct cause-and-effect relationship: It may not be possible to demonstrate, with complete empirical rigor, that Person A killed Person B because Person A watched Movie C. But the virtual violence does have an indirect and corrosive effect on morality. Its endless stream of fantasies of solitary omnipotence and open-ended violence cannot help but undermine those ethical and psychological mechanisms of self-restraint which a civilized society must ingrain in all its members.

According to Charles Mandel, a journalist specializing in the entertainment culture, a recent study shows that "roughly one in four children is addicted to [video] gaming (specifically, 24 per cent play between seven and thirty hours a week)." And what games they are. How many parents, Mr. Mandel asks, know what their kids are playing on the computer? Here's an example:

> Duke Nukem runs forward, grabs the shotgun and pumps a round into the chamber. "Groovy," intones the video-game hero in his gravelly voice, just before he starts blasting alien scum into a gory pulp.

Sound violent? Mandel continues:

> Not to some video-game developers, apparently. Major U.S. software companies are about to make such infamous "splatter" games as Duke Nukem and Doom seem like child's play as they prepare to release a new

wave of titles this fall that enable players to manipulate photorealistic images of humans into acts of torture, mutilation and even—if you can believe it—prostitution.

One of the innovators in digitalized carnage is Interplay Productions, whose sales for the previous six months had been $81 million. Now you don't have to proceed directly to massacring your enemies. You can have some extra fun by torturing them first! Mandel goes on:

> Interplay Productions proudly promotes its Wild 9 as the first-ever ac-
> tion game that encourages players to torture enemies. Shiny Enter-
> tainment, a subsidiary of Interplay, is completing work on Messiah, a
> game in which a cherub tries to cleanse the world of corruption. "Ever
> seen a body with 10,000 volts run through it?" the game's advertising slo-
> gan teases. "Want to?" Not to be outdone, Virgin Interactive is set to re-
> lease Thrill Kill, a series of gladiator-style battles between demented
> characters that bite and tear at each other in a torture-chamber setting.

Lieutenant Colonel Dave Grossman, a retired infantry officer and an expert on the psychology of violence, has labored tirelessly to alert parents to the corrosive effects of what he calls "television's virus of violence." He believes there is a direct link between television's glamorization of violence and the search for recognition by alienated boys through rampage killings of the kind that took place at Columbine High.

What disturbs him the most is the resemblance he sees between television violence and techniques used by the Marines and other military organizations to desensitize soldiers to the moral impact of inflicting death in combat. Killing loses its horror when it becomes a repetitive act carried out against enemies whom you are conditioned to regard as completely alien to yourself. However, while the military uses these techniques only in the dire situation of war, the last resort of national self-defense, television and other electronic media desensitize young men to the existence of their own fellow citizens, schoolmates, and parents. And, of course, while professional soldiers are taught to direct their ability to kill beyond U.S. borders, restricted to those comparatively rare episodes when foreign combatants imperil Americans, the climate of violence fed by the entertainment culture spreads indiscriminately to target one's own fellow citizens.

By a strange coincidence, Jonesboro, Arkansas, where one of the school shootings took place, is Colonel Grossman's hometown. It is a cruel irony that his worst fears about the "virus of violence" spread among young men by the entertainment culture were played out in the ghastliest way in the small town to which he returned after retiring from the Marines. He writes:

> Before retiring here, I spent almost a quarter of a century as an army infantry officer and a psychologist, learning how to enable people to kill. Believe me, we are very good at it. And just as the army enables killing, we are doing the same thing to our kids—but without the military's safeguards.

He believes that violence has been trivialized by its prevalence on television, to the point where the young people watching it cannot distinguish between the fantasy version and the real thing:

> The TV networks are responsible for traumatizing and brutalizing our children as they watch violent acts—a thousand a month, according to the latest research financed by the cable industry itself—at a young, vulnerable age when they cannot tell the difference between reality and fantasy. Children really only know what they have been taught, and we have taught them, ever so cleverly, to laugh and cheer at violence. In Jonesboro, we saw an indication of just how good a job we have done.

Even when they confront it directly, children can confuse real-life violence with something they've seen on a screen and react as if they were detached spectators enjoying a completely fictitious act of carnage. Grossman witnessed this creepy spectacle firsthand in the aftermath of the Jonesboro incident:

> I spent the first three days after the shooting at Westside Middle School, counseling teachers, students, and parents. One high school teacher told me about the reaction she got when she informed her students that someone was shooting at their little brothers, sisters, and cousins in

the middle school. "They laughed," she told me in amazement. "They laughed." We have raised a generation of barbarians who have learned to associate violence with pleasure, like the Romans who cheered and snacked as the Christians were slaughtered in the Colosseum.

As accounts like this one make disturbingly clear, before we can think about how best to prevent young men from committing acts of pointless violence, we have to think about why they may be psychologically prone to them. We must pose the disturbing but crucial question: Is warlike aggression natural to man? Only if we know why men are warlike will we know how to direct their courage toward good aims and away from bad ones.

Even posing this question goes against a powerful grain in our academic culture and the opinion elites influenced by it. Some believe that the use of force is always regrettable—that there is no ethical distinction between using force for just and unjust purposes. People holding this view are often drawn to the idea that warlike behavior can be explained only by an involuntary biological drive in males, since it falls beyond the pale of rational discussion or moral justification under any circumstances. Typical of this reductionist approach is a recent study by the psychologists Neil Wiener and Christian Mesquida. "How do you explain the universality of war?" Dr. Wiener asks. "It's ubiquitous." Using demographic data provided by the United Nations to compare war zones in El Salvador, Northern Ireland, Croatia, Kosovo, Albania, and Chechnya, he and his colleague came up with a single answer: "Wars are not triggered by ideology or religion, but by a society that has too many young, unmarried men."

This kind of broad empirical generalization has the seductive appeal of providing a single answer for the occurrence of violence everywhere in the world. Unfortunately, upon reflection, I believe it obscures rather than clarifies the nature of war and courage. Drs. Wiener and Mesquida begin by setting aside the complex conditions that make each war zone they analyzed unique. They take what is in fact the least interesting and informative characteristic in every one of these cases—the predominance of unmarried males under thirty years old—and elevate it to the most interesting and informative characteristic. But in each case studied, what is primarily motivating the belligerents is their conviction that they are fighting for honor, justice, and the dignity of their people or faith. These views are in turn rooted in complicated competing views of the histories of the opposing sides—how each side interprets the cultural, religious, and ethnic experiences of its people, perceptions of oppression, insult, and grievance, culminating in a feeling on both sides of justified zealotry and the need to reestablish dignity and freedom. In short, contrary to what the researchers maintain, wars *are* "triggered by ideology and religion." Any psychology of male aggression must be able to comprehend those deeper motives.

In order to arrive at the simplistic and reductionist conclusion that all wars are "caused" by young males, we have to set aside our entire accumulated knowledge of history, politics, and civilizational clashes. We have to ignore the reasoned opinions that belligerents advance to justify their cause in favor of the view that wars are driven by a dumb subrational compulsion akin to the need to eat. Above all, the empirical approach prevents us from arriving at a substantive conception of male psychology that includes an understanding of courage as a virtue connected to the aspiration for honor and the service of justice. When we look at war and violence from that perspective, we find that the predominance of young males is not the *cause* of war but its *effect*. Men don't fight wars because they're young. Men fight wars because a desire for justice, honor, and human dignity is intrinsic to human nature, and that desire is often threatened, challenged, or derided by other people or by external events. Fighting wars for those reasons requires young men. Wars are caused by the need to fight for justice.

IS WAR NATURAL?

Of all the traditional virtues, none is more directly connected with manhood than courage in war. Indeed, in both ancient Greek and Latin, the words for courage are synonyms of the words for manly virtue in general. *Andreia*, the Greek word for courage, is derived from the word for a "manly man"—*aner*, somewhat like the Spanish word *hombre*. A manly man is understood in contrast with a mere "human being" (*anthropos*), the undistinguished mass of mankind, including women, children,

slaves, and others who did not have the privilege of bearing arms. As for
Latin, the word for a manly man (*vir*) is connected to the term for virtue
of any kind (*virtus*), as if all excellence of character can be summed up
under the heading of manly courage.

Now, to be sure, the full story of the traditional morality of manhood
is a good deal more complicated. The ancient philosophers argue that
courage is a necessary but not sufficient condition for becoming a fully
virtuous man. Every man needs to acquire courage in order to defend
his country in war. According to the Western tradition, bravery in a just
war is entirely to be admired and deserves public honor and commemo-
ration in art and literature. From pagan philosophers like Aristotle
through the great Christian theologians including St. Augustine and St.
Thomas Aquinas to the present day, a just war has meant the defense of
one's country from an unprovoked attack or the defense of the weak and
innocent in another land against an external or internal oppressor. (The
Clinton administration's action in Kosovo to rescue the minority Muslim
population from genocide, for example, would certainly qualify as the
latter.) Courage in this kind of war was deemed virtuous. By contrast, the
deliberate slaughter of noncombatants, unprovoked attacks on a country
that has done you no palpable harm, and sneak attacks on civilian targets
with no military significance have been deemed unjust wars and ignoble
acts. Fighting on that side was a vice, no matter how much ferocity or
cunning you displayed, or even if you risked your life. The same is true of
the great religions of the world. All of them have an honored place for
courage in a just cause, and all of them decry wars of unprovoked aggression and the deliberate killing of noncombatants.

At the same time, however, these traditional authorities are also
pretty much unanimous in ranking courage as being among the lowest
virtues. If we educate boys and young men only to be courageous, they
say, we run the risk of rearing savages who are fit only for fighting. When
they lack a foreign foe, they will turn on their own kind rather than live
in peace. That is why Aristotle's praise of Sparta, for example—of all
Greek city-states the one most completely dedicated to honoring the
"manly men"—was so lukewarm. The Spartans were good soldiers. But
they lacked the higher virtues that made a man in full—moderation,
generosity, pride, justice, civic-spiritedness, and a liberal education in

the civilizing influences of poetry, science, and history, all combining to engage in informed deliberations about the common good. Pericles, the great wartime leader of Athens during its long geopolitical rivalry with Sparta, makes a similar point in his famous Funeral Oration praising Athenian democracy. Our foes, the Spartans, he says, know only how to fight. Otherwise, they're crude, ignorant, intolerant, xenophobic, distrustful of intellectuals, don't know how to enjoy themselves, and can't converse—a bit like Klingons. (That's my comparison, not that of Pericles.) We Athenians, by contrast, have a gracious way of life, we enjoy the pleasures of the senses, we admire beauty, wit, and learning, we support culture and the arts—and we can still whip the Spartans' butts any time we feel like it.

So the praise for courage in the Western tradition is limited. It's the baseline qualification for being a true man. But it's not an end in itself—it's more like a starting point for building a deeper and broader strength of character. Even so, it would never have occurred to these traditional authorities to argue that we could do entirely *without* educating boys to be courageous, or that a healthy society could deliberately *avoid* honoring its brave soldiers. Unlike our contemporary doctrines of behavior modification, it was not a question of getting rid of the "competitive" traits in boys—their spontaneous desire to wrestle, yell, and play army. Instead, it was a matter of channeling those spontaneous energies away from bad purposes—criminal violence, vendettas, dueling over a woman, picking fights about some imagined slight—and channeling them toward the proper goals of battlefield courage on behalf of the common good.

Moreover, it was recognized that the raw courage required of a soldier in combat could provide the emotional basis for the more subtle kinds of courage required of a good citizen in later life—the *civic* courage to aid fellow citizens in danger or distress, go against the dictates of an unjust government (even a democratically elected one), or combat unjust laws and social practices. Courage is not confined to the battlefield. It would be hard, for instance, to imagine battlefield combatants braver than the firefighters and rescue workers at Ground Zero in Manhattan, or, back in the sixties, the Mississippi Freedom Riders, including the idealistic young Northern college students who tried to help them, facing bullwhips and truncheons wielded by the legal authorities in order to change an unjust law.

And yet, there is perhaps no manly virtue so poorly understood today or with so mixed a reputation as courage. When I was a student at Yale in the 1970s, I remember hearing students argue seriously that Vietnam veterans should not be allowed to vote in elections because their earlier participation in the "mindless violence"of that war had made them permanently unstable. The students hadn't actually met any veterans. But endless television shows like *Hawaii Five-O* and *Mannix* had taught them that a "disgruntled ex-Vietnam vet" was always the likeliest suspect in a murder or robbery. Fortunately, society's attitudes about public honor for military valor have improved enormously since then. Nevertheless, throughout my adult lifetime, our opinion elites have continued to show a pronounced tendency to see no intrinsic difference between courage well employed and courage badly employed.

For many of these people, all forms of aggression or force boil down to the category of "violence," which is considered to be the same phenomenon with the same psychological origins whether it occurs in combat, street crime, or child or spousal abuse. Yes, they would concede, it may be necessary at times—although regrettable—for military and police force to be employed. But the last thing we want to do is draw attention to military courage or praise it as the basis for other virtues of character. After all, that would be to "glorify violence" and encourage "militarism," "patriotic fervor," "hysteria," or a "war spirit" in the populace. This tendency became deeply entrenched during the Vietnam War. The coolheaded systems managers and Boston Brahmins who planned that war regarded popular fervor, including pride in the military, as dangerously vulgar passions that might fan a "war spirit" in the uneducated masses and distract the planners from their flowcharts. They wanted to wage a war for experts, a war with strategic objectives that the soldiers fighting it, and the electorate at large, could not possibly be expected to understand. As a consequence, when the troops began to come home, they found a public that, in contrast with World War II or even the Korean conflict, had been carefully insulated from any atmosphere of hero worship for the military. Instead, students at Yale and other such bastions of privilege often regarded them as "baby killers."

The technocrats' distaste for popular patriotism is one reason for our deep-seated ambivalence about courage. But there's an even deeper reason, which goes to the core of the Western tradition. Try asking yourself the following question: Is it natural or unnatural for human beings to want war? This is the central issue. It has a profound if often unconscious and unrecognized influence on the way in which our opinion elites assess international conflict.

Let's assume for the sake of argument that it's natural for human beings to be warlike. If you take this view, does it necessarily mean that all men are motivated to be warlike all the time? Obviously not—that doesn't follow, either logically or from observation. People could have varying intensities of a warlike disposition, from almost none to a great deal and everything in between. Does it mean that our warlike tendencies are necessarily beyond our control? Again, that does not follow from taking the view that humans are naturally warlike. The traditional authorities I began with all believe that men do have an innate and ineradicable disposition to be warlike, but that education can go a long way to moderating aggressive traits and harnessing them to constructive goals.

It's all a question of knowing when to fight and why—in other words, the doctrine of the just war that I've already outlined from Aristotle to the theologies of the monotheistic faiths. Not only is it impossible to eradicate the warlike side of human nature but if we are in our right minds, we shouldn't even *want* to, for a country needs those aggressive traits to defend itself from external and internal predators. Otherwise, we will suffer the same fate as the foolish sheep in Aesop's fable who agree to sign a peace treaty offered by the wolves. Theodore Roosevelt, a great American warrior and statesman, perfectly comprehended the traditional view of courage as it had evolved in the American national experience. In a letter to his son, he admonished him never to be a bully, never to run from a fight when bullied, and to fight if another boy needed protection from a bully. In a nutshell, that is the American code of military honor.

Moreover, in the traditional view, for people who can't be persuaded by education or moral exhortations to avoid pointless or shameless violence, there's always the rule of law and the fear of legal retribution. In other words, to recognize that human beings have a natural disposition—among their other dispositions—to fight does not mean necessarily to approve of it on all occasions, much less to be "glorifying" it, or to regard war as inevitable or necessarily a good thing. The very fact that most law-bound and democratic societies are not usually plunged into anarchy or civil war, and that most states are not usually at war with each other, is sufficient proof that a natural predisposition to be warlike can be moderated, chastened, and sublimated by the forces of civilization. To concede that there is a warlike side to human nature is in no way to preclude the existence of higher and nobler dimensions to human nature. As all the traditional authorities maintain, courage can and should be governed by faith, civic virtue, prudence, and learning.

Believing in the naturalness of war, however, *does* lead one to adopt a very different perspective on the sources of violence and conflict around us, in contrast with those who believe that war should never be considered an innate human tendency. In order to see how this is so, let us now turn to the other side of the debate—the assumption that we have no innate tendencies to violence and aggression, that war is unnatural. If that is so, where do these traits come from? One answer often given is social conditioning according to those long-standing traditions that honor certain forms of courage—the very traditions I have been recommending as a guide for manly virtue. If you believe human beings are—or can be encouraged to become—naturally unaggressive, then even the carefully qualified kind of praise given by Aristotle for courage in a just war poses the risk of stimulating a passion for conflict that might otherwise not occur to people spontaneously. This is the reasoning, conscious or unconscious, behind the view that any form of public honor for courage is tantamount to "glorifying violence." It corrupts our natural pacificity. This is a very deep strain in the heritage of modernity and the Enlightenment, as we will later consider in more detail. According to Hobbes, Voltaire, and other modern thinkers, the very praise of martial honor going back to Homer, Plato, and the Bible, far from decreasing crime and tyranny by distinguishing legitimate courage from illegitimate violence, increases violent tendencies by giving those whose naturally peaceful natures have already been corrupted some rhetorical camouflage for their thrusting ambitions. As Hobbes puts it, "young men mad on war" love to read the Greek and Roman classics because those books teach them how to disguise their passion for power and glory as a virtuous aspiration to serve the common good. The young man who claims to want to imitate Marcus Brutus and protect the Republic from tyrants secretly yearns to be a tyrant himself once he makes it to the top.

If people are naturally peaceful, why, then, do crime and war exist at all? The general response is that people don't feel aggressive by nature, but everyone wants the basic material necessities of life and the economic wherewithal to pursue whatever vocation or value they see fit, and the ability to pass this freedom on to their children. If people are violent, it's because they are being denied these basic freedoms. If we give them these freedoms, or prevent them from being curtailed, their aggressive traits will melt away, and their natural pacifism will flower. In the words of Schiller's "Ode to Joy," all men will be brothers.

In the pacifistic view of the world, peace is the normal condition, and war is the perversion. True, at any given time there may be a number of wars going on, and many conflicts brewing or barely suppressed. But that's only because of the distorting influences on human nature introduced by poverty or by baleful cultural conditioning in old-fashioned militaristic bombast. Peace is still normal in the sense that it's the underlying reality, an ideal that can be brought to the surface if only the distorting influences of history, politics, competition, and power seeking are curtailed. When war occurs, it is an abnormality that can be reversed if certain basic utilitarian goods are provided to the combatants. Human beings may think they enjoy the glory and honor of combat and martyrdom for their God or soil. But this is just a displacement of their pain at being deprived of their reasonable freedoms, and a rationalization for the fear and anxiety they are actually experiencing behind their bravado. Bring them the benefits of economic prosperity and personal liberty, and their hatreds will melt away. Give them *Baywatch,* DVDs and SUVs, and they'll hang up their Kalashnikovs.

What are the practical consequences of this debate over the naturalness of war? If you believe the second proposition—the view that humans are not naturally warlike—you will have a tendency to dismiss the actual claims of the combatants as mere rhetoric, or as a confused state of mind. They may say that they are fighting for the honor and dignity of their people and faith, and that they want to destroy the interlopers who currently occupy their sacred soil or corrupt their daughters. But you know that what they *really* want is a Western standard of living, and that, once this is within reach, religious and ideological hostilities will evaporate in the sunny uplands of Western prosperity, personal freedom, and entertainment. If, however, like me, you believe the first proposition— that war is an innate natural propensity in mankind—you will have a much more pessimistic view of the prospects for world peace.

If you share my view, you will desire peace just as fervently as those who believe peace is the natural human condition. But you will also put more faith in national security, the balance of power, and the deterrent effect of military preparedness as the perhaps regrettable but necessary real-world basis for whatever limited cooperation between combatants is possible. Moreover, you will also put more faith in the power of liberal education, the jewel in the crown of the West's achievements, not to eradicate violence from the world but to persuade young people that there are many ways of fighting—shameful and noble, despicable and admirable. And that requires a careful study of the psychology of manly courage in both its destructive and its admirable dimensions. Only if we know how to spot the potential predator and tyrant will we have any prospect of nipping those aberrant violent impulses in the bud and rerouting those passions toward the service of a just cause and the common good.

Obviously, these reflections have a bearing on the disaster of September 11, 2001, and the ongoing struggle against terrorism by the democracies. In my discussion of patriotism in Chapter 5, I'll return to that most recent example of the just war and suggest how the traditional teaching about courage as it has evolved in a specifically American context might illuminate our understanding of it. In the rest of this chapter, though, I want to examine the psychology of courage in broader strokes, from Homer to the present.

TAMING THE WARRIOR

Throughout much of the Western tradition, the puzzle about courage has been how to rechannel it away from lawless violence and toward justice, moderation, and the common good. The West's original model for courage—in both its good and its bad dimensions—was the beautiful young Greek demigod, king, and war hero Achilles. In a sense, taming this type of young man became the chief project for civic education beginning with the ancient Greek and Roman moralists, continuing through the Renaissance and the Enlightenment, and well into the twentieth century (including American heroes who wrote about courage like Theodore Roosevelt and JFK). Our chief source for the legend of Achilles is Homer's great epic of the war between the Greeks and Trojans, the *Iliad*. Through Achilles' example, Homer shows that righteous wrath is necessary in a warrior. But when that wrath is driven by jealousy and wounded pride, it can create dangerous instability for the common good.

Ostensibly, the main theme of the *Iliad* is the war between the Greeks (or, as Homer calls them, the Achaians) and the Trojans, sparked when the Trojan prince Paris abducts Helen, the legendarily stunning wife of the Mycenaean king Menelaos. Menelaos's brother Agamemnon, the preeminent Greek king, assembles a multinational force to conquer Troy, recover Helen, and avenge the insult against his brother. But the deeper theme of the *Iliad* is the war within the war—the feud between Achilles, the Greeks' greatest fighter, and his overlord Agamemnon. When the king of kings deprives Achilles of his war prize (yes, I'm afraid it's a young woman), the young warrior withdraws in fury from the army, depriving his comrades of their best warrior. A king in his own right, Achilles has believed all along that he is a better man than his commander in chief. Having been mortally insulted by this feeble superior, he is ready to sacrifice the safety and success of his own side to avenge his wounded pride. It's an age-old conflict between an impetuous youth and a more cautious older superior—a conflict, at bottom, between the natural, as-yet-unrecognized merit of the young and the established authority of older men resting on their laurels. For his part, Agamemnon has long resented Achilles' disregard for his supreme rank, as their heated argument makes plain. In Homer's dialogue, you can hear them spitting the words out between clenched teeth as they square off:

Then glowering at him Achilles spoke:

O clothed in shamelessness, you of the crafty mind, how shall any Achaian obey you with all his heart, whether it be to go on a journey or to fight the foe bravely in battle?

Achilles has nothing against the Trojans, he says. The whole war is nothing but an ego trip for Agamemnon as he avenges a slight to his less than impressive brother (Homer hints strongly that Helen might not have been an entirely unwilling captive of the dashing Paris). Achilles rages on:

I did not come here to fight because of the Trojan spear-men, for they have done me no wrong. . . . It was for *your* sake, you shameless one, that we all followed you here to please you, you dog-face, by avenging your honor and Menelaos' against the Trojans.

I've done most of the fighting, Achilles claims, while you get most of the loot:

My reward is never as big as yours, but whenever the Achaians sack any populous citadel of Trojan men, my hands bear the brunt of furious war. But when the booty is divided, your share is always far greater; I go back to my ships with at least some small thing I can call my own when I am exhausted from fighting. But I am no longer willing to stay here in dishonor while I pile up riches and wealth for you.

Like a CEO who is being challenged by a junior executive, Agamemnon responds with equal hostility to this cocky young upstart:

Then Agamemnon king of men made answer to him:

Run away, yes, by all means, run, if that's what you're set on doing. I won't beg you to stay for my sake. I have others by my side who honor me. By Zeus, lord of counsel, you have always loved strife and war and quarrels. So go home with your ships and your companions. I don't care about you, and I could care less about your anger.

The result of Achilles' desertion of the Greeks is just what he hoped for—the Trojans come close to defeating the Greeks. As the Greeks' best warrior sulks in his tent, Achilles' best friend Patroklos, shamed by his friend's desertion, dons Achilles' armor and dies taking his place in battle. In this way, Homer teaches us, excessive anger and pride are due for a fall. Achilles wanted the Greeks to suffer so they would realize how much they needed him, and to show up Agamemnon as a mediocre commander when deprived of Achilles' superior prowess. He got his wish, but at an awful price—his best friend's life. As Homer intones, "Thus the will of Zeus was fulfilled." The gods even things out in ways that mortals can never anticipate.

Achilles remains the original model of manly honor for the ancient Greeks. When Plato discusses in the *Republic* how ambitious young men might be educated to channel their love of honor into serving the common good, Achilles is the main example he has in mind. But for Plato, the restless, moody, and beautiful young demigod is mainly a negative example. Careening between extremes of frenzied daring and hopeless despair, Achilles represents everything that should be avoided in educating a young man. Socrates dwells disapprovingly on the passages in the *Iliad* that depict the headstrong youth as being so filled with irrational fury that he tries doing battle with a river, or even threatens the gods with punishment if they get in his way. In Plato's depiction, Achilles is a good deal more like an angry teenager slamming his bedroom door when he's been grounded than a formidable general.

Much of Homer's own portrait of Achilles confirms Plato's view of him as narcissistic, self-absorbed, prone to self-pity, oblivious to the existence of others, and with a hair-trigger temper—in other words, a typical adolescent. Manly pride and honor have both good and bad potential. The good potential is for a vigorous service of the common good. The bad potential is for hubristic ambition, arrogance, and tyranny. The same aggressiveness and boldness that can invigorate public service and courage on behalf of a just cause can also, if not properly guided, lead to war, imperialism, and crimes of passion. Achilles betrays his own fellow Greeks while they are fighting for their lives against a deadly enemy because of a purely personal vendetta against his commander. He is willing to sell out his own side because he resents Agamemnon for stealing his loot and his woman.

Much of the subsequent Western tradition is dedicated to exploring the problem so vividly illustrated by Achilles: How can masculine ambition be deflected away from tyrannical and exploitive behavior, and redirected toward honorable citizenship? Properly shaped, battlefield courage can lay the foundation for civic courage, vigor of mind, and boldness of thought. The key to this transformation is what the Greeks called *paideia*, usually translated as "education." Although it eventually came to stand for all learning and culture in general in the ancient world, originally and literally it meant the rearing of male youths (from *pais*, the word for boy).

At this point, before looking more closely at the classical ideal of *paideia*, we should pause to note the parallels with other traditions, particularly religious traditions. The Hebrew Bible, for example, displays a deep ambivalence about kingship and martial prowess. Both are necessary in order to defend the Israelites against their oppressors and enforce God's law over His chosen people. But the Israelites were troubled by the feeling that in elevating one of their own to the same heights of power and prestige exercised by the unbelievers around them—the bellicose and arrogant Egyptian and Assyrian monarchs—they would offend God by giving too much grandeur to a mere mortal. If God is the true king, they wondered, ruling His people directly through His covenant and laws, is it right to have a human monarch like the idolaters, full of pomp and pride? By looking to the prophet Samuel to give them a king, the Israelites tried to make the royal authority come as much as possible from divine revelation, rather than from mere human ambition, military might, or pragmatic calculations based on power politics and international relations.

The story of that first king, Saul, and his relationship with the future king David perfectly parallels the dilemma explored by Homer, Plato, and other ancient philosophers: how a young man's valor can serve his ruler but also threaten his authority. But while Achilles bears much of the blame for his feud with Agamemnon, David is the undeserving victim of Saul's jealousy and suspicion. David meant only to serve his country by slaying Goliath and through his other victories. But Saul feared that David's exploits as a commander, and the soldiers' love for him, might fuel the young man's ambition to overthrow Saul and make himself king. The Bible vividly evokes the paranoid atmosphere of Saul's royal household:

> Next day an evil spirit from God seized upon Saul; he fell into a frenzy in the house, and David played the harp to him as he had before. Saul had his spear in his hand, and he hurled it at David, meaning to pin him to the wall; but twice David swerved aside. After this Saul was afraid of David, because he saw that the Lord had forsaken him and was with David. He therefore removed David from his household and appointed him to the command of a thousand men. David led his men into action, and succeeded in everything that he undertook, because the Lord was with him. When Saul saw how successful he was, he was more afraid of him than ever; all Israel and Judah loved him because he took the field at their head.

There's no question that Saul's jealousy and suspicion toward David are completely unfounded, the product of his own arrogance and having grown too addicted to absolute power, just as the pious had feared might happen when they first approached Samuel to choose a king. Even Saul's own son and heir Jonathan takes the side of his friend David against his father:

> Saul spoke to Jonathan his son and all his household about killing David. Jonathan spoke up for David to his father Saul and said to him, "Sir, do not wrong your servant David; he has not wronged you; his conduct towards you has been beyond reproach. Did he not take his life in his hands when he killed the Philistine, and the Lord won a great victory for Israel? You saw it, you shared in the rejoicing; why should you wrong an innocent man and put David to death without cause?"

In the next chapter, which deals with pride, I'll return to the issue of biblical revelation and the serious argument to be made that it is a better source for the manly virtues than any kind of secular reasoning, even the stalwart defense of the moral virtues undertaken by the ancient Greek and Roman authors, including Plato, Aristotle, and Cicero. But let's dwell for now on the classical approach to taming ambition. Achilles must be replaced with a new model for young men—what Socrates in the *Republic* describes as a moderate "Guardian" of the common good, whose gracious repose and consistency mirror the rationality of the cosmic order. Being a Guardian probably isn't as much fun as being the wild, moody, beautiful, and charismatic demigod of youth, Achilles. Socratic manliness may not match the glorious excesses of Achilles' daring, but it also doesn't plunge into his adolescent self-pity, fury, and pointless aggression. For Socrates, a real man will never do battle with a river or any other god or disobey his lawful commander. Just as reason governs the cosmos, Socrates argues, an orderly soul must govern the passions. And since the soul is common to human beings regardless of physical differences—including the physical differences between men and women—everything Socrates proposes for the education of young men applies to young women as well.

Thus, under Socrates' influence, "courage"—which, as we've seen, in ancient Greek was literally a synonym for "manliness"—becomes primarily a quality of soul, mind, and will, not of brute strength or martial prowess. Plato derives a distinct masculine psychology from a more widespread trait he calls "spiritedness." Spiritedness is not necessarily the same as courage. Spiritedness is a zeal common to all living organisms, and to both sexes. Battlefield courage is only one of its manifestations. Socrates wants to discourage us from confusing spiritedness with a gender-specific trait. Women have it, too.

At its crudest level, spiritedness is a passion for struggle provoked in us by a feeling of vulnerability in the face of enemies or opposition. When we're cornered, we lash out like an animal terrified into a spasm of rage as the only alternative to extinction. Socrates wants to channel this raw emotion by educating it to become moral zeal guided by the intellect in the service of the common good. Our aim should be not the tyrannical mastery of others, he suggests, but the inner mastery of our own base impulses on behalf of the rule of law and justice. This ethic of self-mastery leads away from imperialistic conquest to a more inward-looking politics devoted to domestic affairs. If a people lust to conquer other peoples, they will need to equip their fellow citizens with enormous military powers. More likely than not, those commanders, swollen with victorious pride from their conquests abroad, will turn on their former fellow citizens and become their masters. Untamed courage fed by tyrannical ambition and inflamed desires can lead to catastrophe for everyone—wars of imperialistic aggression abroad and the subversion of lawful government at home. In order to stave off such threats to the well-being and happiness of both individuals and communities, courage must be carefully defined and circumscribed within the bounds of justice.

COURAGE DEFINED

Following upon Plato, Aristotle and his student Theophrastus sum up the classical teaching on courage, one that has been profoundly influential even to the present day. Courage is a mean, they say, between the extremes of cowardice and mad daring. "It holds the middle place between those vicious extremes," Aristotle writes. "It is calm and sedate, and though it never provokes danger, is always ready to meet even death in an honorable cause." Moreover, Aristotle continues, you have to experience fear in order to be brave. If I can kill my enemy by flicking a switch on a console a thousand miles away, or by leaving a bomb in a pizzeria timed to explode when I'm safely out of range, I may be smarter or better trained technically than he is. But I'm not courageous, because I don't feel fear. I have no low passion to overcome when confronted by another determined warrior, thereby demonstrating my courage by standing my ground.

According to Aristotle, that's why a raw recruit heading into battle, whose guts are melting at the sight of the enemy's guns, is more courageous than a general miles behind the lines moving pins on a map. Of course, in making such a judgment, Aristotle expects us to bear in mind that the general has seen combat many times himself in his younger days, and shown his courage on those occasions. Now, as an older man directing younger men who are risking their lives in the fighting, the general is fulfilling graver, broader, and more important responsibilities that involve the overall plan of the campaign, the safety of all the troops, and probably even the war's impact on political and civilian life at home. As we will see in the chapter on pride, there are higher virtues than courage, and for Aristotle they are summed up by *prudence,* the mark of a truly distinguished leader. A young man can ascend over time from courage to prudence, but he can't begin that way. Prudence is born of age and experience. Only mature older men can possess it.

A brave man, Aristotle tells us, is "unshaken and dauntless, subjecting the instinctive emotions of fear to the dictates of reason and honor." But while a coward "lives in continual alarm, and is therefore spiritless and dejected," we must also avoid the opposite extreme: "an excess of courage called rashness, a boastful species of bravery . . . which is nothing but madness, a most stupid insensibility that can make any man preserve, amidst earthquakes and inundations, that unshaken composure which has been ascribed to the Celts." (As a descendant of Welshmen, I will ignore the philosopher's last remark.)

According to Aristotle's student Theophrastus, whose sense of humor was considerably better than that of his teacher, cowards tend to be rather bad companions on a cruise:

> On shipboard the coward is the sort of man who mistakes a rocky headland for a pirate brig, and who asks if there are unbelievers aboard when a big wave hits the side. Or he will show up suddenly alongside the helmsman, trying to find out what the weather means or if they are halfway yet; and he explains to the nearest listener that his fright was caused by a dream.

Cowards also have a way of disappearing when things get hot on the battlefield:

> Suppose, again, that he is on active duty. As the infantry advances into battle, he shouts for his friends from home to come over by him. He wants them to stop for a look round before they go farther, it's a job he says, to tell which is the enemy. And as soon as he starts hearing the shouts and seeing men drop, he explains to those on either side of him that all the excitement made him forget to take his sword. So back he runs to the tent, then he sends his orderly out on reconnaissance, hides the sword under a pillow, and takes his time pretending to hunt for it.

The Aristotelian teaching about courage as a mean between cowardice and rashness sums up the ancient approach to the psychology of the warrior and ties it to the doctrine of the just war. The psychology of courage and the ethical limitations on war go hand in hand. If soldiers are rash, they will undertake wars based on trivial slights, vendettas, or a lust for plunder, or because they confuse battlefield honor with mad daring, frenzy, and an orgy of bloodshed. If they are cowardly, they will find ways of avoiding combat even when directly threatened by an unscrupulous aggressor, like the Italian city-states in the Renaissance that employed foreign mercenaries because they had grown too used to the pleasures of peacetime. These mercenaries fought only for money, and so of course routinely took the money and ran without fighting, or took the money and promptly changed sides so they could collect another fee.

If a just war is limited to self-defense or aiding the oppressed, it is because citizens have already been educated to avoid these extremes of cowardice and rashness, and to choose the peacetime domestic affairs of virtuous self-government over imperialistic expansionism. They won't go to war unless provoked. But then they will fight in an orderly and steadfast way until they repel the invader. Depending on the circumstances, a good leader must encourage a peaceful spirit in his people on some occasions, a warlike spirit on others. A nice example of the appropriate rhetoric is to be found in Shakespeare's *Henry V*, as the young hero-king rallies his troops before the walls of Harfleur, where they have come to wrest back their lands lost to France:

> *Once more unto the breach, dear friends, once more;*
> *Or close the wall up with our English dead!*
> *In peace, there's nothing so becomes a man,*
> *As modest stillness, and humility;*
> *But when the blast of war blows in our ears,*
> *Then imitate the action of the tiger;*
> *Stiffen the sinews, summon up the blood,*
> *Disguise fair nature with hard-favored rage.*

To visualize the difference between the sober, self-disciplined courage recommended by Aristotle and the extreme of rashness, picture those silent closed ranks of Roman legionaries in the movie *Gladiator*, moving as a single unit, never flinching as spears pour down on them, tramping relentlessly forward. Rashness, by contrast, is summed up by the barbarians in the film—who look, by the way, as if they came directly from filming *Braveheart*. They run forward pell-mell, a disordered mob screaming and waving battle-axes, each individual thinking he can kill a million Romans. Guess who wins.

But does the doctrine of the just war, and the psychology of courage as a mean between extremes on which it is based, cover all cases? Here is where things can get messy. If a neighboring country shows no overt signs of attacking you but has steadily built up its military might and conquered other countries, are you justified in launching a preemptive strike before they are strong enough to roll over you? Machiavelli, the Renaissance-era founder of the Realpolitik school of warfare, argues that the traditional doctrine of the just war handed down by the ancient and Christian authorities leaves us helpless in the face of this kind of threat. For if, in obedience to Aristotle, St. Thomas, and the other traditional just war teachings, we wait until actually attacked, the enemy will already have beaten us.

According to Machiavelli, the Romans professed to believe in those fine Aristotelian virtues of moderation and self-control, but fortunately for their empire, they didn't practice what they preached. That's why they ended up with a world empire, while the Greeks had only a collection of piddling little city-states. The Romans were always ready to go to war at short notice in order to avoid having a war forced upon them later at a time not of their choosing. Above all, they were always willing to strike a preemptive blow now, in order to knock out a potential enemy before he got too strong, thereby avoiding a longer war on worse terms down the road, a war that they might lose and that would result in much greater death and suffering for both sides. As Machiavelli observes, exercising preemptive force in the present often maximizes the chances for greater peace in the long run—whereas avoiding combat because of Christian scruples about love and charity can end up plunging your country into the horrors of invasion and conquest. He sums up—and savors—the paradox by concluding that, for a leader, sometimes cruelty is the most compassionate course of conduct, while a preference for being compassionate can subject your people to the cruelty of defeat, conquest, or civil war. A leader may have to be ready to sully his reputation in order to be successful in pragmatic terms.

These reflections may be unpleasant, but unfortunately they have been confirmed time and again by events. When Hitler sent German troops into the Rhineland in 1936, taking back a piece of German territory annexed to France by the Versailles treaty ending World War I, some two hundred divisions of the French army and its allies stood idly by. The force Hitler sent into the Rhineland was purely symbolic—a single division—and at the time the entire Wehrmacht totaled fewer than ten divisions in all. They had orders to withdraw at the first sign of French retaliation. We know from records captured after World War II that Hitler's generals thought he had lost his mind to do something so rash. If France and England had made any move to expel the German contingent—which they could have done easily—there's a good chance the German high command would have deposed Hitler rather than risk an Allied invasion at a time when the German army was still quite weak.

Because Hitler's rash gamble worked, his prestige soared among the military, particularly the bolder young officers, who were eager for the glories of war (including the medals and promotions) and tended to side with the Fuehrer's view of the generals as timid and weak-willed. It also convinced Hitler that the Allied leaders were irresolute and lacking conviction, which emboldened him to grab more and more territory (Austria and the Sudetenland) in a series of bloodless victories that played upon the French and British leaders' desire to avoid war at any price. After Munich, where they sanctioned his rape of Czechoslovakia, he would always say of them: "These men are ghosts. I saw them at Munich." By failing to expel the Germans from the Rhineland when they had the overwhelming military superiority, the Allies emboldened the most bellicose elements of the Nazi regime, and hastened a war that eventually consumed millions of lives.

YOUNG MEN MAD ON WAR

Beginning in the seventeenth century, with the rise of representative government, commercial free enterprise, and the Enlightenment, there was a conscious effort to pacify the ambitions of what Thomas Hobbes termed "young men mad on war" and make them into orderly private individuals devoted to the peaceful arts of moneymaking. This was an enormous shift. As we've seen, the earlier tradition of the West had argued for the right kind of civic education to rechannel courage and the other aggressive traits of boys and young men. With the rise of modernity, for the first time serious efforts were made to get rid of manly honor altogether. Hobbes began the line of reasoning that denies there is any independent capacity for honor seeking in the human soul.

It is still an enormously influential position, one of the important sources for the pacifistic side of the debate we considered earlier over whether and to what extent warlike leanings are innate to human nature. According to this view, the pursuit of honor is reducible to a frustrated desire for material prosperity, stemming from our anxiety about staying alive and resentment toward those who are better off. For Hobbes, the solution is to encourage people to gratify their desires through peaceful economic enterprise, protected from one another's tyrannical impulses by an all-powerful benevolent despot. In effect, Hobbes takes the famous Aristotelian definition of courage as a golden mean between cowardice and rashness and says, When you look at the real world, there is no golden mean—all we see are cowards or the insanely rash. If you praise courage as a virtue, all you're accomplishing is providing usurpers, revolutionaries, and would-be tyrants with nice-sounding rhetoric to disguise their lust for power. Since, in the real world, there are only the cowards and the rash, according to Hobbes, it's better to be a coward. If we all come to realize that self-preservation and fear of death motivate everything we do, we'll lose any pretensions to male bravado and settle down to the peaceful art of making money. Glory seekers are nothing more than muggers and thieves on a grand scale.

With his stigmatization of "macho" pretensions to glory, fed by reading the ancient authors and historians of valorous deeds, Hobbes is one of the forebears of modern feminism. Unfortunately, he's also the first Western political theorist to endorse despotism openly as a necessary instrument for crushing the pretensions of the "vainglorious" to heroic honor. Basically, he recommends equipping one vicious S.O.B. with a big enough club to keep all the other S.O.B.'s in line. While social peace was being preserved through the monarch's capacity to strike terror in the other S.O.B.'s in case they were thinking of usurping him, the universities (as Hobbes hoped) would begin educating the young in his new psychology of materialism, nipping up-and-coming S.O.B.'s in the bud by convincing them that it was far better to act on their ambitions by becoming Bill Gates than by becoming Julius Caesar. One man gets to be the boss. The rest of us get to be retail clerks and burger slingers.

Here begins a dilemma about the place of courage in the modern world that we have yet to resolve. In order to banish the dark side of manliness, must we get rid of it altogether, through a blend of terror and indoctrination, as Hobbes recommends? If we look back over the entire course of modernity, especially the catastrophically destructive wars and totalitarian tyrannies of the twentieth century, it might seem as if the human race has increasingly fallen into one or the other of the extreme versions of courage—excessive pacifism or excessive violence, just as Hobbes said was the case when you forsook the Aristotelian ideal for the real world. But maybe it's a self-fulfilling prophecy. Perhaps this division into extremes of timidity and rashness is the price we have paid for following Hobbes in abandoning the golden mean—the classical view of courage as the restrained exercise of force on behalf of a just cause. Hobbes's therapy for "vainglorious" young men anticipates the treatment in *A Clockwork Orange* of Alex, a modern Alcibiades who identifies masculinity with mayhem, crime, and rape, because none of the traditional outlets for honorable courage are available to him. Since he isn't pacified by the banal material comforts and entertainment culture into which he is born, the state has to rob him of his masculinity altogether through a torture regimen of psychotropic drugs and Pavlovian reconditioning. Seeing the movie today, one can't help but conclude that what Stanley Kubrick depicted in 1971 as a grotesque futuristic fantasy has in many ways been normalized by the widespread use of Ritalin to rewire the brain circuitry of young boys in order to cure them of their excessive boyish aggression and lack of concentration.

Hobbes hoped to see the world rid of "young men mad on war." But their numbers seem to have increased during the last thirty years. When I first saw *A Clockwork Orange* in 1971, people stalked out of the theater in disgust at the infamous rape scene, in which Alex and his fellow "Droogs" invade the trendy pad of a rich, cultured couple and chase them with a huge dildo. At that time, the movie seemed mainly a nasty dystopian fantasy, pumped up with exaggerated and gratuitous violence.

But in some ways it only mirrored disturbing cultural trends that were already under way, such as the Manson Family's eerily similar slaughter of a house party of privileged celebrities a few years earlier, or the Rolling Stones' horrifying performance at the Altamont Music Festival, where the Hells Angels beat a young man to death before Mick Jagger's eyes. These trends only grew worse with time. In England, with the rise of the punks and the soccer thugs, it was as if the Droogs from *A Clockwork Orange* were stomping off the screen straight into the real world. The punks, with their fascistic leather gear, shaved heads and snarling demeanor, were reacting to the reigning hippie Establishment, with their combination of self-satisfied privilege and smug other-worldliness, rolling their joints in the Jacuzzi and listening to meditation tapes in their Jags (crystallized by Paul Simon's wonderful turn as the rich, laid-back, too-hip-for-thou West Coast producer in *Annie Hall*).

The punks' crude, three-chord thrash rock, with its deliberate avoidance of melody and deliberately irritating nasal wailing, was designed to be a cruise missile aimed at the increasingly precious, sanctimonious, and overblown art rock of the High Late Hippie era (with its "suites" and "operas"). Their early cinematic manifesto, *Rude Boy,* a vérité chronicle of the rise of the Clash interwoven with scenes from the deepest punk recesses of East London, made a brilliant gesture toward *A Clockwork Orange* by placing its protagonist—a punk rock lover and fringe member of the skinhead fascist scene—in exactly the same kind of dreary public housing complex that Stanley Kubrick had chosen for his Alex. In this way, the punks were saying, it's all come true in one short decade—the Droogs are here.

And that, of course, brings us right to the present—and to the opening pages of this book. The characteristic dichotomy brought out by *Fight Club* between the wimp and the beast was already at work in the war between hippie and punk culture, and this in turn was deeply rooted in the original Hobbesian argument that there is no middle ground for manly combativeness in the real world of passion and self-interest. There are only pacifists and the insanely daring; those unwilling ever to fight, and those always ready to fight for no sound purpose.

THE MODERN AMBIVALENCE ABOUT COURAGE

Now, to be sure, there are more balanced approaches within the modern tradition than the Hobbesian strain, approaches that seek to marry traditional notions of courage to the new civilization of democracy and the elevation of the commercial virtues over the old knightly codes of valor. Few avatars of the Enlightenment shared Hobbes's taste for extremes. According to them, the fact that we want to get rid of the retrograde side of the old martial culture doesn't mean we think that war is going to disappear forever, or that soldiering can't still be an honorable profession. The eighteenth-century poet Alexander Pope, for example, believed that Homer's *Iliad* and *Odyssey* should still be the models for manliness in the modern age, precisely because the increasing emphasis on self-interest and material prosperity needed tempering with a reminder about heroic valor, duty, and self-sacrifice.

By contrast, later modern thinkers like Rousseau and Marx began to maintain that war is completely unnatural because humans actually have no spontaneous desire for competition at all. Whereas Hobbes thought you had to be either a warrior or a coward, the socialist school went further, contending that all human beings are peaceful. When you remove the distortions that cause war—class, inequality, religion—war will vanish forever. This heady brew of different moral perspectives in the modern West about the role of courage has much to do with why we are so ambivalent about it today. We know we can't do without courage. But we can't endorse it completely without seeming to oppose progress and peace.

One of the ironies often noted by historians and moralists is that, as the values of democracy, free enterprise, and the Enlightenment spread throughout the nineteenth and twentieth centuries, proclaiming the impending brotherhood of all mankind, war, revolution, and violence have actually intensified rather than withered away or even decreased. Once again, it seems as if we might reluctantly have to concede the prescience of Hobbes. Given the terrible wars and genocide unleashed by totalitarianism in the twentieth century, an unprecedented level of barbarism that emerged in the very heartland of the liberal, enlightened, democratic, and prosperous West, again it seems as if real-life history has offered an ever more worrisome division between the pacifists and the fanatics. While the Enlightenment and liberalism have preached the message of peace, tolerance, and reconciliation, in practice the democracies time and again have had to mount extraordinary military efforts against the resurgence of tyrannies of the Left and Right, and most recently against terrorist zealots and their state sponsors.

As a consequence, and not surprisingly, while psychology, sociology, political science, and other academic disciplines have been ill-equipped during much of the twentieth century to give a nuanced account of courage that does not simply stigmatize it or wish it away in accordance with the socialist ideal of universal peace, actual statesmen and commanders from the twentieth-century's wars have provided some of the best contemporary insights into the meaning of courage. In truth, reading de Gaulle, Churchill, or John F. Kennedy on courage makes us realize how impoverished and reductionist the academic and professional psychological literature is by contrast. While modern behaviorists like Harold Lasswell and other conventionally celebrated academic experts on aggression could offer little more than a rehash of Hobbes and a pious hope for a future utopia of peace, their contemporaries in the real world of warfare reached into the richest insights of the Western tradition to make some sense of the terrible conflicts of the democratic age.

Among the best of these are Charles de Gaulle's writings on the soldier's virtues and the good and bad sides of war. De Gaulle argues that we cannot imagine life without military force—and that we should not want to. Why? Because human nature cannot change. More important, although ambition and pride can do evil things in the world, it's equally true that nothing noble or just can be accomplished without these same qualities:

> Hope though we may, what reason have we for thinking that passion and self-interest, the root cause of armed conflict in men and in nations, will cease to operate; that anyone will willingly surrender what he has or not try to get what he wants; in short, that human nature will ever become something other than it is? . . . Is it possible to conceive of life without force? Only if children cease to be born, only if minds are sterilized, feel-

ings frozen, men's needs anaesthetized, only if the world is reduced to immobility, can it be banished. Otherwise, in some form or another, it will remain indispensable, for, without it, thought would have no driving power, action no strength. It is the prerequisite of movement and the midwife of progress.

In war, we can observe men's basest passions of cruelty and revenge. But we can also observe their finest aspirations to self-sacrifice and duty. While war can serve exploitation and domination, it can also defend the oppressed and spread the ideals of civilization and religion:

> War stirs in men's hearts the mud of their worst instincts. It puts a premium on violence, nourishes hatred, and gives free rein to cupidity. It crushes the weak, exalts the unworthy, bolsters tyranny. . . . But, though Lucifer has used it for his purposes so, sometimes, has the Archangel. With what virtues has it not enriched the moral capital of mankind! Because of it, courage, devotion, and nobility have scaled the peaks. It has conferred greatness of spirit on the poor, brought pardon to the guilty, revealed the possibilities of self-sacrifice to the commonplace, restored honor to the rogue, and given dignity to the slave. It has carried ideas in the baggage wagons of its armies, and reforms in the knapsacks of its soldiers. It has blazed a trail for religion and spread across the world influences which have brought renewal to mankind, consoled it, and made it better. Had not innumerable soldiers shed their blood there would have been no Hellenism, no Roman civilization, no Christianity, no Rights of Man, and no modern developments.

Whether we enjoy facing it or not, de Gaulle is saying (like Machiavelli before him), military conquest can have beneficial consequences. The supreme example of this sometimes disturbing paradox is de Gaulle's legendary predecessor Napoleon, the founder of modern French military honor. The traditional just war doctrine had restricted military action against another country to self-defense or rescuing the oppressed. Beginning with Napoleon, however, war could be waged for the modern ideals of the rights of man and representative government. Those ideals could be taken to justify invading not only countries that are obviously tyrannical but even those that, by any traditional standard, do not oppress or menace their subjects. All must be reformed into democracies in which the People and the Rights of Man are sovereign.

On a personal level, Napoleon was motivated by an insatiable craving for victory and glory. He dreamed of matching and even surpassing the exploits of Alexander the Great and Julius Caesar. But as the war leader of revolutionary France, Napoleon used his victories to spread the ideals of liberty, equality, and fraternity. His defeat of the European powers was not just an old-fashioned victory for French territorial and dynastic ambitions of the kind that European states had always fought. His victories also brought about the collapse of the old feudal order, and gave the Enlightenment parties in those countries a chance to foster the cause of constitutional democracy, civil liberties, and individual self-advancement through commercial enterprise. Napoleon was a liberal imperialist, a progressive conqueror. To this day, liberal democracies remain troubled by the question of how far we are justified in imposing our military will on other countries, not merely to restore peace or rescue them from an aggressor but to reform them into our own kind of pluralistic liberal democracy. This is a complication we must frankly confess the traditional just war doctrine did not envision.

As for Napoleon himself, this complex genius who spread death and destruction to millions in order to make them free, one of the best portraits of his good and bad sides comes from an unexpected source: the American Transcendentalist and clergyman Ralph Waldo Emerson. Like de Gaulle writing a century later, Emerson sees the value of military might when it is allied with the spread of freedom and the rule of law. But not being a man of war himself, he is perhaps more sensitive than the French general to how military ambition can distort the soul of a man who devotes himself to it above all else:

> Here was an experiment, under the most favorable conditions, of the powers of intellect without conscience. Never was such a leader so endowed and so weaponed; never had a leader found such aids and followers. And what was the result of this vast talent and power, of these immense armies, burned cities, squandered treasures, immolated millions of men, of this demoralized Europe? It came to no result. All passed away like the smoke of his artillery, and left no trace. He left

France smaller, poorer, feebler, than he found it; and the whole contest for freedom was to be begun again.

At the end of the day, Napoleon sacrificed everything—the ideals for which the armies of revolutionary France were fighting, and finally France herself—to his unquenchable thirst for glory:

> Men found that his absorbing egotism was deadly to all other men. It resembled the torpedo, which inflicts a succession of shocks on any one who takes hold of it, producing spasms which contract the muscles of the hand, so that the man can not open his fingers; and the animal inflicts new and more violent shocks, until he paralyzes and kills his victim. So this exorbitant egotist narrowed, impoverished and absorbed the power and existence of those who served him; and the universal cry of France and of Europe in 1814 was, "Enough of him"; *"Assez de Bonaparte."*

The paradox of the liberalizing conqueror Napoleon draws together a number of themes in our examination of courage. The old just war doctrine made a distinction between the just and moderate employment of courage, limited primarily to a country's self-defense, and unjust wars of imperialistic expansion. With Napoleon, we get something new and unanticipated—an imperial conqueror who spreads democratic justice. It is as if the vainglorious young man "mad on war" decried by Hobbes as the source of all upheaval drew his sword on behalf of Rousseau and Marx. As pacifists and socialists, we must condemn this throwback to the blood-soaked empires of the past. But as believers in progress, we applaud his overthrow of reactionary feudalism. Once again, it proves devilishly difficult to find the golden mean between the extremes of passivity and rashness.

Nowhere are these paradoxes of modern courage better explored than in the novels of Tolstoy. *War and Peace* unforgettably portrays the attractions and drawbacks of a life devoted to martial valor and patriotic service and the more retiring, inward-directed life of a family man, husband, and father. The novel's main character, Pierre Bezukhov, sums up all the ambivalence of the modern liberal about war and conquest, an ambivalence later to be repeated over Stalin, Mao, and other self-proclaimed liberators of mankind. Pierre is a decent and well-meaning man, a member of the aristocracy who believes in progress, tries to be a benevolent master to his serfs, studies the social sciences and agronomy in order to modernize production on his estates and spare his serfs back-breaking labor, and longs for the simple pleasures extolled by Rousseau of a life in the country with his wife and children. He abhors violence. And yet he is thrilled by the advance of Napoleon across Europe, and mesmerized by the emperor's charisma. As a liberal who believes in the rights of man and the inevitable moral victory of representative government, he cannot shed tears over the reactionary Prussian and Austrian monarchies being crushed by the French. Pierre wonders constantly: Is Napoleon a liberator or a tyrant? In truth, he is both, for only a tyrant could have imposed the Enlightenment on the old regimes.

In contrast with Pierre, his friend Prince Andrei Bolkonsky is a professional soldier devoted to martial honor and patriotic service. He longs for a cause in which to sacrifice himself, and the art of war provides the surest means. His father, the old Prince, is modeled on Voltaire, lost in his books and telescopes, sleeping in different rooms of his palace every night as he rummages restlessly through his manuscripts and collections. But the son is not content with a life of peace and learning; he longs for conflict. In this way, Tolstoy shows us that the Enlightenment's credo of peace, liberal education, and the satisfactions of private life are not for everyone. To use the Platonic term, a young man's *thumos*—his zeal and daring—cannot always be repressed or tranquilized by family life or the enjoyment of prosperity. Some men are born warriors. When Napoleon invades, he provides both Pierre and Andrei with a solution for their inner conflicts: loyalty to the Russian fatherland. The war of national defense gives the restless Andrei an outlet for his courage. For his part, Pierre finally realizes that, if he has to choose between liberalism imposed by a foreign conqueror and a Russia that is imperfect but still free, he will choose the latter.

America has experienced its own version of the paradox that conquest is sometimes the only means to freedom. During the Civil War, Abraham Lincoln was compelled, with infinite regret but inflexible purpose, to wage war on the half of his own country that refused to part with slavery, the most intolerable contradiction to democratic values imaginable. Stephen Crane's novel about that conflict, *The Red Badge of*

Courage, is the classic American story of a young man coming of age on the battlefield. As it begins, its hero, Henry Fleming, recalls his excitement at enlisting in the Union army. Although he had been taught to regard warfare as the vestige of a bygone age, happily left behind by the modern march of progress, like most young men, he secretly fantasized about being in battle:

> He had, of course, dreamed of battles all his life—of vague and bloody conflicts that had thrilled him with their sweep and fire. In visions he had seen himself in many struggles. He had imagined peoples secure in the shadow of his eagle-eyed prowess. But awake he had regarded battles as crimson blotches on the pages of the past. He had put them as things of the bygone with his thought-images of heavy crowns and high castles. There was a portion of the world's history which he had regarded as the time of wars, but it, he thought, had been long gone over the horizon and had disappeared forever.

Like all young men about to taste combat for the first time, he cannot escape a nagging question: Will I run? In his first encounter with the enemy, he does in fact flee. But in the second battle he stands his ground and, in Crane's words, becomes a "war-devil." He had passed the test of manhood, surprising himself with his own ferocity:

> These incidents made the youth ponder. It was revealed to him that he had been a barbarian, a beast. He had fought like a pagan who defends his religion. Regarding it, he saw that it was fine, wild, and, in some ways, easy. He had been a tremendous figure, no doubt. By this struggle he had overcome obstacles which he had admitted to be mountains. They had fallen like paper peaks, and he was now what he called a hero. And he had not been aware of the process. He had slept and, awakening, found himself a knight.

TERRORISM, TOTALITARIANISM, AND THE PERVERSION OF COURAGE

Napoleon was a new kind of conqueror, a democratic Caesar who destroyed for the sake of peace. Adding a new twist to the old doctrine of courage as a mean between two extremes of rashness and pacifism, he exercised limitless daring on behalf of an ideal of perfect brotherhood. Napoleon thus anticipates the even more catastrophic ideological wars of the twentieth century, in which brutal despots like Hitler and Stalin justified the conquest and murder of tens of millions on the grounds that, once the impediments to the brotherhood of mankind were finally exterminated, a thousand-year kingdom of heaven on earth would reign. And well-meaning Western intellectuals, bewitched by these charismatic tyrants speaking the language of millenarian happiness, experienced the same ambivalence about them as Tolstoy's Pierre Bezukhov does about Napoleon; initially starstruck, they would later grow profoundly disillusioned and disgusted.

Totalitarianism and terrorism have spawned an extreme perversion of courage. As we know only too well from the last century and the opening years of the new one, the attraction of young men to struggle and glory has been perverted to serve some of the worst tyrannies known to human history. What leads young men to murder innocents for the sake of a cause? How does a man come to the point where he is rigging a bomb to explode on a school bus full of children, or aiming a machine gun at a line of naked women in front of a mass grave? There are, of course, many theories. A psychological profile presented at the French trial of Carlos the Jackal (his real name is Ilich Ramirez Sanchez), the notorious terrorist who masterminded the 1972 Olympic Village massacre and many other acts of bloodshed, suggested that he was revenging himself on bourgeois society for taunts he had received as a child for being overweight and unathletic. This interpretation has its attractions. In a sense, it would be morally satisfying to believe that cowardly sneak attacks by a sniveling nonentity on unarmed civilians stem from a desire to feel powerful; that performing terrorist acts masks a deep sense of inner weakness and worthlessness, a worm trying to convince himself that he's a lion by killing children.

But it would be simplistic to leave it at that. For one thing, not all terrorists are cowards in the ordinary sense of the traditional definition going back to Aristotle. The men who destroyed the World Trade Center in September 2001 were neither rash nor cowardly in the obvious meaning of those terms. They did not act on an impulse of spasmodic fury but planned their action methodically for months, including all the necessary technical training. And then they deliberately sacrificed their own lives as the necessary guarantee of success in attaining their objective. This was evil, but it was not cowardly or rash.

Such observations don't invalidate the traditional distinction between courage and cowardice. They only demonstrate that courage itself is not the most important criterion for evaluating honorable and dishonorable action. When terrorists act on principle, they need to be condemned not primarily for their lack of courage but for the moral bankruptcy of their principles. Murdering innocent civilians, even when it requires courage, is nevertheless dishonorable because it is unjust and despicable, the act of a soul twisted and scarred with resentment, intolerance, and hatred. Terrorists may not be lacking physical courage in the narrowest meaning of the term, but their war is unjust.

The two worst totalitarian systems of our age, Nazism and Bolshevism, were brought to power by terrorist movements made up of young men with the same twisted psychology and perverted idealism as the cadres of al-Qaida, Hizbollah, or fringe radicals like Timothy McVeigh. Both Nazism and Bolshevism appealed strongly to young men and encouraged a bizarre idealism whereby they could convince themselves that wars of aggression and mass murder served a shining ideal that would bring about a golden age for all mankind. The leading Bolsheviks who served under Lenin, including Stalin, Trotsky, and Bukharin, were surprisingly young when they took power. As for the Nazis, one of the first demographic groups to join their ranks as a bloc in the 1930s were university students, which is why the Nazis were often simply referred to as the *Jugendbewegung*, the youth movement. The Hitler Youth traced its origins to a hippielike "back to nature" movement beginning around the turn of the century known as the Ramblers (*Wandervogelin*). Mostly middle-class and well off, they liked to hike, camp, and sing around the campfire as a way of asserting their opposition to materialistic bourgeois life. First regularized by the Nazis as the boy troops we see in Leni Riefenstahl's famous propaganda film *Triumph of the Will*, the Hitler Youth formations often passed directly into the SS, the elite ideological warriors who carried out the Holocaust.

Young men are attracted to revolution because it appears to justify heroism, valor, and self-sacrifice, which have few permissible outlets in modern democratic society. Capitalism often corrodes premodern traditions of patriotism and faith, and if it doesn't succeed in bringing about the prosperity it promises and isn't accompanied by genuine democratic reform, it can provoke a backlash in the name of national dignity against the Enlightenment's entire civilizational project of individual liberty, tolerance, and elected government. This backlash helps to explain the appeal of third-world socialism and what the Chinese Communist ideologue Lin Piao termed the revolt of "the backyard of the world" against the wealthy West. V. S. Naipaul makes the same observation about the appeal of Islamic fundamentalism to young men in the Muslim world. It begins with the unsatisfactory progress of economic modernization in developing economies and harnesses that resentment to the deeper anger over the loss of a traditional collective identity, so that war against the West simultaneously avenges what is seen as the West's economic exploitation and roots out its corrupt secularizing values.

Western intellectuals have often displayed an armchair voyeurism about this kind of revolutionary violence. Those who are most addicted to the vision of a future utopia of perfect peace have often been among the most fervent apologists for terrorism in the present, as long as it is aimed at destroying corrupt bourgeois society (the same liberal democratic civilization that provides their professorships and villas). From Sartre to Foucault, French leftist intellectuals rarely encountered a form of revolutionary terror they didn't like. Sartre's hit parade of genocidal pinup boys included Stalin and Mao. Foucault effused about the Ayatollah Khomeini as "a mystic saint." Closer to home, American intellectuals have sometimes displayed a similar ambivalence about violence, decrying it as a general ideological position while being attracted psychologically to it as a matter of personal voyeurism and aesthetics.

A leading example is Norman Mailer. He has argued that twentieth-century military technology removes glory from combat because it allows us to kill anonymously by raining bombs from the sky. In this view technology both insulates us from the perils of combat and restricts our freedom for brave deeds by making us cogs in the wheel of mechanized and computerized destruction. In my view, this was always an exaggerated claim. One would be hard-pressed to deny the many acts of battlefield bravery by the soldiers of the democracies during the Vietnam War, the Gulf War, or the wars of aggression launched on Israel. There was no dearth of battlefield bravery and honor, including air combat. One suspects Mailer of shedding crocodile tears over something he'd loathe if it were accorded more public recognition and gratitude. When commentators claim to bemoan the loss of glory in combat, it is often in order to justify doing nothing warlike in the present. This was particularly evident during the air campaign against Kosovo, when the odd view was aired that the bombing of a genocidal regime was somehow unworthy because no one on our side ran the risk of being killed. People who regarded military honor with suspicion in principle were suddenly arguing that only if American combat troops were "blooded" would the war against Milosevic be worth fighting. And yet military doctrine from Julius Caesar to Dwight Eisenhower—not to mention common sense—has held that the purpose of war is victory at the smallest possible cost in lives.

In the case of Mailer, his professed admiration for an allegedly long-departed creed of truly manly combat—in contrast with the allegedly "bloodless" and "technological" war of today—also justifies an unhealthy and self-indulgent hero worship of criminal violence and revolutionary fanaticism as a legitimate protest against bourgeois complacency. Mailer experienced his own personal little Vietnam when he lionized a convicted murderer, Jack Abbott, helped him to publish his prison memoirs, and obtained his release from prison by speaking to the parole board on his behalf. Mailer gave Abbott a research job and introduced him to celebrities and literati around Manhattan. Mailer seemed to believe that this heartless sociopath was a genuine "homegrown" revolutionary, our version of those brave freedom fighters under Ho Chi Minh or the Red Guards. Mailer's voyeuristic thrill ended when, six weeks after his release, Abbott stabbed a young man to death outside a Manhattan restaurant for the wrong choice of words. When you lionize a murderer and help him get out of prison, is it surprising that the first thing he does is murder another innocent, because he was enraged at an imagined petty slight?

Mailer and intellectuals like him perfectly illustrate Aristotle's point, at least in their heads and from the safety of their privileged enclaves.

They are incapable of seeing courage as a golden mean between extremes. Either they are pacifists and one-worlders or they worship mad daring and fanaticism, often because of a patently ludicrous belief that a world of peace can be brought about by bloodshed and terror. In the face of such stubborn resistance to common sense, one wonders if their utopian ideology of global peace doesn't mask and excuse the vicarious love of violence and fantasies of revenge by cloaking them in a humanitarian motive. Foucault's Marxism was largely based on the writings of Georges Sorel, a worshiper of vitality and struggle against the complacency of materialistic bourgeois wimps; Sorel's writings are widely viewed as one of the inspirations for fascism. Sorel influenced Mussolini, and his vision of manhood can be seen in both fascist and Bolshevik poster art, those brawny titans whose more benign American descendants are comic book heroes like the Hulk or the actor-acrobats of World Wrestling Entertainment. When academics grow effusive about hip and daring young warriors against the West, such as Che Guevera, it's hard not to wonder if their enthusiasm doesn't stem from a long-standing desire to be one of the guys, as if they had found a way in adult life finally to be chosen for the football team.

OUR SQUEAMISHNESS

As I observed earlier, modern theories of motivation from Hobbes down to Harold Lasswell and the contemporary social sciences are frequently unequipped to account for and make sense of this depraved version of the warrior spirit, because the theories reduce human behavior to material self-interest. The traditional wisdom about courage as a mean between rashness and cowardice has never been more relevant than during the century just past and the century just begun. From Stalin and Hitler to al-Qaida, totalitarian and terrorist movements force us to abandon this pedestrian theory of human motivation, which ignores the capacity for glory, honor, and self-sacrifice, and return to the full-blooded evocations of male aggression and tyranny found in Plato and Aristotle. Before we can redirect these darker masculine passions, we have to begin by admitting they exist, and recovering the richness of the traditional psychology of manly valor. Until we do, we will be doomed to veer endlessly between pacifism and fanaticism or, as Aristotle would have put it, between cowardice and rashness.

The obstacles to recognizing the traditional wisdom about courage are formidable. They involve sacred cows that our opinion elites and universities cling to in defiance of all known historical experience and common sense. Let's consider a few of those delusions. Since the 1960s, we have witnessed a relentless campaign to demystify and demythologize war and martial valor. In university courses on international relations, wars of the past are almost always reinterpreted in light of the war in Vietnam. Hence all war is reduced, as we saw earlier, to the moralistic abstraction of "violence." This abstraction ignores the substantive differences between good and evil causes, and leaves little room for a legitimate role for manly honor. Even the history of World War II, the best example of a clear-cut battle between good and evil, can be rewritten by academic theorists of international relations as another lamentable expression of a universal "patriarchal" impulse toward "hegemony" rather than as something caused by the unjust ambitions of Germany and Japan. This kind of vapid moralizing, which is so fastidious and embarrassed about making judgments as to which sides are just or unjust, leads to a view of history as driven by impersonal forces and universal abstractions rather than by virtuous and vicious men.

As a consequence, it has become increasingly impermissible to extol or even explore masculine martial prowess or statesmanship. Partly out of a distaste for martial honor, partly out of an overfastidiousness about giving offense by describing male psychology, universities increasingly opt not to teach the narrative history of war, statesmanship, and diplomacy in international relations courses. All events are explained in terms of global economic trends and dependency theory. War is treated as an aberration or a selfish power agenda, and rarely judged as honorable or dishonorable depending on the cause for which it is waged. The memoirs of Lloyd George, Churchill, Acheson, or Kissinger are less likely to be found in the course syllabus than something along lines of "a Foucauldian analysis of international dependency theory with special attention to patterns of gendered aggression, supplemented by queer theory and a Derridean deconstruction of neocolonialist hegemony." Genuine military and diplomatic achievements go uncelebrated, for fear of stimulating the alleged latent warmongering spirit of the American people.

As a consequence, we have come perilously close during the last thirty years to losing the sense that war can be ennobling. Whereas our victory in World War II produced a long celebration and reflection on the evils of totalitarianism, the victory over the equally evil Soviet regime produced no comparable national dialogue. In the case of both victories, fine work has been done by scholars for the benefit of other specialists. But there is no Cold War equivalent of the hugely popular middlebrow epic of World War II, William Shirer's *Rise and Fall of the Third Reich*. When I was growing up, it seemed like almost every household had this book on display, often alongside Churchill's memoirs of the war. For the most part, the works of major scholars of the Soviet era, such as Robert Conquest, have not crossed over into best-sellerdom, as did, say, Alan Bullock's study of Hitler. No sooner was victory over the evil empire in view than liberal commentators such as Michael Kinsley were rushing to warn us against taking any credit or feeling any sense of pride in the achievement. It was "inevitable," they constantly proclaimed, it would have happened anyway and in no way confirmed the moral superiority of American democracy to Soviet Communism or (God forbid above all) the sagacity of the Reagan administration's statesmanship.

And yet the victims of Soviet totalitarianism, who had seen it up close and felt the wolf's hot breath on their necks, usually took a very different view. Andrej Sakharov was a notable case in point. A Nobel laureate and one of the creators of the Soviet Union's nuclear capability, he was also an indefatigable critic of the regime and its human rights abuses, and had suffered a long internal exile in harrowing conditions before being pardoned by Gorbachev. Interviewers sometimes asked him about his opinion of Ronald Reagan, confident that, like educated people in the West with their horror of Reagan's "simplistic" distrust of the Soviet leadership and lack of a "nuanced" approach to the "ambiguity" of international relations, he would decry this "cowboy" for provoking the Soviet Union by departing from the "bipartisan" approach supposedly embodied by Jimmy Carter.

Sakharov's reply? He endorsed Reagan's policies. Sakharov favored U.S. and NATO deployment of Pershing and cruise missiles in Europe as a necessary countermeasure to the Soviet Union's relentless pursuit of nuclear superiority. As he knew from long experience of the Soviet system, its rulers, not Reagan, were to blame for escalating the arms race. In standing up to the Soviets over their attempt to block placement of the new missiles, Reagan had delivered a timely check to their bullying bluff. As for the peace movement, Sakharov sympathized with its ideals but criticized its naïveté in blaming only the United States while swallowing Soviet propaganda hook, line, and sinker.

There is a widespread perception among American opinion makers that to discuss the psychology of violence and tyranny at length is in some way to indulge in a taste for it. This is rather like concluding that Alan Bullock and Robert Conquest must have had a secret hankering to *be* Hitler or Stalin because they wrote such brilliant biographies of the tyrants. This discomfort with distinguishing dishonorable from honorable motivations for the use of force has increasingly sapped our ability to recognize tyranny for what it is, along with our ability to distinguish between legitimate regimes ruled by law and despotisms that maintain their dynamism through saber rattling and aggression.

When the innate and ineradicable male taste for contest and command is stigmatized and repressed in public life and expelled from respectable academic debate, not surprisingly it is deflected to the trivia of private life, like computer games, or worse, the murderous nihilistic fantasies of a Timothy McVeigh. An underfathered and lonely misfit, McVeigh came to see the real world as a series of video targets ranged against himself, until he blew up the building in Oklahoma City containing what he perceived to be hundreds of little stick men and women who deserved death for making the world a frustrating place for him.

As we observed at the outset of these reflections, certain strains of popular entertainment culture contribute to the narcissism exemplified in its most extreme form by McVeigh. They flatter the young male ego into thinking that one can be a hero without knowing anything about the past, or about the substantive policy debates of the present. Technological wizardry and game playing foster the illusion that precocious young men can do without the moral and intellectual education that was the traditional hallmark of manliness. For example, in the movie *WarGames,* the teenage hacker played by Matthew Broderick can't keep his room clean and changes his grades by hacking into the school computer. He knows nothing about the Cold War, but through these same value-neutral game-playing skills, saves the world from nuclear destruction. In many schools, history now is taught through video games; in one that I've seen, a kid with a skateboard shows up at various disconnected historical crisis points (for example, Lincoln pondering the Emancipation Proclamation) and solves the problem with a few flippant remarks about everybody's need to chill out.

These trends only reinforce the wisdom of Aristotle's view of courage as a mean between two extremes. Often it seems as if we're either too passive or too wild—there's no middle ground. In the world beyond the United States, the weakening of the nation-state combines with the parody of masculinity as nihilistic violence to produce a cult of "road-warrior" ethnic tribalism. As the empirical research we touched upon earlier shows, these wars are being fought by young men in their teens and twenties—but not because of a biological drive. They are warriors in the revolution for nihilism. In Rwanda, the Balkans, Somalia, and Afghanistan, they have been acting out in real life the creed of violence for the sake of violence that Edward Norton's character fantasizes about in *Fight Club* through his creation of his blond beast of an alter ego, Tyler Durden. (What's more, the Rambo kids in many of these third-world murder zones are probably watching the movie between killing sprees.) In his book *The Warrior's Honor*, Michael Ignatieff revealingly describes the "militias" in Rwanda and the Balkans: "The young warriors on both sides wear the same international uniform: the tight-fitting combat fatigues, designer shades and headbands popularized by Sylvester Stallone's Rambo." As globalization erodes substantive differences between peoples, the remaining small symbolic differences are blown out of all proportion, a trend that Ignatieff sums up perfectly as "the narcissism of minor differences." One tribe wants to kill another simply because it's another group, or over some imagined slight or rumored injury. The lines blur between patriotism and the mentality of the Cosa Nostra. It's as if Tyler Durden ruled a country.

The degeneration of military tradition into sociopathic thuggery yields a conclusion diametrically opposite to the one advanced by Neil Wiener and Christian Mesquida, the psychologists whose survey research on the causal connection between young males and international conflict we discussed earlier. The rise of the road-warrior militias on the crumbling margins of failed or stalled modernization, where traditional communal values of self-restraint and peaceable deliberation have been undermined without being successfully replaced by the civilizational project of the secular Enlightenment, points not to the absence of "ideology and religion" as causes of conflict but to their *intensification* in an increasingly morally debased and intellectually vulgarized form. The doctrine of the just war, with its mooring in the psychology of virtue, once gave different faiths and ethnic communities at least a chance to converse in common terms about the sources of enmity between them, and agree that limits were imposed on the use of military force by all civilized societies. The languishing of those traditions, however, reduces war to the most naked, historically ignorant, and hate-filled clash of Us against Them. It's not the continued influence of traditional concepts of manly honor that has made the wars of our era so dismally pitiless and stupid but the absence of those concepts.

All of these observations converge in a single overwhelming conclusion: You can't get rid of the male character, you can only drive it underground, where it will assume a distorted shape and sometimes resurface as a monster. During the same period that real wars and martial prowess were being demystified and stigmatized, martial pride was steadily deflected to the realm of entertainment fantasy (*Star Wars, Star Trek, Rambo, The Terminator*), becoming one of America's most profitable businesses at home and for export. In this realm, our admiration for courage can safely reemerge, because it is detached from an explicit defense of the United States, liberal democracy, and the West. The Star Wars trilogy was a revealing case in point. Faithfully viewed by millions over a ten-year period, it amounted to a Baby Boomers' Ring Cycle. In it, the same generation that prided itself on leading the peace movement and preaching "love not war" was able vicariously to scramble on the flight deck and risk their lives against a tyrannical aggressor, the Empire. That empire was a transparent stand-in for *the* Empire, the source of all oppression—the superpower the New Left had delighted in branding, with a gesture to Kafka's tales of faceless bureaucratic oppression, "Amerika." By deriving the warrior spirit from a New Age concoction of

California Zen and hippie mysticism, Star Wars was covertly exploring the fantasy of an armed counterculture battling the Nixonian Darth Vader—a longing for honorable combat that its real-life counterparts could not express.

The deflection of the suppressed taste for warfare and honor to the entertainment culture can have positive dimensions. Some video games, movies, and television series do appeal to a boy's wish to be a hero in a constructive way, engaging his imagination in solidly researched historical adventures that hone his thinking skills. In the second Star Trek series, for example, we get a nice illustration of the argument in Plato's *Republic* that reason should govern spiritedness. Riker, the second in command, is courageous in a steady, sober, and dutiful way. He is the ideal combat officer, subordinating himself willingly to the larger strategies of Picard, an exceptionally cerebral and reflective captain whose favorite off-duty relaxations include archaeology, the piano, and reading Klingon philosophical commentaries on the shortcomings of Kant's system of ethics. Star Trek comes closer to exploring traditional masculine themes of bravery, self-sacrifice, insubordination, republican virtue, and imperialism than a good deal of contemporary schooling. Its elaborate pseudohistories of peoples like the Klingons embody warrior virtues that are politically incorrect to attribute to human beings today. It's a way of studying them on the sly.

Still, the majority of video games and combat movies stress endless death, battle, and destruction bereft of historical context or redeeming moral purpose—and our civic culture pays a heavy price for this flight into fantasy. As the memoirs of de Gaulle and other modern soldiers reveal, the study of actual military history shows us how the material and physical conditions of the empirical world—together with our human limitations, virtues, and character flaws—temper our expectations of military prowess and how much can be achieved by relying on it. This is why the history of war is a such valuable component in the history of manly virtue—not because it "glorifies" war but because, on the contrary, military history moderates the warrior spirit and brings it under the guidance of courage tempered by prudence and knowledge. Anyone who has met high-ranking military men knows that, if anything, they tend to be unusually restrained, reflective, and moderate about the use of military force. War is too lethal a business to revel in. By contrast, much of our entertainment culture stimulates an onanistic fantasy of the solitary power to destroy, severed from the experience of relations with one's fellow citizens or from the defense of any honorable public aim. Game culture is ultimately infantilizing, like giving an angry child a howitzer.

THE HAPPY WARRIOR

As recently as JFK, a president could still openly praise courage in the full-blooded traditional language we have recalled in this essay. I wonder if much of our distorted thinking about courage doesn't stem from the still-tragic hole his assassination left in American life. An unquestionably brave war hero, he turned to public service and as president represented a generation of veterans in a way that served the highest ideals of liberal progress at home and liberal internationalism to oppose tyranny abroad. His death brought to power men who sometimes had not fought but were willing to send the next generation of young men to their deaths in a war which they were ashamed to declare openly and which privately they neither believed in nor thought winnable. This moral vacuum placed veterans in a difficult position. Although they honored their own service, they couldn't always blame their sons for not wanting to fight a war waged in secret and with no convincing justification or strategy for victory. More than one World War II vet who began by being ashamed of his son for protesting the war and avoiding service ended up by admiring his courage in taking a stand, even risking jail.

JFK's crucial point was that, however much we admire battlefield courage, its highest vindication is that it can help to instill the psychological temperament needed for moral courage. There is an intrinsic connection between battlefield courage and the courage of democratic citizenship. As he wrote in the conclusion to *Profiles in Courage*:

> To be courageous, these stories make clear, requires no exceptional qualifications, no magic formula, no special combination of time, place

and circumstance. It is an opportunity that sooner or later is presented to us all. Politics merely furnishes one arena which imposes special tests of courage. In whatever arena of life one may meet the challenge of courage, whatever may be the sacrifices he faces if he follows his conscience—the loss of his friends, his fortune, his contentment, even the esteem of his fellow men—each man must decide for himself the course he will follow. The stories of past courage can define that ingredient—they can teach, they can offer hope, they can provide inspiration. But they cannot supply courage itself. For this each man must look into his own soul.

JFK was something of an Anglophile, and the English poet Wordsworth's poem "The Happy Warrior" is very much in the spirit of Kennedy's reflections. So perhaps that is a good place for this exploration of courage to come to rest. The taste for battle—on behalf of justice and ideas—can ennoble us. Anything worthwhile we want to do in life requires bravery.

> *Who is the happy Warrior? Who is he*
> *That every man in arms should wish to be?*
> *—It is the generous Spirit, who, when brought*
> *Among the tasks of real life, hath wrought*
> *Upon the plan that pleased his boyish thought:*
> *Whose high endeavors are an inward light*
> *That makes the path before him always bright:*
> *Who, with a natural instinct to discern*
> *What knowledge can perform, is diligent to learn;*
> *Abides by this resolve, and stops not there,*
> *But makes his moral being his prime care . . .*
>
> *Rises by open means, and there will stand*
> *On honorable terms, or else retire*
> *And in himself possess his own desire;*
> *Who comprehends his trust, and to the same*
> *Keeps faithful with a singleness of aim;*
> *And therefore does not stoop, nor lie in wait*
> *For wealth, or honors, or for worldly state.*

This returns us to our opening reflections. Courage on behalf of a good cause is honorable and necessary, but it is not among the very highest virtues. It needs to be governed by higher virtues of moderation and prudence. Its chief justification is that it provides a man with the moral energy and strength of will to fight for what is right in our larger civic culture. Public service is higher than military glory, for it calls on us to exercise higher moral and intellectual faculties. Ultimately, the noblest form of courage is the struggle to defend and extend justice and to overcome our own baser instincts. And that requires pride—our next topic in the search for the manly heart.

III.

PRIDE

THE QUESTION OF PRIDE BRINGS US TO THE CENTRAL ISSUE IN OUR search for the code of man. How should a man live in order to be proud of himself and to make his family and friends proud of him? Or is pride a quality we should even want to cultivate? Does encouraging men to feel pride in themselves simply encourage male aggression, including arrogance and insensitivity toward women?

Not everybody thinks so. The terms of the debate are perhaps most clearly revealed when we look at the rearing and education of boys. A growing number of psychologists have begun to express concern that attempts to suppress boyish high spirits, competitiveness, and aggressiveness may do far more harm than good in the long run. In almost every measurable sphere of behavior, boys today are doing worse than girls. Boys and young men are five times as likely to commit suicide, four times as likely to be diagnosed as emotionally disturbed, and six times as likely to have attention deficit disorder; across the board, they perform considerably worse in school than their sisters. Since these disturbing measurements coincide with the increasing influence of feminism over a thirty-year period, a few experts have dared to ask whether there might be a cause-and-effect relationship between the project of curtailing "gender specific" male traits and the steady rise in male dysfunction. They deplore the tendency in our educational institutions to treat boyishness as a pathology requiring treatment with powerful psychotropic drugs like Ritalin. As they see it, medication and behavior modification have taken the place of the traditional way of moderating boyish excesses—shame and exhortations to goodness.

Unfortunately, this is still a minority view. While the academic and psychiatric establishments have begun to notice the increasing problems of boys and young men, their usual answer is to expand and intensify the social experiment of extending feminism to men, as a way to cure what the Harvard psychologist Carol Gilligan terms their masculine "willfulness." As Professor Gilligan puts it, "Just as adolescent girls struggle with their socialization toward cultural constructions of femininity, boys may experience a similar struggle in early childhood." Studies reveal "parallel symptoms of psychological stress among boys—depression and evidence of struggle and conflict." The cause? According to Professor Gilligan, it all starts when young boys "are faced with heightened pressures to conform more rigidly to cultural constructions of masculinity." In other words, whereas the solution for girls' problems is to encourage the flowering of their gender "difference" (the favored postmodernist term), the solution for boys' problems is to do everything possible to get rid of *their* distinct differences as males. The "cultural construction" of "masculinity" is still the common foe, the common obstacle to progress. But after three decades of precisely this kind of "socialization" of boys to forestall their masculinity, doesn't it make sense to wonder whether the very attempt to repress their natural energies is contributing to "depression and evidence of struggle and conflict" in boys? Why not, instead, encourage a constructive flowering of distinctively masculine "difference" to parallel what has already been done with such great success for girls? Justice is not a zero-sum game in a society of open opportunity like America. Letting boys be themselves need not endanger the gains made by girls.

A more benign version of Professor Gilligan's position has been argued by Dr. William Pollack in a series of popular books about the psychology and behavioral problems of boys. His passion and sincerity are admirable, and his anecdotal descriptions of how boys cope with everyday life are of great value. But his analysis suffers from the same flaw. Dr. Pollack begins with the same empirical evidence of boys' increasingly poor academic performance and behavioral and psychological disorders. He, too, argues that these problems are caused by social pressure on boys to be tough and unfeeling and to repress their sensitive and emotional sides. But to read Dr. Pollack, one might think boys were still living in the grim world of switchblades and chicken races from *Rebel*

Without a Cause, instead of in the sunny uplands of BoBo tolerance that are the reality for the middle-class majority today. Society has already spent decades on an ever-intensifying campaign to pressure boys to renounce that old tough-guy code and extend to them the alleged blessings of the feminist project, conditioning them to give up their masculine traits and become more caring, consensual, and sensitive. If, during that same period, levels of depression and dysfunction among boys have soared, then again we are compelled to ask whether the very project Pollack advocates may be contributing to the problems he so accurately and feelingly diagnoses. There is every reason to wonder whether the extension of the feminist project to boys is contributing to their depression by making them deny their true natures.

The campaign to stigmatize and eradicate the distinctive features of male psychology—thereby eliminating the only basis upon which men could take pride in their own distinctive natures—has provoked a backlash, veering to the opposite extreme of the "men's consciousness" movement. Modeled on the earlier social movements promoting black and gay pride, the men's movement attempts to depict men as another minority or victim group—in my view, with the same danger of sectarian isolation that can attend all such victim groups, and with far less justification than in the case of ethnic minorities or gays. In reality, it's not possible for an entire gender to be oppressed in the same way as it is for a racial or sexual minority.

This is true for several reasons. Since each gender makes up half of the human race, both men and women have access to almost limitless possibilities for individual advancement through talent and hard work. Within these two broad divisions of the human race, we find that the equality of individual opportunity for an earned inequality of result—the hallmark of American democracy—generates an almost infinite variety of levels of success and choice of vocations. It is therefore impossible for either men or women to be classified in a single sweeping generalization as victimized or oppressed. Moreover, far fewer people have an irrational hatred for men or women as a gender than is the case with the unfortunately large number of idiots who hate black or gay people. To the extent that the men's movement portrays the male gender collectively as victims, it is aping the most narcissistic excesses of feminism itself.

The men's movement is symptomatic of a larger problem facing American civic culture—its disintegration into a kaleidoscope of single-issue advocacy groups at the cost of any overarching sense of citizenship. Over the last thirty years, the concept of pride has too often been distorted into a stubborn assertion of group identity, as if this were necessarily something good in itself. I'm proud to be me, I'm proud because I exist, proud because I have one defining identity—gender, sexual preference, or ethnicity. This new tribalism began in the Nixon era, when the rise of black consciousness was paralleled by the rise of the "new ethnics." Films like *The Godfather* reflected the growing belief that family and clan were more meaningful and worthy of loyalty than the broader civic culture. It was a reaction against what was increasingly seen as the bloodless universalism of the melting pot, and the idea that Americans had more in common as citizens than as members of subcultures. At its best, this kind of group pride can invigorate our wider civic life with the unique perspective and kinship ties of an ethnic or religious heritage. But at its worst, it can degenerate into mere tribalism, a crude and narrow-minded code of Us against Them.

Pride has to be more than an unquestioning loyalty to our own group, for after all even our own people, families, children, and coreligionists sometimes behave shamefully. Indeed, pride comes fully into its own when we begin to transcend such group loyalties and blood ties in favor of universally admired standards of justice, goodness, and wisdom. True heroes belong to all mankind, not only to their own people, clan, or faith. Much as we admire, say, Aleksandr Solzhenitsyn and Nelson Mandela for their courage against tyranny, what's even more impressive is their ability to rise above even the most justified partisanship on behalf of their own people and speak to the conscience of the entire world—displaying what Thomas Jefferson termed "a decent respect to the opinions of mankind." Both Solzhenitsyn and Mandela reached a spiritual epiphany when, after decades of brutal imprisonment and persecution, they emerged victorious over their oppressors—and then urged their fellow victims to forgive their tormentors and reconcile with them. Mandela wanted to free both black South Africans from the oppression of apartheid and white South Africans from its moral stain on their souls. Similarly, when Martin Luther King delivered his unforgettable speech on freedom at the Lincoln Memorial, he spoke for poor whites as well as for blacks. With men such as these, giants whom we all admire, we know we are in the presence of something even more rare and admirable than justice and courage. This is nobility.

Noble conduct justifies pride in others and in ourselves. But what, then, is the source of pride in a man's character? What is its psychological makeup? The answer given for most of the last three thousand years of Western civilization is that pride is built upon a well-ordered soul—a balance of active and contemplative virtues. Men have a code of honor to live up to, including all the cardinal virtues of courage, justice, wisdom, compassion, and generosity. To the extent that they strive with all their power to reach that goal, they are entitled to feel proud. This is why Aristotle, for example, says that pride is the ornament of all the moral virtues. You can be courageous or compassionate without experiencing pride. But if you are truly entitled to take pride in yourself, you cannot be lacking in courage, compassion, or any other virtue of character. And, because men are capable of aspiring to proud conduct, it is equally important that they have a capacity for shame at failing to live up to that code.

According to the traditional teaching, men do not need to choose between excessive harshness and excessive sensitivity. We aren't forced to be beasts or wimps—to choose between Adolf Hitler and Rod McKuen, or between Tyler Durden and his lame alter ego. Physical courage is the necessary but not sufficient condition for pride. As we saw in the last chapter, courage points beyond itself to higher virtues, furnishing the energy for moral and intellectual vigor and a relish for reasoned debate. A man's pride does not consist of mere willfulness. That would be to mistake pride for stubbornness. A mule isn't proud, it's just set in its ways. However, and with all due respect to Professor Gilligan, there's nothing necessarily wrong with masculine willfulness. It isn't a problem that has to be eradicated. Like every other moral energy, willfulness is neither good nor bad in itself. It all depends on whether it's used for base or for noble purposes. If we accept, then, that strength of will is the minimal condition for pride, there's no reason to call for a moratorium on masculine willpower. What we need is to rechannel it toward goals of which we can be proud.

THE CODE OF MAN

PRIDE OR FAITH?

But can a man be proud without being arrogant and overbearing? In modern times we often tend to think not. Moreover, the major religious teachings have always stressed that faith rather than pride is the core of a good life, and that humility before the greatness and mercy of God is the foundation for all the moral virtues. It's not so much that Islam, Judaism, Christianity, Hinduism, and the other faiths are simply opposed to pride. On the contrary: their scriptures and theologies believe that a man who walks in the ways of righteousness and obeys God is truly honorable. Their objection is that an emphasis on purely secular, this-worldly honor can lead us astray. If we believe we can achieve anything honorable by ourselves, unaided by God's grace, our pride is in reality a kind of vanity, arrogance, and vainglory. In the rest of this essay, we'll look at some of the main features of this profound debate over the sources of happiness.

The ancient philosophers believed that a justified pride in one's accomplishments can be the basis for good behavior toward others, a teaching that has endured through the centuries until just yesterday. The classic definition of pride, echoed by authorities throughout the Renaissance, the Enlightenment, and down to the twentieth century, comes from Aristotle's *Nicomachean Ethics*. The word he uses for pride literally means "greatness of soul." A proud man will not stoop to treat others unjustly or unkindly, because doing so would reveal his need for others as objects of exploitation. It is a source of shame to be dependent on others, especially for the gratification of coarse and uncontrollable appetites. A proud man is generous and decent toward others precisely because he doesn't need anything from them.

Aristotle tells us that pride is the crown of all the moral virtues, including courage, self-control, and generosity. The proud man is the source of his own self-esteem, amply confirmed by the honor he receives from his fellow citizens. He disdains the humdrum issues of everyday politics, reserving his extraordinary talents for the gravest challenges of war and peace. He'll nod off over a position paper on the capital gains tax, but the prospect of a major international conflict will bring him quickly back to life. One thinks of men like Lincoln, Churchill, Franklin

Roosevelt, de Gaulle, and other great leaders who did not fully shine until called upon to conduct a war against an unjust cause, and who were often not as successful in dealing with the more ordinary economic and social issues of domestic political life. For Aristotle, being a proud man means cultivating moral and intellectual virtues that achieve real results in our service to the common good, our families, and our friends. Virtue is not just a good intention or a state of bliss—it is a deed. A virtuous man needs friends with whom he can cooperate in honorable enterprises, friends whose honor is worth having because they are honorable as well.

There is probably a bit of tongue-in-cheek in Aristotle's description of "greatness of soul." The proud man, he tells us, "is moderately delighted by great honors when they are bestowed by the deserving, as being his due." However, "he only accepts such honors if nothing better can be bestowed." It's as if, when being informed that you had simultaneously won a Pulitzer Prize and the Congressional Medal of Honor, you blandly replied: "Yes, of course. How nice. Thanks. But . . . what about the Nobel?" The proud man, Aristotle goes on, will react to "wealth, power, good or bad fortune" with "the same dignified composure, neither elated with prosperity nor dejected by adversity." Ed McMahon and Dick Clark should avoid this guy when they bring a camera crew to record the reaction of sweepstakes winners. He's definitely not going to scream and jump up and down. When handed that million-dollar check, he'll pause for a moment, then say: "Right. Thanks. Could you call my accountant?"

Like a lot of great statesmen—Lincoln and Churchill come to mind—proud men can often be mediocre politicians when politics is restricted to everyday domestic affairs, rising to greatness only when war and destruction loom. Only the greatest challenges and the greatest opportunities for achievement and honorable public service rouse their full interest. Otherwise, like Churchill during his "wilderness years" out of the limelight, they'd rather stay up until four in the morning with a snifter and a good Havana, rise at noon, and host lunch for twenty as the sun sets. The proud man, Aristotle says, is "slow in action and averse to exertion, except when great honor may be obtained or great actions are to be performed, not busied about many things, but confined to those which are great and splendid." Aristotle's description makes one think of the Gary Cooper type in Westerns, who resolves to hang up his guns and be a peace-loving family man but who dons them once again to save the town from a clear and present danger.

A proud man can be unnervingly frank. If he's your friend, he'll pay you the compliment of assuming you want to be told the truth, however unpleasant. If he despises you, he'll tell you so to your face. "A proud man," as Aristotle puts it, "is as open in his hatred as in his friendship; for concealment is the part of fear. He regards truth more than opinion, declaring his mind with full freedom, which indicates both his own love of truth and his contempt for the opinions of others." University administrators, stay away from him!

Finally, the proud man prefers beautiful and useless possessions to practical items. Don't try to engage him in a conversation about the comparative merits of drill bits or lawn mowers. He'd rather buy a painting: "His possessions are distinguished for their beauty and elegance rather than for their fruitfulness and utility." He won't run for the bus—he'd rather miss it than make such a spectacle of himself. He's the guy who would rather drive out of his way for hours than ask for directions. And since he prefers to be silent when he has nothing original to say, he'll be a flop on a book tour: "The gait of a great-souled man is slow," Aristotle continues, "his tone of voice grave; his pronunciation firm. A man is seldom in haste when he deems few things worthy of his pursuit." Not suitable for *The O'Reilly Factor*.

Much of this standard goes against the grain of democracy. But we still experience pride and appeal to it. Pride and dignity can console us when we are the victims of injustice. Pride stops us from stooping to do evil. But pride must be tempered by wisdom in order to avoid degenerating into arrogance. Therefore pride is necessarily connected to wisdom. We need the wisdom to distinguish between good and bad reasons for feeling proud. And a life of mature reflection and spiritual fulfillment is the life of which we can be proudest, more so than a life spent making money or acquiring fame and power.

PRIDE AND WISDOM

Everyone would admit that there is some connection between pride and wisdom, since wisdom is one of those attainments in which we take the greatest pride. But the connection is not easy to define, and it has sparked a lively and even fierce debate over the centuries. For, after all, what do we mean by wisdom? On one level, it can be taken to mean a purely intellectual, abstract kind of reasoning—the grand contemplative speculations and metaphysical systems of philosophers from Plato to Hegel, the search by natural scientists for ever greater clarity about the universe, the mental beauties of pure mathematics, the jeweler's-eye precision of the logician.

But is there any *necessary* connection between this kind of intellectual prowess and the manly virtues? Does a man have to participate in philosophic or scientific wisdom in order to be wise in the affairs of state, or a good husband and father? Not necessarily. The word *wise* suggests a kind of human quality different from that indicated by words like *brilliant* or *smart*. As Aristotle tells us, a young man can be a brilliant logician or mathematician but does not possess enough experience of the world to be wise in civic affairs, family relations, and ethical behavior. You can be wise in this sense of the word without having the IQ of a Stephen Hawking. By contrast, someone can be a brilliant entrepreneur and technological wizard and still have the character of a child. We know of cases like this—men who become fabulously wealthy through some cybernetic innovation and spend gazillions on a house that looks like an airport terminal and is filled with giant-screen images of cartoons and other childish drivel. Some of them even write embarrassing books presuming to show the rest of us the way to the future—a philosopher with a Mickey Mouse watch.

Wisdom—as opposed to mere braininess or technological brilliance—suggests a mature character, tested and tempered by time, honed by adversity, and fortified by the earned insights of experience. Wisdom is not possible without moderation, a word which in ancient Greek meant literally a "sound mind." A young man can be a mathematical or musical prodigy but lack common sense about practical affairs. The latter comes only with age. An older man with little formal education but a solid character and experience can usually handle a difficult situation better than can a callow youth with straight A's. We've all observed this. The best recipe for happiness, according to the ancient thinkers, is the right balance of contemplative and active virtues gradually achieved over a lifetime of experience in the trials of public and private life. It's a teaching that weaves a golden thread throughout every period of reflection on the meaning of manliness down to the present.

The stern Roman moralist Cato the Elder once said that wise men learn more from fools than fools do from wise men, because wise men can learn from observation to avoid the errors of fools while fools rarely profit from the examples of the wise. This sharp distinction between the wise and the foolish does not sit well with our democratic instincts, but it is often amply justified by our everyday experiences. Wise men don't grow on trees. When you find one, you want to hold on to him. And again, wisdom is by no means necessarily a function of formal education. Only those who know academic life from the inside can have a full sense of the breathtaking naïveté, shallowness, vanity, and utter lack of common sense of which Ph.D.'s can be capable. I generally get more out of talking with my barber than out of conversations with many of my colleagues at the university, and far more out of talking with my students. (As you might gather from this, I'm also very fond of Aristotle's discussion of pride.)

Traditionally, and in our own experience as well, a wise man is known for being cautious and for taking nothing for granted, whether about ideas or people. Wisdom involves foresight about private and public life, a sense of timing that stems from an ability to discern prudently the likely pattern of events in the future and to trust those judgments. This ability to see future patterns is connected with open-mindedness and a capacity to look beyond the conventional wisdom of the status quo. As Thoreau puts it, "The wisest man preaches no doctrines, he has no scheme, he sees no rafter, not even a cobweb, against the heavens. It is clear sky." Being open-minded also implies rising above one's own prejudices and not mistaking one's present opinion for a fixed and unalterable truth. In this sense, wisdom is intrinsically connected with intellectual modesty. Echoing Socrates, Thomas Jefferson wrote that a wise man is the best expert on his own weaknesses and failings, for he understands how little he *really* knows when measured against the vastness of time, history, and the cosmos.

Just as important, wisdom has always been associated with the ability to live a simple life, a life of inner spiritual riches rather than outward material wealth. The wealth of the mind and spirit is more firmly entrenched, more securely possessed, than material goods, for while bad luck, illness, and other reversals of fortune can take our material goods away, the treasures of the soul can endure almost any degree of illness, poverty, or sorrow. This reliance on inner rather than external riches makes a wise man cosmopolitan—not in the negative sense of having no attachments to family and country but in the positive sense that he is less dependent on an economy devoted to maximizing material wealth than is someone whose only goal in life is to acquire "the biggest toys." Because his pleasures are spiritual rather than material, his soul is free to soar above bodily and material limitations, visiting all parts of the world and all eras of history through his books (and, of course, through the mind-broadening impact of actual travel to the cultural treasures of other lands, always an important part of liberal education). "Go where he will," as Emerson observes, "the wise man is always at home."

Finally, as always in our reflections on pride, we must remember that there is a special kind of wisdom conferred by faith. As the Ecclesiast tells us, true wisdom comes from submitting to the will of God. A young man is entitled to feel his oats—to enjoy his youth and the graces peculiar to that age. But he must always remember that God will judge him for how he makes use of those youthful energies:

> Rejoice, O young man, in thy youth; and let thy heart cheer thee in the days of thy youth, and walk in the ways of thine heart, and in the sight of thine eyes: but know thou, that for all these things God will bring thee into judgment. Therefore remove sorrow from thy heart, and put away evil from thy flesh: for youth and the prime of life are vanity. Vanity of vanities, saith the Preacher; all is vanity.

Among the vanities to which young men often succumb, the Ecclesiast warns, none is greater than the foolish belief that human nature can achieve wisdom entirely on its own, in purely worldly terms, without God's guidance. In the biblical view, human wisdom ultimately takes us further from the truth, not closer to it:

> And furthermore, my son, be admonished: of making many books there is no end; and much study is a weariness of the flesh. This is the end of

the matter; all hath been heard: fear God, and keep his commandments; for this is the whole duty of man. For God shall bring every work into judgment, with every hidden thing, whether it be good or whether it be evil.

Faith adds a new dimension to our discussion of the manly heart—touching on not only what it means to be wise in the affairs of one's fellow citizens and loved ones but also what it means for a man to embark on an *inner* journey of self-awareness and spiritual evolution from reflecting on life's hardships, disappointments, and puzzling reversals.

So, again, this is the question to bear in mind as we look to traditional sources for understanding the role of pride in a man's character: Does happiness come from worldly achievements or from faith? It's the old debate between pride and humility. If you firmly believe that faith is the answer, it's not hard to see the proud man whom Aristotle praises as the paragon of all the virtues gradually growing horns and exuding a whiff of brimstone as he morphs into Milton's Lucifer, the former angel who is cast out of paradise because his arrogance made him compete with the Lord. Do we do our duty out of pride, as the ancients maintained, or out of humility, compassion, and piety, as the Bible teaches? Should I refrain from being cruel because to oppress the weak is to lower myself, to put a stain on my own noble character? Or should I refrain from being cruel because God commands it and because one man's cruelty to another blasphemes God's infinite compassion for us all? Once again, we are led from the question of pride back to that larger question: How should I live? What should I respect, in others and in myself? How can I achieve inner wholeness, the right balance of personal and public commitments, the right balance of energies for work, family, and citizenship?

Because of such questions, pride is inseparable from the two virtues we've already considered, love and courage. Indeed, love and courage take their direction from pride. For pride guides us in our choice of the right people in whom to repose our love and affection, and in picking the right time to fight on behalf of a just cause.

The dependence of love and courage on the leadership of pride is captured in the beautiful image with which I began this book, one that originates in the Vedic teachings of early Hinduism and reappears in the

West in Plato's dialogue the *Phaedrus*. It bears repeating here as we begin to see how the five paths to manliness connect with one another. In this image, the soul is likened to a chariot. The charioteer represents the intellect, while the chariot is sped by two powerful horses, representing love and courage. As the soul makes its celestial journey through the heavens, the charioteer of the intellect must be firmly in control, guiding the chariot toward the realm of eternal bliss. If the horses are allowed to have their own way, if the charioteer loses the reins or relaxes his grip, those mighty steeds will drag the chariot downward, plunging the soul into a chaos of ungoverned lust and fury. But, by the same token, the charioteer can't take the chariot anywhere without the mighty power of the horses. The intellect must control love and courage. But without the energies of those passions, the soul cannot complete its ascent to happiness. Pride is this balance of mind and desire.

THE MASCULINE AND THE FEMININE

An important ingredient in this balance of mind and desire is a balance of the masculine and feminine parts of a man's character. In ancient Greek mythology, the gods Apollo and Dionysus represented the masculine and feminine sides of human nature. Dionysus himself was a later male version of an even earlier divinity, the Earth Goddess Gaia, worshiped since prehistoric times. As we saw in Chapter 1, Apollo's chief cult site at Delphi was originally associated with Gaia. We should return for a moment to the legend surrounding it, because just as the symbiosis between Apollo and Gaia is an important early symbol for the Western tradition of manly love, it also symbolizes the correct proportions of intellect and passion in the Western tradition of pride. According to the legend, Apollo began as a harsh warrior god from the distant North who invaded the Mother Goddess's sanctuary and slew the giant python protecting her. Instead of destroying her or driving her away, however, Apollo in effect invited her to remain and she became his priestess and oracle. Because of her association with the python—snakes were symbols of wisdom in many Mediterranean and Near Eastern cultures— Apollo's main oracle, always a woman, is called "the Pythia," and he is worshiped there as Pythian Apollo, the Apollo of the snake.

The legend of Delphi is the archetypal male encounter with the feminine at the earliest origins of the West, an intertwining of Apollo and the earth mother. Initially a crude and barbaric marauder, Apollo is deepened and beautified by his encounter with the Mother Goddess, becoming the paragon of classical Greek manliness, patron of the fine arts and good government. His interaction with the forces of the goddess and her python makes him sensuous, gracious, and subtle, sublimating his aggressive passions by putting them at the service of the arts. The stern and static Pharaonic and Assyrian features of the earlier male gods, once they are flooded with the fecundity of the Earth Goddess, soften into the rounded curves and almost polymorphous thighs and breasts of the ever young, ever gracious Apollo. In this way, the legend of Delphi shows how male and female traits can deepen and strengthen each other both in their differences and in their common humanity. Men and women possess the same virtues and vices, but they are manifested and expressed differently in temperament and action. Apollo's sublimation of the Dionysian is another expression of pride as that balance of virtues captured by the image of the chariot of the soul—a sublime intellect guiding the passions of love and daring.

With Homer's epic poems the *Iliad* and the *Odyssey*, we encounter the first full literary exploration of this balance of the Apollonian and the Dionysian as the key to a fully developed man. Achilles, the hero of the *Iliad,* is the archetypal man of war, while Odysseus, the hero of the *Odyssey,* is the archetypal man of peace. I don't mean by this that Odysseus always behaves peacefully, much less that he is a pacifist. In both poems, he is a formidable warrior. But whereas Achilles is somewhat one-dimensional, relying on physical strength and bravery in combat, Odysseus is a more complicated mix of masculine and feminine traits. He is brave but also prudent, a persuasive orator, a lover of riddles, subtle, curious, and intuitive, like his special patroness among the Olympians, the goddess Athena. Indeed, it is she who calls her human favorite *polytropos,* the man of many turns. She recognizes that he shares many of her own quicksilver and quick-witted qualities.

In the last chapter, we saw Achilles at his worst, insubordinate toward his commander and deliberately sabotaging the Greek side in the Trojan War out of personal spite. But during the course of the *Iliad,* he evolves into a fuller man. Although he is generally alone in his solitary magnificence, Achilles' narcissism is softened by his love for his best friend, Patroclus. When Patroklos is slain by the Trojan hero Hektor, Achilles returns to battle to avenge his death. Facing his chief rival among the Greeks at last, even the brave Hektor loses his nerve and begs for his life. But Achilles is implacable. After killing Hektor, he remains so consumed with rage that he refuses to return the Trojan hero's body for a decent burial. Instead he mutilates the corpse, dragging it around the walls of Troy tied to the back of his chariot. Achilles' mother warns him that the gods are angry at this show of disrespect for a worthy adversary, a man honored by the gods for his piety. The gods admire manly pride, but they demand that worthy men honor one another even in enmity. By treating the fallen Trojan so savagely, Achilles is exercising a vengeance reserved for the gods themselves.

The aged Priam, Hektor's father and the king of Troy, comes under a flag of truce to the Greek camp to beg Achilles for his son's body to be returned. When the old man falls to his knees and clings to the young man's legs like a supplicant, Achilles' heart melts as he thinks about the death of his friend Patroklos and of his own elderly father far away at home. Priam's willingness to humble himself to retrieve his son's body reminds Achilles of his own father's love for him. Achilles lifts the old king to his feet, and they embrace, weeping together at all they have lost. In a larger sense, the Trojan king and the Greek hero are weeping over all the victims of their terrible ten-year war, all the dead sons. Achilles finally learns moderation and a more mature manliness through his reconciliation with Priam, father of his best friend's killer. For a moment, the sorrow of their losses renders Achilles and Priam a surrogate son and father to each other, an unexpected reconciliation between foes. As the poem draws to a close, Homer has shown us another side of Achilles. At the eleventh hour, he matures and he is deepened. Hektor gets his burial rites, as the *Iliad* ends with funeral games for Patroklos and the other fallen warriors.

This solemn, pious closing for a poem that has been largely concerned with vengeance and the glory of combat reminds us that what unites us as humans through a consciousness of our mortality, reverence for our departed loved ones, and submission to the gods is more important than what divides us through the pursuit of power and honor. Achilles is finally humanized by his ability to enter into the suffering of someone other than himself. Moved by the mourning that transcends the divisions of war, and particularly by a father's love for his son, Achilles is a man in full at last.

The *Iliad* points to its sequel, the *Odyssey*, because Odysseus, the hero of the postwar era, shows a kind of heroism superior to that of the valiant but isolated, self-absorbed Achilles. Odysseus's journey home from the war to his kingdom of Ithaca and his wife and son is also an inner journey of the spirit, guided by Athena, the goddess of wisdom. The poem teaches that the peacetime virtues of the intellect, good government, and domestic life are ultimately more impressive than warrior prowess.

Indeed, Homer's *Odyssey* is perhaps the single most satisfying account in the Western tradition of manliness as a balance of courage and intellect, passion and self-restraint. Odysseus is courageous and wrathful when justice demands that evil be punished. In the harrowing final revenge he takes against the nobles of Ithaca who have menaced his wife and treated his son with contempt during his long absence, Odysseus does not cease shooting his arrows until a hundred and fifty of them lie dead in a banquet hall slick with blood. But Odysseus is also subtle, curious, and open to all variety of new experiences. He is dignified but clever, amusing, and good company. Highly erotic, he even has a few flings on his way back home. (Not all of them are voluntary: the sorceress Circe gives him a choice between acting like a swine by cheating on his wife or being made into one.) But despite these lapses, he remains committed throughout his ten-year exile to returning to his wife and son, resisting a string of queens and sorceresses who try to get him to give up the hardship of the voyage and settle down with them. Penelope is his match in every way, but her virtues manifest themselves differently as a queen, wife, and the mother of a sensitive and troubled adolescent boy. Odysseus shows how a man can combine the best of male and female characteristics in which both dimensions are strong, and not a bland synthesis leading to androgyny or a transgendered personality.

CIVIC PRIDE

The most practical consequence of this balance of active and reflective virtues was found in the ancients' ideas about virtuous citizenship and statesmanship. Achilles' narcissistic ambition and glory seeking gave way to an ideal of calm and steady service of the common good in exchange for public honor. Young men were not expected to turn away from politics and fame but to rechannel their energies into the cultivation of civic virtue and the pursuit of wisdom.

There was another compelling reason for enlisting manly ambition on behalf of the common good. For the ancients, tyranny was always a danger in political life. As one of Aesop's fables has it, some men are wolves. Predators by nature, tyrants will always find a pretext for aggression and exploitation of others:

> A Wolf meeting with a Lamb astray from the fold, resolved not to lay violent hands on him, but to find some plea, which should justify to the Lamb himself his right to eat him. He thus addressed him: "Sirrah, last year you grossly insulted me." "Indeed," bleated the Lamb in a mournful tone of voice, "I was not then born." Then said the Wolf, "You feed in my pasture." "No, good sir," replied the Lamb, "I have not yet tasted grass." Again said the Wolf, "You drink of my well." "No," exclaimed the Lamb, "I never yet drank water, for as yet my mother's milk is both food and drink to me." On which the Wolf seized him, and ate him up, saying, "Well! I won't remain supperless, even though you refute every one of my imputations."

Societies ruled by law must always be on the lookout for such wolves. Men ambitious for public honor—men who, if not properly educated, might have gone on to be tyrants themselves—are needed to defeat the would-be tyrants and protect the citizenry.

Again and again, the classical authors teach that honor, fame, and power are good only insofar as they enable us to demonstrate our virtues. Pride must always be guided by wisdom. In Plato's utopian community, the Republic, the producers of material goods are ruled by the warriors, while those proud men are ruled in turn by the wise. This tripartite hierarchy, in which learning is ranked above civic honor and civic honor is ranked above material wealth, is one of the oldest recipes for the true meaning of pride in both the individual and the healthy organization of society. Versions of it are found in Vedic and Muslim teachings and in many other cultures. According to Plato, the wise man is the best ruler precisely because he doesn't care unduly about political honor and power, much less about bodily pleasures. He is too absorbed in the pleasures of learning to be tempted by the lesser pleasures of glory, wealth, and hedonism. His rule is therefore benevolent and unmarred by self-interest, because the passions which in lesser men would be absorbed in material goods and sensual pleasures are sluiced off into the pleasures of the mind.

The ancient Greek and Roman authors offer many variations on this fundamental classical ideal of citizenship, which identifies true manliness with the sobriety, thoughtfulness, and steadfastness required by civic affairs and a respect for learning. To be a man one must demonstrate civic virtue, including battlefield courage, in the service of one's country, thereby reaping the reward of public honor. But worthy as the civic virtues and public honor may be, the life of learning, art, and culture is even higher. Just as a chariot needs a charioteer, the virtues of the mind should govern the active virtues of courage and public service so that the soul's moral and intellectual riches might flourish in harmony. In Cicero's *On the Commonwealth,* in part a commentary on Plato's *Republic,* the Roman statesman and thinker describes this balance of active and contemplative virtues as "everything that entitles a man to praise." He writes:

> Let us count those who treat the philosophy of life as great men—as indeed they are—let us count them as scholars and teachers of truth and excellence. But at the same time let us admit the existence of an art—whether discovered by statesmen who have faced the vicissitudes of public life or studied even by your philosophers in scholarly retirement—an art which comprises the theory of politics and the government of peoples and which, in truth, is by no means to be despised. . . . What, indeed, can be more glorious than the union of practical experience in great affairs with an intelligent enthusiasm for the liberal arts? . . . I hold that a man who has been able and willing to combine

these two interests, and has disciplined himself both in the ways of his ancestors and in liberal culture, has attained everything that entitles a man to praise.

Political and military honor that might otherwise make a man too harsh and arrogant will be tempered by their subordination to the nobler virtues of learning and culture. A true man is strong, but in a quiet way. He is modest, generous, and affable, not a boaster or a bully. This ideal of statesmanship as a balance of active and contemplative virtues endures throughout all the ages of the West, down to the American Founding Fathers (as we'll see in Chapter 5) and great men of the twentieth century, such as Winston Churchill.

This ideal is portrayed vividly in Cicero's depiction of Scipio Africanus the Younger, the great Roman general and statesman. Scipio perfectly embodies the classical hierarchy of active and contemplative virtues. He is a brilliant success as a commander and statesman. But he reserves his greatest respect for the life of the mind. To be a real man is not only to be vigorous in serving the common good but to absorb the sublime beauties of art, music, and philosophy, softening the harsh edges of the warrior's spirit with the light of the eternally good and true. Indeed, Cicero's portrait of the magnificent young Roman consciously echoes the Apollonian ideal that was first elaborated by Homer. Scipio is a warrior when war is necessary, but he is also subtle, gracious, and refined. In the "Dream of Scipio," which ends *On the Commonwealth,* Cicero depicts Scipio as taking the same celestial journey we saw in the Vedic and Platonic image of the soul as a heavenly chariot speeding through the stars. While Scipio is sleeping one night during his campaign in Africa against the Carthaginians, his dead father comes to him in a dream and gives his noble son a revelation of the afterlife. Scipio's father promises his son that celestial bliss will be his eternal reward for serving his fatherland and family here on earth:

> Strive earnestly, and be assured that only this body of yours, and not your real self, is mortal. For you are not the mere physical form that you appear to be; but the real man is the soul and not that physical body which men can point to. Know, then, that your true nature is divine, if indeed it is a divine principle which lives, feels, remembers, and foresees, and

which rules, guides, and activates the body beneath its sway, even as the supreme god directs the universe. And as the world, which is in part mortal, is stirred to motion by God Himself, who lives forever, so the frail body is quickened by an immortal soul.

Every man has a duty during his lifetime to cultivate the divine spark in his soul through service to the common good of his country. By exercising our highest faculties in the service of the common good, we enhance the immortal part of our souls, and prepare ourselves for the celestial bliss of union with the gods after we shed the mortal shells of our earthly bodies. But if, by contrast, we neglect our duties while we are alive, and allow carnal desires to drag us down into the lowest and most bodily aspect of our natures, we will remain chained to the earth after we die, fallen souls unable to rise toward the light of eternity:

> Now the noblest concerns of the soul have to do with the security of your country, and the soul which is employed and disciplined in such pursuits will fly more speedily to this abode, its natural home. This journey it will make the swifter, if it looks abroad, while still imprisoned in the flesh, and if, by meditating upon that which lies beyond it, it divorces itself as far as may be from the body. For the souls of men who have surrendered themselves to carnal delights, who have made themselves as it were slaves of the passions, and who have been prompted by lust to violate the laws of gods and men, wander about near the earth itself, after their escape from the body, and do not return hither until they have been driven about for many ages.

The core of what Scipio learns from his father's revelation from beyond the grave is that our mortal life is a test in which we prove our fitness for immortality and the immortal fame of a good reputation for the life we lived on earth. Many classical writings on pride as a balance of mind and desire stress this need for a man to be tested. For instance, Seneca, another eminent Roman moralist, lays great emphasis on the value of adversity as a catalyst for virtue. Only when we are put to the most severe tests will we know if we have the capacity for noble conduct:

> Success comes to the common man, and even to the commonplace ability; but to triumph over the calamities and terrors of mortal life is the

part of a great man only. You say you are a great man. But how do I know it if Fortune gives you no opportunity of showing your worth? True worth is eager for danger and thinks rather of its goal than of what it may have to suffer, since even what it will have to suffer is a part of its glory. Warriors glory in their wounds and rejoice to display the blood spilled with luckier fortune. Those who return from the battle unhurt may have fought as well, but the man who returns with a wound wins the greater regard. God, I say, is showing favor to those whom he desires to achieve the highest possible virtue whenever he gives them the means of doing a courageous and brave deed, and to this end they must encounter some difficulty in life.

Far from lamenting our afflictions, we should be grateful for them as an opportunity to prove our mettle:

Disaster is Virtue's opportunity. Justly may those be termed unhappy who are dulled by an excess of good fortune, who rest, as it were, in dead calm upon a quiet sea. . . . Cruel fortune bears hardest upon the inexperienced; to the tender neck the yoke is heavy. The raw recruit turns pale at the thought of a wound, but the veteran looks undaunted upon his own gore, knowing that blood has often been the price of his victory. In like manner God hardens, reviews, and disciplines those whom he approves, whom he loves. No proof of virtue is ever mild.

The Stoic author Plutarch, perhaps the best-known moralist of the Imperial Roman period, offers Marcus Brutus as another model for the combination of active and contemplative virtues. Student of philosophy, defender of the Roman Republic against ambitious usurpers like Julius Caesar, he was blessed with an extraordinary wife, Porcia, with whom he shared his secrets and his perils. She followed the same Stoic code of integrity and fortitude under adversity as her husband, and although he tried to protect her from the dangerous consequences of his political activities, she would gladly have shared her husband's perils in defending the cause of the Republic against Caesar and his party, even marching with him into death.

For his part, Brutus was inclined by nature to prefer peaceful study and reflection to warfare and political ambition. In the midst of his bat-

tles on behalf of the Republic against the would-be despot Caesar, he
had books of philosophy read to him in his tent in the evenings. He was
not a naturally warlike or glory-seeking man; on the contrary, he steeled
himself to face military peril and political intrigue out of a pure sense of
duty to his country. Even Brutus's enemies on the Caesarean side, such
as Mark Antony, admired his nobility of character and the sincerity of his
convictions. Of all the men who plotted and carried out the assassination
of Caesar on the Ides of March, Caesar's followers credited only Brutus
with having acted on principle, not out of jealousy of Caesar or a desire
for a share of the political spoils. Plutarch writes:

> Brutus took pains to moderate his natural instincts by means of the cul-
> ture and mental discipline which philosophy gives, while he also exerted
> himself to stir up the more placid and passive side of his character and
> force it into action, with the result that his temperament was almost ide-
> ally balanced to pursue a life of virtue. So we find that even those men
> who hated him most for his conspiracy against Julius Caesar were pre-
> pared to give the credit for any redeeming element in the murder to
> Brutus. Brutus' enemies never accused him of betraying his principles,
> and indeed Antony was heard by many people to declare that Brutus was
> the only one of the conspirators who was moved by the splendor and
> what he believed to be the nobility of the deed, while all the rest plotted
> against Caesar because they envied and hated him. It is plain too from
> Brutus' letters that he put his trust in the virtue of his cause rather than
> in armed force.

One of the most impressive summations of the classical code of virtue
comes from the *Meditations* of the great Roman emperor and Stoic
philosopher Marcus Aurelius. "A man must stand erect," he tells us, "not
be kept erect by others." Happiness comes from understanding that a virtuous soul participates in eternity, while everything else—power, riches,
prestige—vanishes with our mortal shells. True strength is the inner
strength of self-mastery. A man who knows this will neither be intoxicated
by his earthly authority nor overwhelmed by its frustrations and failures.

> Every moment think steadily as a Roman and a man to do what thou hast
> in hand with perfect and simple dignity, and feeling of affection, and

freedom, and justice; and to give thyself relief from all other thoughts. And thou wilt give thyself relief, if thou doest every act of thy life as if it were the last, laying aside all carelessness and passionate aversion from the commands of reason, and all hypocrisy, and self-love, and discontent with the portion which has been given to thee. Since it is possible that thou mayest depart from life this very moment, regulate every act and thought accordingly.

At the end of the day, worldly prestige, like all things mortal and fleshly, is doomed to perish. Only through contemplation can we enhance that small part of our earthly lives—the divine spark in the soul—that points us toward eternity:

> Of human life the time is a point, and the substance is in a flux, and the perception dull, and the composition of the whole body subject to putrefaction, and the soul a whirl, and fortune hard to divine, and fame a thing devoid of judgment. And, to say all in a word, everything which belongs to the body is a stream, and what belongs to the soul is a dream and vapor, and life is a warfare and a stranger's sojourn, and after-fame is oblivion. What then is that which is able to conduct a man? One thing and only one, philosophy.

MODERN NOBILITY

The classical idea of pride as a balance of mind and passion, and an intertwining of masculine and feminine, is not as far away from us as it first might appear. Indeed, the positive tradition of manliness is readily available to us through the influence of its modern followers, including Thomas Jefferson, Alexis de Tocqueville, Theodore Roosevelt, and Winston Churchill, all of whom were steeped in the ancient wisdom; they were also modern-day exemplars of the very virtues they had read about and admired in others. That influence still shapes us, even if we are suffering from a temporary amnesia about its exact whereabouts and its day-to-day connection with life in the present. Our interest in manly pride isn't just a matter of antiquarianism or museum culture. We still need to draw on those energies, in both our personal and our public lives. As Jefferson writes in his *Notes on the State of Virginia*, the citizens of a democracy must be given a liberal education in the same moral and intellectual virtues praised by the ancients if they are to be on guard against potential demagogues and tyrants. Modern men still need to absorb the lesson of that charming fable by Aesop, and learn to spot the wolves in our midst. As long as free peoples and self-governing republics exist, they must encourage noble public service and discourage tyrannical ambition.

We saw in the last chapter that some of the greatest soldiers and statesmen of the twentieth century discussed courage in terms familiar from the traditional Western teachings going back to the ancients. The same is true of pride. These same outstanding men, both in their careers and in their reflections, vindicate the classical idea of a balance of virtues and the importance of what Aristotle calls "greatness of soul" in the major affairs of the day.

In Winston Churchill's brief, eloquent 1935 essay on T. E. Lawrence, "Lawrence of Arabia," we encounter one hero praising another in precisely these terms. Churchill narrates the main elements of Lawrence's astonishing life—his legendary prowess and daring as a military commander in the Arab world, and his official role as a broker along with Churchill of the conflicts in that region. Particularly striking, though, is Lawrence's personal charisma, "the generous majesty of his nature"—his immense quiet charm, his air of effortless command, the modesty that came not from humility but because he would not lower himself to boast or plead. Whether he was dressed like a gentleman for his London club or more magnificently in his Arab robes, Lawrence's handsome features and flashing eyes shone forth: "He looked what he was, one of Nature's greatest princes."

Lawrence was a brilliant general and leader of men. But even more admirably, from Churchill's viewpoint, he was an outstanding scholar and author, "a savant as well as a soldier." The author of *The Seven Pillars of Wisdom*, Lawrence was also an archaeologist and a classicist best known for his translation of Homer. Not untroubled in his personal life, haunted by some nameless melancholy, Lawrence nevertheless sublimated his darker side in a seamless harmony of public service, poetry, and intellect: "An epic, a prodigy, a tale of torment, and in the heart of it—a Man." Churchill's praise of Lawrence could almost have been written by Aristotle or Cicero, so closely does it adhere to the tradition of manly refinement and honor that stretches in an unbroken pedigree back to antiquity. In some ways, writing only sixty-five years ago, Churchill has more in common with the classics than he does with us.

As for Churchill's own career, it is very much like Aristotle's depiction of the proud man. Churchill regarded the threat posed by Hitler to the free world as providing him with the ultimate test of his own best qualities. Never more than a mixed success when dealing with the quotidian issues of domestic politics—trade issues, budgets, and the like—he lived to see his mission to defeat the Nazis bring him into the same hallowed ranks as Pericles, Washington, Wellington, Lincoln, Franklin Roosevelt, and other defenders of free government. Without a trace of bombast or false humility, Churchill simply *knew* he was the best man to lead his country in its hour of greatest peril. Upon being made prime minister following the collapse of Chamberlain's government in the wake of Hitler's flagrant violation of the Munich Accord, Churchill recalls that he slept soundly for the first time in years, secure in the knowledge that the best man was finally in charge:

> During these last crowded days of the political crises, my pulse had not quickened at any moment. I took it all as it came. But I cannot conceal from the reader of this truthful account that as I went to bed at about three o'clock in the morning, I was conscious of a profound sense of relief. At last I had the authority to give directions over the whole scene. I felt as if I were walking with Destiny, and that all my past life had been but a preparation for this hour and for this trial.

His less than spectacular performance as a peacetime politician in the 1920s turned out to be a blessing in disguise: forcing him into retirement, it allowed him to devote himself single-mindedly to warning his countrymen about the danger posed by Nazi aggression. He writes,

> Eleven years in the political wilderness had freed me from ordinary party antagonisms. My warnings over the last six years had been so numerous, so detailed, and were now so terribly vindicated, that no one could gainsay me. I could not be reproached either for making the war or with want of preparation for it. I thought I knew a good deal about it

all, and I was sure I should not fail. Therefore, although impatient for the morning, I slept soundly and had no need for cheering dreams. Facts are better than dreams.

Charles de Gaulle, Churchill's counterpart on the French side in the struggle against Nazi tyranny, writes with great eloquence and psychological subtlety about the special role that "the man of character" must play in the affairs of his nation. (I may be going out on a limb here, but I suspect he may have had himself in mind as a primary example.) According to de Gaulle, although the man of character serves a democracy and defends its values, in crucial respects he is undoubtedly superior to the vast majority of those around him. He is their equal insofar as he possesses the same rights under the law and must respect the rights of others. But in terms of intellect and depth of vision, he stands apart. Others look to him for guidance and inspiration. His calm self-assurance exercises a charismatic effect on the demoralized or the timid.

Like Aristotle's description of the great-souled man, de Gaulle's man of character hates to be dependent on anyone else for advice:

> When faced with the challenge of events, the man of character has recourse to himself. His instinctive response is to leave his mark on action, to take responsibility for it, to make it *his own business.* . . . It is not that he wishes to turn a blind eye to orders, or to sweep aside advice, but only that he is passionately anxious to exert his own will, to make up his own mind. It is not that he is unaware of the risks involved, or careless of consequences, but that he takes their measure honestly, and frankly accepts them. Better still, he embraces action with the pride of a master; for if he takes a hand in it, it will become his, and he is ready to enjoy success on condition that it is really *his own,* and that he derives no profit from it. . . . In short, a fighter who finds within himself all the zest and support he needs . . . a man who pays his debts with his own money lends nobility to action. Without him there is but the dreary task of the slave; thanks to him, it becomes the divine sport of the hero.

Echoing Aristotle, Cicero, Seneca, and many other traditional authorities on greatness of soul, de Gaulle's man of character welcomes only the greatest challenges and the most severe adversity. They alone give him a test that will enable him to display his full abilities:

> The man of character finds an especial attractiveness in difficulty, since it is only by coming to grips with difficulty that he can realize his potentialities. Whether or not he proves himself the stronger is a matter between it and him. He is a jealous lover and will share with no one the prizes or the pains that may be his as a result of trying to overcome obstacles. Whatever the cost to himself, he looks for no higher reward than the harsh pleasure of knowing himself to be the man responsible.

He can certainly be overbearing. But that is the flip side of his self-confidence and willingness to lead:

> Those under his command mutter in whispers about his arrogance and the demands he makes. But once action starts, criticism disappears. The man of character then draws to himself the hopes and the wills of everyone as the magnet draws iron. When the crisis comes, it is him they follow, it is he who carries the burden on his own shoulders, even though they collapse under it.

The man of character feels an obligation to those who follow him. He wants to succeed as much for their sake as for his own:

> The knowledge that the lesser men have confidence in him exalts the man of character. The confidence of those under him gives him a sense of obligation. It strengthens his determination but also increases his benevolence, for he is a born protector. If success attends upon his efforts he distributes its advantages with a generous hand. If he meets with failure, he will not let the blame fall on anybody but himself. The security he offers is repaid by the esteem of his men.

Aristotle tells us the great-souled man is kind to inferiors but rather stiff and thin-skinned with those whose rank or social status is conventionally superior to his own. As a lieutenant, he knows that the beribboned old general set above him is a mediocrity and timeserver compared with his own dazzling talents. De Gaulle says much the same thing about the man of character:

In his relationship with his superiors he is generally at a disadvantage. He is too sure of himself, too conscious of his strength to let his conduct be influenced by a mere wish to please. The fact that he finds his powers of decision within himself, and not imposed upon him by an order, often disinclines him to adopt an attitude of passive obedience. All he asks is that he shall be given a task to do, and then be left alone to do it. He wants to be the captain of his own ship, and this many senior officers find intolerable.

The man of character simply wants to be left alone to do the best job he can. But that's precisely what the mediocrities and timeservers find so infuriating. He exposes the fact that they aren't really needed:

> And so it comes about that the authorities dread any officer who has the gift of making decisions and cares nothing for routine and soothing words. "Arrogant and undisciplined" is what the mediocrities say of him, treating the thoroughbred with a tender mouth as they would a donkey which refuses to move, not realizing that asperity is, more often than not, the reverse side of a strong character, that you can only lean on something that offers resistance, and that resolute and inconvenient men are to be preferred to easy-going natures without initiative.

In ordinary times the man of character is often ignored or denied advancement, precisely because his natural superiority makes his undeserving superiors uncomfortable; he reminds them that their own privileges and positions of authority are unmerited, the result of being agreeable and pliant team players. But when disaster strikes and national survival is at stake, they are only too happy to hand over the reins of power so that he'll save their bacon:

> But when the position becomes serious, when the nation is in urgent need of leaders with initiative who can be relied upon, and are willing to take risks, then matters are seen in a very different light, and credit goes to whom credit is due. A sort of a ground swell brings the man of character to the surface. His advice is listened to, his abilities are praised, and his true worth becomes apparent.

There have been few more eloquent modern champions of Aristotle's view that humility is a vice rather than a virtue, and that nothing great can be accomplished on behalf of justice and a nation's success and prosperity without men of extraordinary ambition:

> This rallying to character when danger threatens is the outward manifestation of an instinctive urge, for all men at heart realize the supreme value of self-reliance, and know that without it there can be no action of value. In the last resort, we must, to quote Cicero, "judge all conduct in the light of the best examples available," for nothing great has ever been achieved without that passion and that confidence which is to be found only in the man of character. Alexander would never have conquered Asia, Galileo would never have demonstrated the movement of the earth, Columbus would never have discovered America, nor Richelieu have restored the authority of the crown, had they not believed in themselves and taken full control of the task in hand.

PRIDE OR HUMILITY?

While it's true that the ancient ideal of pride has been influential right down to the twentieth century, it's equally true that not everyone has admired it. Having looked at the secular account of manliness as a balance of reason and passion, we now need to pick up the other half of the debate, the perspective of faith.

With Christianity, a new understanding of man's foremost duties emerged in the West. Godliness and humility were viewed as far more important than a concern with this-worldly success and intellect. We recall that the classical ideal of manhood, summed up by Plato's *Republic,* subordinated civic virtue and commerce to the life of the mind in a harmonious tripartite hierarchy. But in *The City of God,* St. Augustine insists that one must choose between two irreconcilable ways of life—the city of the flesh and the city of the spirit. A life devoted to worldly ambition is vain, exploitive, arrogant, and restless. A life devoted to God is moderate, modest, peaceable, and allows a man to be at peace with himself. Within Christian civilization, faith becomes the new model for manliness. Being a Stoic, St. Augustine concedes, is preferable to being a hedonist. But both schools of thought are mistaken in believing that wisdom and happiness are possible though man's efforts alone, without faith in God.

With Christianity, we encounter a remarkable reversal of the moral values admired by the Greeks and Romans. For Aristotle, pride was a mean between the extremes of vainglory and humility—between the arrogant, empty belief in a superiority unmatched by one's actions and a paralyzing lack of self-confidence or conviction even when the ability is genuine. There could hardly be a greater measure of the distance between the secular and religious understandings of virtue than the realization that Aristotle regarded the chief Christian virtue of humility as a vice. For Aristotle, it was simply unintelligible that a man would deliberately not lay claim to honor for virtues he actually possessed. For him, humility could be explained only as "smallness of soul," often translated by that wonderfully contemptuous old English word *pusillanimity.*

For St. Augustine and many Christians, by contrast, there is no difference between pride and vainglory: pride is *always* arrogant, empty, and unjustifiable, while humility is the true mark of a man of faith. Whereas the ancient philosophers would have distinguished between better and worse forms of authority, St. Augustine tends to dismiss *all* forms of government as sinful, power hungry, and idolatrous in comparison with the otherworldly City of God. He asks of his pagan Roman readers:

> Is it reasonable and wise to glory in the extent and greatness of the Empire when you can in no way prove that there is any real happiness in men perpetually living amid the horrors of war, perpetually wading in blood?—Does it matter whether it is the blood of their fellow citizens or the blood of their enemies? It is still human blood, in men perpetually haunted by the gloomy specter of fear and driven by murderous passions. The happiness arising from such conditions is a thing of glass, of mere glittering brittleness. One can never shake off the horrible dread that it may suddenly shiver into fragments.

Compared with the perfection of the otherworldly City of God, all merely human authority looks tawdry. All human honors, including the achievements of Scipio, Marcus Brutus, and the other heroes of antiquity, are cheap tinsel and hollow baubles. Even the best intentioned of governments are little better than criminal gangs organized on a large scale:

In the absence of justice, what is sovereignty but organized brigandage? For, what are bands of brigands but petty kingdoms? They also are groups of men, under the rule of a leader, bound together by a common agreement, dividing their booty according to a settled principle. . . . It is smoke that weighs nothing. The reward of the saints is altogether different. They were men who, while on earth, suffered reproaches for the City of God which is so much hated by lovers of this world. That City is eternal. There, no one is born because no one dies. There, there reigns that true and perfect happiness which is . . . a gift of God—toward whose beauty we can but sigh in our pilgrimage on earth.

As this great work of theology so eloquently testifies, the believing Christian must experience a deep ambivalence about any merely worldly or civic account of the manly virtues. Pride, which Aristotle regarded as the crown of the moral virtues and the earned reward of serving the common good, tends to be reduced under the Christian interpretation to a base drive for power and domination. The gentlemanly virtues of liberality and courage, the Ciceronian balance of the active and the cultured temperaments, are often diminished in the Christian account to "fleshly" drives for hollow worldly prestige.

But of course it would be a mistake to think that Christianity has no positive conception of manliness and manly honor. Early on in the history of the faith, the saint provided a new model for manliness, a spiritual courage on behalf of Christ and a deepening of the soul through penance, chastity, and self-abnegation. As we saw in Chapter 1, during the Middle Ages the Christian tradition of courtly love sublimated and refined manly passion in the service of an ideal lady who reflected the purity, gentleness, and compassion of the Virgin. The medieval knight provided a new ideal of courage, the soldier of Christ. In Bulfinch's version of the oath sworn by King Arthur's Knights of the Round Table, the perfect knight combines the valor and splendor honored by the pagan tradition with the compassion, humility, and piety emphasized by Christianity:

Then the king established all his knights, and to them that were not rich he gave lands, and charged them all never to do outrage nor murder, and always to flee treason; also, by no means to be cruel, but to give mercy unto him that asked mercy, upon pain of forfeiture of their worship and lordship; and always to do ladies, damsels, and gentlewomen service, upon pain of death. Also that no man take battle in a wrongful quarrel, for no law, nor for any world's goods. Unto this were all the knights sworn of the Table Round, both old and young.

In ways such as these, Christianity tried to strike a compromise between its central vision, which was otherworldly and took notice of our earthly sojourn only as a preparation for salvation and eternal life, and the inescapable reality that men had to continue fighting and ruling.

In the legends of Alfred the Great, Charlemagne, and other great medieval kings, the ideal Christian monarch combines courage with learning and piety, a blend of the classical and Christian virtues. As the Victorian historian John Richard Green sums up Alfred:

> [He] was the noblest as he was the most complete embodiment of all that is great, all that is lovable, in the English temper. He combined as no other man has ever combined its practical energy, its patient and enduring force, its profound sense of duty, the reserve and self-control that steady in it a wide outlook and a restless daring, its temperance and fairness, its frank geniality, its sensitiveness to action, its poetic tenderness, its deep and passionate religion. Religion, indeed, was the groundwork of Alfred's character. His temper was instinct with piety. Everywhere throughout his writings the name of God, the thought of God, stir him to outbursts of ecstatic adoration.

In addition to his saintliness, though, Alfred possessed that love of learning and that balance of active and contemplative virtues which, going back to Cicero's praise of Scipio, was the hallmark of the virtuous prince:

> His intellectual activity breathed fresh life into education and literature. His capacity for inspiring trust and affection drew the hearts of Englishmen to a common centre, and began the upbuilding of a new England. And all was guided, controlled, ennobled by a single aim. "So long as I have lived," said the King as life closed about him, "I have striven to live worthily." Little by little men came to know what such a life of worthiness meant. Little by little they came to recognize in Alfred

a ruler of higher and nobler stamp than the world had seen. Never had it seen a king who lived solely for the good of his people. Never had it seen a ruler who set aside every personal aim to devote himself solely to the welfare of those whom he ruled. It was this grand self-mastery that gave him his power over the men about him.

As the High Middle Ages give way to the early Renaissance, Christian writers become more interested in the worldly affairs of government on their own terms, and not merely as something to be put up with while we dwell in this fallen realm in our prisons of flesh. The fifteenth-century Christian humanist Erasmus argues that faith is important not only because it prepares us for eternal life—the core of the traditional Augustinian message—but because it is the source of all *worldly* courage and virtue as well. Government and worldly affairs are no longer seen as an entirely fallen realm—"smoke that weighs nothing," as St. Augustine had put it—standing across a great divide from the hereafter. Instead, God is now seen to intervene directly in worldly affairs to provide moral guidance for citizens and rulers. St. Augustine had viewed distinctions between legitimate and illegitimate government as paltry in comparison with the City of God's perfection; but for Erasmus and other humanists, Christians have a duty to make such distinctions, in order to support good government and decry tyranny. The traditional classical distinctions made by Plato, Aristotle, Cicero, and the Stoics between the nobility of public service and the baseness of tyranny are now ascribed directly to God and become a part of Christian teachings. In detailing the education of a young prince, Erasmus sums up the maxims of Christian statecraft:

> Let the teacher paint a sort of celestial creature, more like to a divine being than a mortal: complete in all the virtues; born for the common good; yea, sent by the God above to help the affairs of mortals by looking out and caring for everyone. Let the tutor point this out as the picture of a true prince! Now let him bring out the opposite side by showing a frightful, loathsome beast, formed of a dragon, wolf, lion, viper, bear, and like creatures; with six hundred eyes all over it, teeth everywhere, fearful from all angles, and with hooked claws; with never satiated hunger, fattened on human vitals, and reeking with human blood; never sleeping,

but always threatening the fortunes and lives of all men; dangerous to everyone, especially to the good; a sort of fatal scourge to the whole world, on which everyone who has the interests of the state at heart pours forth execration and hatred; which cannot be borne because of its monstrousness and yet cannot be overthrown without great disaster to the city because its maliciousness is hedged about with armed forces and wealth. This is the picture of a tyrant.

Renaissance humanism returned gradually to an open advocation of ancient Greek and Roman notions of manly pride and civic-spiritedness, in order to counteract what some saw as the destabilizing effects of Christian pacifism and otherworldliness on real-life politics, especially the weak and fractious city-states of sixteenth-century Italy. Ambition on behalf of the common good was praised once again. The Renaissance humanists revived classical principles for the education of young men as virtuous citizens and princes. The "mirror of princes" genre, best known through Castiglione's *Book of the Courtier,* returns to the writings of Xenophon, Plato, Aristotle, and Cicero on good government and gentle-manly character. The Ciceronian ideal of a balance of virtues embodied in the life of Scipio is revived by Petrarch, Vergerius, and Pico della Mirandola, among others.

But with Machiavelli, a darker side of the Renaissance emerges. He asks: Are there *any* limits on what a ruler must do to make his people se-cure and prosperous? As he writes in *The Prince,* his famous manual of Realpolitik, "Many have imagined republics and principalities which have never been seen or known to exist in reality; for how we live is so far removed from how we ought to live, that he who abandons what is done for what ought to be done, will rather learn to bring about his own ruin than his preservation." In this swipe at "imagined republics," Machiavelli is repudiating both the classical *and* the Christian traditions of manliness as being hopelessly unrealistic; too good for this world. His criticism takes in not only the *Republics* of Plato and Cicero but also St. Augustine's *De Civitate Dei,* most often translated as *The City of God* but more literally rendered as "The Republic of God." As he dryly sums up the deluded idealism shared by both pagan and Christian moralities, "A man who wishes to make a profession of goodness in everything must necessarily come to grief among so many who are not good. Therefore it is necessary for a prince, who wishes to maintain himself, to learn how not to be good, and to use his knowledge and not use it, according to the necessity of the case."

Shakespeare's history plays show the emerging tension between the old ideal of the Christian monarch and the ruthless new Machiavellian prince, the man who will stop at nothing to achieve power. *Richard II*, *Henry IV*, and *Henry V* are rife with tension between the still-influential Christian strictures on worldly honor and manly pride and the thrusting modern Machiavellian ambition to "conquer Fortuna," as Machiavelli had famously put it in his conclusion to *The Prince*. In *Richard II*, Shakespeare shows us the contrast between the Christian king by divine right, Richard II—a dismally incompetent ruler but given to poetic Augustinian soliloquies about the emptiness of a man's life in the prison of his flesh—and the cold-blooded pragmatic young Machiavellian prince, Henry Bolingbroke, the future Henry IV. In Henry IV's son Hal, Shakespeare shows us the growth of a young man from the life of a wastrel into a mature and vigorous young monarch, an ideal Renaissance blend of courage, intellect, prudence, and chivalry. Torn between his flawed real father, the usurper and regicide Henry, and his flawed surrogate father, the libertine Falstaff, he is educated by his grave responsibilities as the new king and outgrows them both.

Machiavelli takes the Renaissance's liberation of manly honor and ambition from Augustinian restraints to its furthest extreme—the liberation of princely willpower for the conquest of nature. God's power to overcome all natural limitations, to create out of nothing, is transferred by Machiavelli to men of "outstanding virtue." Man can burst the bounds of nature, smash the Great Chain of Being, the teleological ordering of the world common to both classical and Christian traditions, and remake the world in order to maximize stability, wealth, and power.

In his notorious remark that "Fortuna is a woman, and prefers her lovers to be hot-blooded rather than cautious," Machiavelli characterizes the natural world as a female object to be subjugated by an impetuous, bold young ruler. The revolutionary project for the conquest of an irrational and hostile "female" nature by an amoral, ruthless, and unrestrained "male" ambition for power and glory repudiates both Christian and classical notions of manly self-restraint, gentlemanly moderation, and friendship between men and women. It destroys the Western archetype of balanced manhood, stretching back to Delphi and Homer, as a partnership of male and female traits. The masculine degenerates from Apollonian sublimity into crude "macho" aggression—Odysseus gives way to Tyler Durden—while the feminine degenerates from the majestic calm, subtlety, and intuitive insight of Athena and Penelope into a spunky lass, the bitch-goddess Fortuna, a wild, untamed virago like Elizabeth Taylor in *Who's Afraid of Virginia Woolf?* If there is any justification for feminist scholarship's identification of the Western tradition with the encouragement of sexist and macho attitudes toward women, symptomatic of a stance of domination toward the world in general, it stems not from the Western tradition as a whole but only from this one dark strain of radical modernity. Philosophically, sexism is a modern phenomenon. There are no more consistent champions of friendship between men and women than the ancients.

The Machiavellian prince must also deeroticize himself so as not to be beguiled by a trust of others. Whereas the classical prescription for citizenship and good government prizes friendship with one's fellow citizens and servants of the common good, Machiavelli encourages paranoia and isolation: "It is better to be feared," he concludes, "than to be loved." This is the beginning of a tendency within modernity to caricature manliness as unrestrained power seeking and cold-blooded exploitation and manipulation. To counteract this dark tendency, however, we must be careful not to throw out the baby with the bathwater. There's no need to identify the entire Western tradition with this deformed version of masculinity. As I've tried to show throughout this book, there are healthier understandings of manhood, and of masculine civility, decency, and restraint, available in all periods of Western literature, history, and thought.

PRIDE IN THE NEW WORLD

The debate between faith and worldly achievement as the key to happiness continues as we move closer to our own era. As we saw in our discussion of love in Chapter 1, the Romantic writers are among the keenest advocates of a renewed sense of the divine within the increasingly materialistic and secular civilization of modernity. Urging a return to the mysteries of faith through poetry, art, and music, men like Rousseau, Schiller, the Romantic poets, and Tolstoy maintained that human reasoning was incomplete without an experience of the divine. Like the Ecclesiast and St. Augustine, they often stressed that relying on human reason alone was an example of the folly of pride. The quandaries and quibbles of philosophy ultimately lead nowhere, leaving us empty and exhausted.

In a moving scene from Tolstoy's *Anna Karenina,* Levin is plunged by the death of his brother after a gruesomely protracted illness into wondering what meaning his life has as a man. He concludes that the philosophy and theology he learned as a youth amount to little more than vanity and conceit. Instead, he realizes that it is his daily obligations as a husband, father, and landowner that give his life meaning—his duty to his wife and children, to their extended families, and to the people who work for him:

> Ever since, by his beloved brother's deathbed, Levin had for the first time looked at the questions of life and death in the light of his new convictions, as he called them, which between the ages of twenty and thirty-four had imperceptibly replaced the beliefs of his childhood and youth, he had been stricken with horror, not so much at death, as at life, without the least conception of its origin, its purpose, its reason, its nature.

His experiences of bereavement and of fatherhood have taught him that faith is a more solid route to peace of mind than any form of modern rationality:

> One thing he had discovered since these questions had begun to occupy his mind—namely, that he had been mistaken in supposing with his contemporaries at the university that religion had outlived its day and was now practically non-existent. The best people he knew were all believers. Moreover, at the time of his wife's confinement an extraordinary thing had happened to him. He, an unbeliever, had prayed, and prayed with sincere faith. But that moment had passed, and he could not allot any place in his life to the state of mind he had been in then.

Finally, the answer to the riddle of life's meaning comes to him in the words of a simple, uneducated peasant, one of his own serfs:

> The words uttered by the peasant were like an electric shock. He felt something new in his soul and took a delight in probing it, not yet knowing what this new something was. "Not to live for one's own needs, but for God! . . . And not only I but everyone—the whole world—understands nothing but this one thing fully: about this alone men have no doubt and are always agreed. . . .
>
> "Yes, what I know, I know not by my reason but because it has been given to me, revealed to me, and I know it with my heart, by my faith in the chief things which the Church proclaims. . . . " He rolled over on his other side and, leaning on his elbow, fell to gazing into the distance at a herd of cattle going down to the farther bank of the river.

As Levin thinks back over his formal education and his interest in the intellectual debates of his day, he realizes that he cannot justify his new belief in living for God in rational terms, no matter which version—liberalism, socialism, science, utilitarianism—he chooses. But it's precisely because he cannot justify this teaching intellectually, yet feels it to be true with every fiber of his soul and all his emotions, that he experiences such a feeling of liberation. Science tells him that the sky is not a beautiful blue vault but instead a mass of atoms. Nevertheless, with every one of his senses and his imagination, he experiences it as a blue vault. The same is true with faith. He cannot justify it rationally. But when he sets aside the claims of reason, every other human faculty proclaims it to be true:

> Lying on his back, he was now gazing high up into the cloudless sky. "Do I not know that this is infinite space, and not a rounded vault? But however much I screw up my eyes and strain my sight I cannot see it except as round and circumscribed, and in spite of my knowing about infinite space I am incontestably right when I see a firm blue vault, far more right than when I strain my eyes to see beyond it. . . ." Levin ceased thinking and, as it were, only hearkened to mystic voices that seemed to be joyfully and earnestly conferring. "Can this be faith?" he wondered, afraid to believe in his happiness. "My God, I thank Thee!" he breathed,

gulping down the sobs that rose within him and with both hands brushing away the tears that filled his eyes.

As our discussion of pride draws to a close, let's bring it closer to home. From its earliest colonial origins, the debate between faith and worldly honor was a deeply American preoccupation. A good example is John Woolman, who spent thirty years traveling the New England colonies during the eighteenth century to preach the Quaker faith, as well as lecturing in favor of temperance and the abolition of slavery. Woolman's recollections of how he found the path to God after overcoming his boyhood temptations to the sins of pride and the flesh have a profoundly Augustinian resonance:

> Having attained the age of sixteen, I began to love wanton company: and though I was preserved from profane language or scandalous conduct, still I perceived a plant in me which produced such wild grapes. Yet my merciful Father forsook me not utterly, but at times, through His grace, I was brought seriously to consider my ways; and the sight of my backsliding affected me with sorrow: but for want of rightly attending to the reproofs of instruction, vanity was added to vanity, and repentance. Upon the whole, my mind was more and more alienated from the truth, and I hastened towards destruction. While I meditate on the gulf towards which I travelled, and reflect on my youthful disobedience, my heart is affected with sorrow.

Plagued by the torments of a guilty conscience, the young Woolman realizes his only hope is to live "under the cross" and give himself over entirely to God:

> I was now led to look seriously at the means by which I was drawn from the pure truth, and I learned this: that if I would live in the life which the faithful servants of God lived in, I must not go into company as heretofore, in my own will; but all the cravings of sense must be governed by a divine principle. In times of sorrow and abasement, these instructions were sealed upon me, and I felt the power of Christ prevail over all selfish desires. . . . While I silently ponder on that change which was wrought in me, I find no language equal to it, not any means to convey to another a clear idea of it. I looked upon the works of God in this visible

creation, and an awfulness covered me: my heart was tender and often contrite, and a universal love to my fellow creatures increased in me. This will be understood by such who have trodden in the same path.

Writing a century later, the Harvard philosopher William James strikes a similarly Augustinian note on the emptiness of human ambition:

All natural goods perish. Riches take wings; fame is a breath; love is a cheat; youth and health and pleasure vanish. Can things whose end is always dust and disappointment be the real goods which our souls require? Back of everything is the great specter of universal death, the all-encompassing blackness.

Any man whose sense of self is based on his worldly prestige, James warns, is bound to be disillusioned in the long run. Even such geniuses as Martin Luther and Goethe, he claims, looked back on their lives with disappointment at the hollowness of their achievements. He concludes:

In short, life and its negation are beaten up inextricably together. But if the life be good, the negation of it must be bad. Yet the two are equally essential facts of existence; and all natural happiness thus seems infected with a contradiction. The breath of the sepulcher surrounds it.

Although Americans could experience faith with the same depth and fervor as their Old World forebears, America was at the same time the first country in history founded on the principles of the Enlightenment and without a feudal heritage. As we saw in our discussion of love, the spread of the Enlightenment changed the meaning of manliness. There was less emphasis on martial and aristocratic pride, and more emphasis on the peaceful arts of commerce. American devotees of the Enlightenment like James Madison and Alexander Hamilton believed that the New World would turn ambition away from the glory of caste and warfare, and direct it toward the creation of wealth in order to better the lot of everyone. The old aristocratic class structure that distinguished a gentleman from the common man—a distinction going all the way back to Aristotle's discussion of pride—would give way to a society based on equal opportunity for individual advancement.

Still, the Enlightenment and its most successful statesmen, the American Founding Fathers, saw no fundamental contradiction between the code of the gentleman and the new egalitarian society. They believed in the possibility of a democratic gentleman who would combine the freedom of the individual with the old standards of probity, candor, courage, and refinement inherited from the ancients. John Locke and Adam Smith, two philosophers who influenced the Founders, championed liberal education because they believed that a society based on commercial free enterprise needed traditional high moral standards to prevent it from taking on an unhealthy and vulgar obsession with moneymaking and material prosperity. As we will see in Chapter 5, Jefferson was the most passionate and eloquent American proponent of liberal education as essential for combining democracy with nobility of character.

Many of the Founders, after all, had received an education at William and Mary, Princeton, and Columbia that stressed the classical teachings we have examined in this chapter, including the distinction between gentlemanly and ungentlemanly conduct. As they defended the new American democracy from its proudly aristocratic foe, Great Britain, colonial gentlemen like Washington and Jefferson often had the classical teachings in mind. They were keenly aware of the honor that came from serving the new republic. But they were also wary of glory seeking and suspicious of their own motives. They wanted to be pure in their desire to serve the common good, and they guarded themselves carefully against the temptation of becoming military usurpers or dictators.

The founding of America, as we'll consider further in Chapter 5, shows the combination of the two profound strains of morality we have been considering here—the classical code of pride and the Christian emphasis on humility. Both were present in the Founders' reflections. They were thinking not only of their Christian upbringing but of classical works such as Sallust's *Conspiracy of Catiline*. Based on Plato's distinction between the statesman and the demagogue, this work warned of how an unscrupulous and ambitious usurper can disguise himself as a champion of the common people. Catiline fed the common people's grievances against the aristocracy of the Roman Republic so that, after emerging as their leader, he could seize tyrannical power in a coup.

Cicero, so influential in his idealization of Scipio as the perfect balance of manly virtues, was also the man who prosecuted Catiline for his crime of attempted usurpation of the Republic. Cicero would also become the foe of another would-be tyrant, Julius Caesar, and the American Founders were keenly aware of how this young generalissimo had hijacked the cause of popular liberty as a vehicle for his ambition for dictatorial power. Just as Marcus Brutus had sat in his tent at night thinking about philosophy while he waged war on behalf of the Roman Republic against the Caesarean faction, the American Founders were prone to philosophical reflections on their own motives even as they fought for their new republic. George Washington thought a great deal about the permissible limits of honor and ambition, and was especially interested in the life of Cato. Alexander Hamilton warned repeatedly that a republic like America must beware of its "Catilines and Caesars." The Founders were determined to model themselves on the citizen-philosopher Cicero and the citizen-soldier Scipio, not on the populist demagogue Caesar.

As we have observed before in these reflections, America has had no lack of "great-souled men." Because of our democratic and religious convictions, however, we are wary of calling them "proud." It's not easy for modern men to use this word in a complimentary way as the ancients intended it, but their deeds live up in every way to Aristotle's criteria for a merited sense of achievement and honor. Men like Frederick Douglass certainly prove the truth of Seneca's teaching that adversity can make a man noble. The same is true of Martin Luther King, Jr., John McCain, and many others.

To these we can add the noble men of our age who have fought for freedom around the world; names such as Solzhenitsyn and Mandela will be spoken by future generations in the same breath as those of the heroes of Thermopylae or Yorktown. Finally, I think of a more recent and deeply moving example: Jim Bowers, the missionary whose wife and daughter were killed when their plane was mistakenly shot down over Peru. As he floated on the plane's wreckage with his one surviving child waiting to be rescued, he had to explain to him that Mommy had gone home to God. There are as many heroes in private life as in the great affairs of state.

Just as with courage, we have a complicated and ambivalent relationship to the old-fashioned virtue of pride. But we still recognize noble conduct, and we are still willing to honor ambition when it is harnessed to a good cause. Noble conduct can be inspired by faith or by a commitment to human justice and dignity, or by both. In reflecting on such actions, we have to distinguish between their sources and motivations. In practice, they come together in those stirring deeds.

IV.

FAMILY

IS IT POSSIBLE FOR A LEADER TO CORRUPT HIS OWN COUNTRY? THAT old-fashioned question took on an unexpected relevance in the closing years of the century just ended. One of the most important issues raised by President Bill Clinton's embarrassing tryst with a young female intern is the connection between family life and the moral tone of our civic culture. Is leadership reducible to a debate about policies, irrespective of the good or bad character of the leader? The president's defenders said so, implying that you can be a swine in private life and remain a first-rate public servant. Then again, on the contrary, is it impossible to stand for the right thing in public if you have a corrupt character in private? Most of our religious, philosophical, ethical, and political traditions would say yes to this latter view. Only in recent decades have the social sciences tended to discount the moral virtues as ephemeral to the process of policy making. Unfortunately for the United States, the error of this assumption played itself out disastrously at the highest level of the nation's affairs and in its symbolic family residence, the White House, whose most august precincts were the scene of a sexual *Hee Haw* show that left even the jaded public of the late 1990s gasping.

The Clinton-Lewinsky scandal emerged against the backdrop of a decade of increasing concern about the decline of the American family, and it was symptomatic of a wider moral corrosion and lack of purpose. Surveys showed a large majority of Americans believed that society had grown too permissive, that civility had declined, that people were too selfish. Above all, they were deeply worried about the disintegration of family life. Barbara Dafoe Whitehead's book *The Divorce Culture* amassed devastating evidence that having an absentee father was the single strongest predictor of crime and severe behavioral and psychological dysfunction among boys, regardless of ethnicity or socioeconomic background. In other words, a boy living in Scarsdale with no experience of a father was at least as likely, if not more likely, to engage in illegal activity or display a personality disorder as a boy in an inner-city neighborhood whose father had always been there for him.

What was particularly devastating for my generation of Boomers was Whitehead's evidence showing that few if any of the claims made back in the 1970s for "elective divorce" had proven true. She observed that, whereas divorce had once been rare and the result of an insuperable conflict between husband and wife, the divorce rate skyrocketed in the 1970s. The Me Decade regarded divorce as an extension of its search for purely personal satisfaction begun in the 1960s, regardless of its effect on the family as an institution. Divorce was now regarded as a "lifestyle" choice. If, after a few years a marriage failed you as an individual in any way—if the sex wasn't as good, if your career prospects were hampered, or even if you just felt like a change—then you owed it to yourself to split.

Sociologists assured us there would be no harmful effects on the kids. After all, weren't they better off living with one parent than with a couple who were at each other's throats? Drawing upon Margaret Mead's alleged discovery of blissed-out happiness among tribal societies who weren't hung up on monogamy, private property, and other middle-class, bourgeois, Nixon-loving fixations, they argued that the kids' lives would be enriched as they were exposed to an "extended family" of stepparents and new siblings. This sophistry dovetailed beautifully with the Boomers' continuing collective obsession with the 1960s, which they looked back upon as a utopia of complete and unfettered self-expression and polymorphous sexuality whose revolutionary spirit they were trying to keep alive in a more conservative age. Although they pursued careers, money, and status, they read New Age potboilers like *The Greening of America* or *The Third Wave*, and believed themselves to be "reforming the system from within." Why not transform the repressive old Ozzie and Harriet family of the 1950s into a hip ganja-drenched tribe spread throughout lofts and beach houses from coast to coast? Thus, they flattered themselves that the "extended" families they were creating through serial divorce were something akin to a hippie commune (but with pasta machines and Jacuzzis), where we all might live groovily together.

As Whitehead's book proved, it was pretty much all bunk. Kids overwhelmingly preferred living with their real moms and dads—even if they didn't get along—to being forced to choose between them, or live with one of them plus a stepparent. Her research revealed that most children of divorced parents never stop missing their original family, never stop feeling betrayed and abandoned by parents whom they feel didn't try hard enough to keep the family together, and generally detest both their "new" moms and dads and "new" siblings. Although we have to sympathize with the many among us who have tasted the bitter experience of divorce, people have come increasingly to feel that the divorce culture has left the social fabric badly damaged.

Given this disastrous project for dismantling the family, it's hardly surprising that contrary yearnings have increasingly expressed themselves through the entertainment culture. Gradually, Americans have been subconsciously yearning for some kind of reconciliation with the patriarchal family pattern of the past. Because it can only be indulged with a guilty conscience, this longing is deflected from the mainstream of public debate to the personal realm of movies, television, and music, because our predominant political and psychological orthodoxies sternly forbid us to flirt with such deservedly outmoded and reactionary beliefs.

Disillusionment and queasiness over the divorce culture set in almost from the start, and mounted steadily over time. Both the Godfather movies and David Lynch's *Blue Velvet* treat the traditional patriarchal family as a lost golden age, a Garden of Eden from which we children of the divorce culture have been expelled. The first Godfather film opens with the wedding scene at the Corleone family compound in the leafier reaches of Long Island, a secure and happy little kingdom managed benevolently by the don and his loyal soldiers. While the children dance and sing on the sunny lawn, the patriarch takes care of the family's business in his darkened office. Having preserved their fortunes for another day, he can then reward himself with some fun at the party, leading an old-fashioned Sicilian waltz with his queen. This is the high point of the Corleone saga. The don is shrewd, successful, and capable of ruthlessness, but he is also prudent, levelheaded, and realistic in his ambitions.

He protects and guides everyone. When he is disabled by a gunshot wound from a rival family, the Corleones are expelled from the garden into a darker world, where Sonny, the overly impetuous heir to the throne, tries to make up for his lack of judgment with brute force.

The Eden motif is even more striking in *Blue Velvet*. The film begins literally with a garden, the peaceful green lawns of the suburbs. Dad is watering the grass, tending his realm. The world is at peace, the children secure in his love and guidance. Suddenly the camera plunges beneath the calm green surface of the garden, showing us the insects and other dark evils that lurk below, as the father keels over from a heart attack. While the father was well, his authority and care for his kingdom kept that dark world of chaos and disordered passions at bay. In his absence, the monsters come out of their holes. His father's rule having collapsed prematurely, the young man in the film is expelled from the garden. He searches for surrogate fathers who can provide him with the security he once knew. He is torn between his girlfriend's father, a police detective who sternly protects the public order, and the creepy-crawler nighttime criminal portrayed by Dennis Hopper, the human embodiment of the dark forces under the grass. The boy is faced with an unsatisfactory choice between a cold and distant guardian of morality and an evil charmer who gives him a twisted kind of paternal affection.

More recently, *The Sopranos* has given us an update on the Mafia myth which is the most unabashedly flattering portrait of the mobster as patriarch we've seen in years. Tony Soprano is an amoral thug. But he is also the protector of his family and the extended family of soldiers and dependents. He is a man of action who, like some Roman commander of old, does what must be done to enemies of the family without flinching. His wife, Carmela, is the earth mother, tolerant of (although not happy about) Tony's infidelities, generally plying everyone in sight with an endless stream of delicious food to keep the hearth fires going.

Of special interest is the suppressed erotic charge between Tony and his psychiatrist, Dr. Melfi. Educated, cool, well-coiffed, and cultured, she is the yuppified Italian who has left Tony's world behind. The Sopranos are far wealthier than she is, but their monster house, with its Kmart furniture and tacky metal wall ornaments of peacocks and musical notes straight from Canarsie, shows they remain hopelessly blue collar in their tastes. By contrast, Dr. Melfi and her husband have all the right toys—the Persian carpets, the antiques, the wine cellar, the sleek clothes. And yet Dr. Melfi finds her husband too bland, too yuppified, as Tony's roguishness and hot temper work their charms. As she enters Tony's world through their therapy sessions, she becomes more and more of a "broad," swearing and drinking, her accent losing its PBS poise and reverting to the flattened vowels of Queens.

When she is brutally raped on the way to her car late at night, she is tempted to tell Tony. That would be a violation of every conceivable ethical guideline for a psychiatrist, because it would break down the division between her personal life and her role as a therapist. But she also knows that, unlike her husband, who is solicitous but ineffectual, Tony would only have to be told what happened in order to have the rapist killed—instantly and without mercy. He would protect and avenge her.

I don't use these examples from popular culture because I necessarily approve of them. The point is this: What cannot express itself in an open public debate will degenerate into nostalgia or a crude and decayed version of an ideal no longer clearly recalled. The reason so many of us indulge a guilty pleasure in admiring Don Corleone or Tony Soprano as effective fathers is that our public orthodoxies have for many years forbidden a rational dialogue that can distinguish between responsible and irresponsible visions of manhood—including a reasoned endorsement of paternal authority as one ingredient in a healthy family life. Movies and television shows are starting points for thinking about our repressed longing for paternal authority as a significant moral element in a balanced family structure, along with the contributions of motherhood, the child's viewpoint, and respect for all family members. But if we want to restore a reasoned public dialogue about the proper balance of authority and freedom within the family, we need to move beyond nostalgic and half-buried reminiscences from the entertainment culture to the real thing—the Western tradition, where a more robust ideal of fatherhood awaits us in all its richness, preserved intact in the Great Books. Here we find that the family household, and the father's role in it, is perhaps the single most enduring social arrangement of the last five millennia. To deny it is to deny our nature as human beings, along with the accumulated experience of our entire historical odyssey.

THE HOUSEHOLD

Throughout most of the history of the West, and for much of the world today, the family has been held to be more important than other ties, including those of citizenship. Clan, blood, loyalty to kin—these have been more meaningful than the more abstract concept that you owe a duty to strangers in accordance with the requirements of citizenship. By family, I don't mean the conventional "nuclear family" of the economically developed liberal democracies. The nuclear family is virtually unique to liberal democracy, and its current predominance in the West already reflects the enormous transformation of traditional living patterns that was achieved by modernity over the course of several centuries. The nuclear family is a much weaker version of the traditional family clan, because since the eighteenth century, the West has chosen individualism as its core value; in order for individualism to win the day both politically (in the form of representative democracy) and economically (in the form of entrepreneurial capitalism), it was necessary for the traditional authority of the father and clan to be weakened. The same patriarchal authority that had placed restrictions on free trade, reserving certain economic activities as privileges for the aristocracy, also refused to share its authority with elected assemblies. The same royal power that governed an entire kingdom was also reflected in the rule of fathers over private households, and those mini-monarchs had similar powers to restrict the economic independence and personal rights of their wives, children, dependents, and clients. The family tribe meant everything, and individual freedom next to nothing.

The gradual triumph of modernity required diluting and undermining the authority of the father, both in his role as ruler over the individual family and in his role as ruler over an entire people as king. For in the premodern tradition, family authority and royal authority are interchangeable. The father is the king of his family, and the king is the father of the family making up his entire people. Moreover, the private family in premodern times and cultures is a vast network of interwoven blood ties, embracing not only the relatives but their servants, clients, and dependents, and the children of those clients. In many tribal patterns of authority, the king is the father of the most prominent clan or family within an extended tribe of blood relatives. The bond between patron and client extends over generations, so that the grandson of a lord continues to have an obligation toward the grandson of his servant, who owes the lord's grandson loyalty in return. Nation and household are one.

In much of the world today, non-Western cultures take a view of fatherhood and family life that is very similar to the premodern views of the West—closer, in many ways, to the premodern traditions of the West than is the West itself. Your duty to your clan is more important by far than your rights as an individual. One of the more ludicrous sights of my lifetime was the spectacle of the feminist writer Kate Millett dashing to Tehran after the fall of the shah, in the belief that she could lecture the leaders of the Iranian Revolution on the need to extend equal rights to women. There was not much chance that the Ayatollah Khomeini would have been friendly to any version of secular individualism imported from the West. It was the hapless shah, in fact, who as a half-hearted modernizer offered Iranian women a freedom to pursue careers that they have rarely known either before or since, although it may be returning now.

A man of traditional faith, Khomeini did not believe in secular human equality, whether between men and women or between men and men, because he believed in God's authority as the divine father of us all. Although this conviction may distress us as citizens of modern secular democracies, it is important to remember that it was the prevailing view in the West until well into the nineteenth and twentieth centuries, including our own major religious teachings as exemplified by figures such as St. Augustine and St. Thomas Aquinas, but also finding stout defenders among the American Founding Fathers, the Victorians, and well nigh down to the present. When Khomeini was asked by a journalist during his exile in France how Iran would be governed if he ever came to power, he replied: "Read Plato's *Republic*." As a theologian steeped in al-Farabi and Averroës, he believed in a tripartite hierarchy, the Muslim version of the Republic, in which the teachers rule the soldiers, and the soldiers rule the workers. Much of the non-Western world, especially as regards family life and other personal relationships, would be in complete agreement with the ancient Greek saying "What's oldest is best."

For the ancient Greeks, the family was taken to reflect an eternal truth about the entire world. The authority of father over wife and children, and of the larger tribe and tribal head over the individual fathers, was taken to reflect the authority of the gods themselves over the clan heads and everyone below them. Just as we honor our fathers, our fathers and their children honor the gods, the fathers of us all. Rights meant very little; duty to your superiors meant everything.

This duty was not something that should have to be enforced. We should do our duty to our clan, father, and king freely and with gratitude, because of all they and our ancestral forefathers in the past have done for us by preserving and increasing the status and prosperity of the household before passing it on to their heirs. Xenophon remarks that the ancient Persians regarded ingratitude as the worst of vices—the first sign of it in a boy was met with a severe flogging. Ingratitude was taken to be a symptom of impiety and shamelessness. Only a shameless, arrogant, and immoderate young man could set his own claims above those of his elders.

The same is true of the Hebrew Bible, which holds that sons must honor and obey their fathers. When Abraham is commanded to sacrifice his son, Isaac, Abraham must obey the father God, and Isaac must obey God through the command of his father, Abraham. God suspends the sacrifice at the last minute as an act of mercy, an unfathomable gift from on high that requires the deepest gratitude. As some of the midrashim teach, the lesson of the story is that God is saying: I can demand this sacrifice of you any time I want to, and I don't have to explain my actions. If I decide not to demand this sacrifice, that's not because my will is constrained by any preexisting set of laws. The law is my gift to you. I created it, so I cannot be bound by it. If I spare you, it's out of mercy and love, not because I can be held to any standard higher than my own will. God is the ultimate paterfamilias. As the source of all justice, he cannot be subordinated to its rules.

This is not the whole story, of course. It's often remarked that, although the Hebrew Bible accepts the patriarchal pattern of authority because it mirrors the fatherhood of God, its depictions of family life are often more vivid than anything to be found in the secular literature of the ancient world, and show how the formal supremacy of the father is relaxed and softened in practice by his love for his wife and his dependence on her as a partner in their experiences as a family. Certainly the Bible features a number of very strong women characters—Ruth, for example, or Abraham's wife Sarah—whose rectitude and intelligence make them the equals of men in practice, if not according to the letter of the law. When Sarah hears that God has promised them a child even though she is ninety, she just laughs. God or no God, she knows a thing or two about being a woman.

By the time of the classical era in Greece and continuing into the Roman Empire, the pure pagan version of patriarchy had also softened somewhat. The fabled authority of the Roman paterfamilias—his ability to act as judge, jury, and executioner over his own family—was largely a memory of a harsher era, preserved mainly in ritual ceremonies. Increasingly, brutality toward wives and children was frowned upon as being beneath the dignity and breeding of a real man. Plato, Aristotle, and the Stoic philosophers argued that the relationship between a husband and a wife should be regarded as a friendship, not as akin to the mastery of servants. Although children were to obey their elders, it was recognized that even they had a share of the moral and intellectual virtues, and that it was better to govern them by persuasion and by appealing to their reason than by fear or force. As we've seen in the earlier chapters on love, courage, and pride, the ancient philosophers were, so to speak, "liberals" in comparison with the prevailing views of their own time. They criticized the harsher versions of manliness that equated it with sheer brute force and argued for an intertwining of male and female characteristics so that manly honor and aggressiveness would be sublimated by female subtlety and balance. Knightly chivalry went further in arguing that love, not force and obedience, should be the main bond between a man and a woman, and that a virtuous woman could provide a man with an ideal for his own self-perfection.

As we'll see in the rest of this chapter, Renaissance humanism stressed that a civilized man should be a friend to both his wife and his children, and that child rearing provided the fullest scope for husband and wife to create a partnership to which each could contribute his and her own specific merits. The Western tradition enshrines family life as the greatest test and the greatest reward for the majority of men. A

happy marriage and the love of his children is a man's reward for pursuing love in the correct way we explored in Chapter 1—as a vehicle for
self-perfection. Starting with Aristotle, and echoed by much of subsequent theology, literature, and philosophy from the Renaissance through
the Enlightenment, the Romantics, and the Victorians, the family is seen
as a natural society providing bonds of friendship and affection within
the much larger and more artificial surrounding civil society—what
Christopher Lasch termed "a haven in a heartless world." Education begins in the family. Children first learn about love, justice, and duty as
they relate to other family members. By learning to be good to our relatives, we can then extend those virtues outward in widening circles to
our fellow citizens. But if we don't first learn those virtues in the family,
where our natural affection for our siblings and parents gives us a direct
and spontaneous motivation to treat them well, those virtues will never
take root in our souls, and we will never evolve into good citizens.

Still, one must not stress *too* much similarity between the modern
liberal view of fatherhood and these premodern philosophical and ethical traditions, however progressive they may appear in comparison with
the prevailing views of their eras. It would be wishful thinking to pretend
to ourselves that all the great thinkers and writers of premodern times
were incipient feminists or egalitarians, the advance guard in the lock-
step march of historical progress. They weren't. From Aristotle to the
Renaissance thinkers, it was taken for granted that human beings were
not equal, that some were ordained by God and nature to rule over others, and that, although men and women could be friends in many respects—and especially in the domestic affairs of child rearing—men
were better suited than women for the responsibilities of public and economic life. As Aristotle put it, the family was like a civic community in
which the offices never rotated—the father was the permanent first
magistrate. True, he should attempt to persuade his wife of the reason-
ableness of his views and not just demand obedience as if she were a servant. At the end of the day, though, his opinion prevailed. In all essential
matters, men were the masters; they alone owned the property, and they
alone could hold public office.

Not until the philosophers of the Enlightenment, and of political liberalism, was a direct assault made on this old patriarchal structure. John

Locke argued that every individual—man and woman alike—is free by nature, and therefore has a right not to be tyrannized by others, including fathers and husbands. Every individual by nature also has the freedom to prosper through economic activity, as well as the freedom to worship as he or she pleases and to live where he or she pleases, and every individual is entitled to equal treatment under the law. For these natural rights of the individual to take effect in reality, the royal authority of the father both as the master of the private household and as the master of an entire nation had to be broken down.

From its earliest days, America, the land where Lockean individualism was most fully put into practice, permitted an equality between men and women, and a casual attitude on the part of children toward their fathers' wishes, that Europeans, still closely bonded to the premodern outlook, found profoundly shocking. Alexis de Tocqueville observed as early as the 1830s that, given the American experience as the world's first fully formed democracy, we can take it as inevitable that, wherever democracy spreads, the authority of the father must decline. As he depicts it, American fathers even at that early stage were more like "pals" to their children than the mini-monarchs of the European household. European conservatives, in contrast with their American counterparts, always distrusted the rise of free enterprise and the equality of individual opportunity for economic self-advancement, because they saw—quite correctly—that these trends were inseparable from an assault on the old feudal and aristocratic conception of the family, and on established authority in general.

It's also fair to say that Americans themselves have often wondered whether we've taken the weakening of the father's authority too far, and whether American families might not benefit from a little more "royal" authority on the father's part. Sitcoms of the 1950s and 1960s like *Bewitched* or *The Dick Van Dyke Show* reflected a feeling that the sexy rogues of the 1930s—the tough-talking Humphrey Bogart type—had degenerated into the blandness of the "man in the gray flannel suit." As the adventure of World War II was replaced by the corporate culture of the 1950s, the roguish independence of the Sam Spade type was no longer viewed with favor. Getting along became the order of the day, as seen in the wimpiness of Darrin in *Bewitched* or Dagwood's hapless subordination to Blondie. Having put in his eight hours at his soul-destroying office job sucking up to the tyrannical Mr. Dithers, all Dagwood wants to do when he gets home is curl up on the couch, while his ex-flapper wife, having exchanged the dance floor for a tract house in the suburbs, manages him and the children with lighthearted ease.

People felt early on that the 1950s' obsession with success in business and commerce was emasculating and leading to too much conformism. The rise of "juvenile delinquency" as a theme of pop culture, as well as earnest policy debate, was widely perceived as a reaction by boys against the wimpiness of their fathers. If their fathers were whipped dogs, ruled at home by Mom and at work by the boss, the boys would revert to being warriors in a nighttime world of switchblade fights, chicken races, and alley-cat sex. Out in the darkened fields beyond the neat suburban tract houses where Mom and Dad were watching *What's My Line*, these leather-clad bad boys were instinctively reestablishing the primitive tribal pecking order of the warrior and his woman, a gum-chewing bad girl similarly outrageously clad in leather, cheap makeup, and huge hair. The rebellion by the juvenile delinquent against the bland father of the 1950s—his instinctive groping toward some primitive version of the patriarchal hierarchy based on prowess in battle—is epitomized in the movie *Rebel Without a Cause*, with the pathetic character played by Jim Backus wearing an apron and doing the dishes to avoid the wrath of his shrewish wife. James Dean, unforgettable as the archetypal juvenile delinquent, is all inarticulate writhing and squirming agony as he surveys his father's emasculated state. He wants his father to take charge of him, to discipline him and make him obey. But his father has learned the lingo of Dr. Spock and just wants to "have a talk" as he clears the dish rack. James Dean despises his father for being too weak to assert his royal authority, to put his virago of a wife in her place, and to make him toe the line. And, of course, he also feels as if his father doesn't care enough about him to discipline him effectively. His emasculated kindness and understanding have the practical effect of neglect.

And that brings us back to our opening observations: The boy in *Rebel Without a Cause* would be much happier with Tony Soprano for a dad. He would become Christopher, Tony's surrogate son and aspiring mafioso, channeling his ferocity into the family business, guided by his stern but affectionate and canny leader. As we've seen so often in these reflections on the manly virtues, nature is trying to speak to us through the primitive and decayed versions of forgotten authority patterns that reemerge in pop culture. The point is not that we should want to be like the Sopranos, or that Tony really is an improvement over Jim Backus. The point is that our guilty pleasure in liking Tony should act as a clue that something is radically deficient about our official orthodoxies and received opinions about fatherhood and family life. We need to get behind the decayed recollections that speak to us through movies and television and encounter the real thing—the Western tradition of father-hood. In terms of moral and psychological satisfaction, it's like moving from junk food to a well-balanced meal.

THE CHALLENGES OF FAMILY LIFE

The family is the source of almost all of the substantial roles a man is called upon to play in his life. As a father, son, brother, or husband, a man finds himself confronted with complex and often competing sets of relations and obligations. Moreover, as a man ages, the nature of those bonds can change dramatically. What distinguishes these relationships from ties outside the family is a unique depth of feeling, a depth both sublime and perilous. The same achingly intense love for a parent, spouse, or child that is at the heart of family life can be the source of bit-ter disappointment, crippling fear, and immeasurable grief.

It is these complexities that make the family a lifelong school in which a man can develop his own character; it is a classroom for the soul. Ideally, the lessons learned coalesce into a comprehensive whole, founded on morality and competence. Aristotle calls it "the proper art of household management." By household management, Aristotle means not only the ability to sustain a family economically but—more impor-tant—the art of raising children in order to prepare them for their future duties as parents and citizens. Indeed, child rearing is the most impor-tant duty of the partnership formed by husband and wife. In the project of nurturing and educating a family, a man finds many of his chief emotional and intellectual satisfactions. And, by persevering in this endeavor throughout the reversals, torments, and puzzles of family love, men are drawn again and again to consider the deeper meaning of their lives.

The risks a man must take in giving his love wholeheartedly—the danger of rejection or betrayal by his spouse or children—cause some men to flee family life altogether, to shake off its obligations and reject its possibilities. For some men, the inherited responsibilities of kinship seem burdensome and restrictive. These men sometimes reject ties of blood and kinship in favor of friendships and loves entirely of their own choosing. But for most men the family is, for better or worse, the best hope for happiness. From the *Odyssey* of Homer to Frank Capra's *It's a Wonderful Life*, it is a recurring theme in Western culture that material prosperity and social status are unlikely on their own to provide a man with a genuine and long-lasting feeling of inner contentment, peace, and success.

Being the father of a family can be likened to governing the affairs of a small, self-contained country. It calls for great reserves of prudence, experience, rhetorical skill, and an ability to mix gentle admonition with candid rebuke. The great French humanist Michel de Montaigne maintained that governing a private family is only slightly less demanding than governing an entire kingdom. It's even more demanding in our era, when we are as reluctant to obey a king in private life as we are in our politics, particularly when our political leaders so often fail to live up to the ethical demands of their own high calling. To govern a family when government itself is often in disrepute calls for the gifts of a Solomon.

FATHERS AND SONS

In the rest of this chapter, let us look at some of the basic relationships making up the family—fathers and sons, husbands and wives, and the duties of child rearing. We'll begin with fathers and sons.

As is so often the case in our reflections on the positive tradition of manliness, we begin with Homer. The *Odyssey* is the first work in the Western tradition to explore a son's search for a father—an outward physical journey that parallels an inward psychological search. The poem is a quest within a quest. As Odysseus makes his slow way home from

Troy to Ithaca, his son, Telemachus, embarks on his own voyage, setting
out from Ithaca on a search for a father who is all but unknown to him,
having left to fight the Trojans some twenty years earlier. Telemachus's
quest is not just for a biological father but for a guide—the spiritual
search for a source of direction in life. In seeking a father who has been
absent for the entire life of his son, Telemachus is searching for a father
who exists for him more as an ideal than as a flesh-and-blood reality.
Telemachus is transformed by this search. As he journeys to find his father, he also journeys into manhood, guided by this ideal. Endeavoring
to become worthy of being this great man's son, inspired by stories of his
father's exploits, Telemachus in effect becomes his own father guided by
this distant ideal. He raises himself. Meanwhile, both Odysseus and
Telemachus are offered advice and protection on their voyages by the
goddess Athena. She is particularly attached to Odysseus. Athena's intelligence, subtlety, and curiosity mirror Odysseus's own. In mentoring
both father and son, in helping them advance on their respective journeys toward each other, Athena progressively reveals to them a rich and
multifaceted vision of manliness, one in which male and female traits
deepen and temper each other.

In the opening pages of the *Odyssey,* the youthful Telemachus
laments the long absence of his father from the royal household. Visited
by Athena, who is disguised as a wandering minstrel, he opens his heart
and shares with the goddess his anxiety about the future. How can he
protect his mother, Penelope, from her greedy and overbearing suitors
from the great clans of Ithaca, who are pressing the queen to admit that
her husband is dead and choose one of them to take his place as her husband and Ithaca's king? Is he man enough to bear the burdens he has inherited? Again and again, as he opens up to the goddess in disguise, his
fears and longings turn to his absent father:

> By far the first to see Athena was the princely Telemachus. For he was
> sitting with the suitors, sad at heart, picturing in his mind his noble fa-
> ther—how he might come back and, throughout the entire house, make
> the suitors scatter, reclaim his rightful place and be master of his own
> possessions. . . . "Good stranger, will you take offense at what I say? All
> they care about are the lyre and the singing. Easy for them when, with-

out making any amends, they eat up the substance of a man whose white
bones now are rotting in the rain, if lying on land, or in the sea they roll
around in the wash of the breakers. Yet if they were ever to see him coming home to Ithaca, they all would pray to be fast on their feet instead of
for stores of gold and clothing. But, instead, he has been taken by some
hard fate, and nothing remains to comfort us, no, not if any man on earth
were to tell us he will return. His day of homecoming has died."

Upon hearing Telemachus's bitter lament, Athena offers him new
hope. She promises that Odysseus is still alive. But even this hopeful news
prompts fresh worries in the boy. He asks himself: Am I really his son?
How can I be certain, when I know so little of him? "My mother says I am
his," he tells Athena. "But I don't really know. Nobody really knows his
own father." This last remark is surely intended to be taken figuratively as
well as literally. Telemachus is admitting something much deeper than
doubts about his legitimate birth, or the fact that sons often have a difficult
time getting to know their fathers. He's wondering whether fathers and
sons are fated *never* to understand each other at all—a feeling often felt, if
not put into words, by both sides of the relationship. Fortunately for
Telemachus, his anxieties prove to be unjustified.

Like so many traditional works about family life, this one is not
merely the personal story of a son's search for a missing father but a
wider saga about a missing king and the perils faced by his young heir to
the throne. To preserve social and dynastic stability in the kingdom of
Ithaca, men from noble families aggressively court Telemachus's mother.
They are convinced that Odysseus is dead, and that his widow must
choose one of them to take his place as husband and king so Ithaca can
return to normal. If the royal household is in disorder, the entire kingdom and all its families are in disorder. If the king is not securely in place
as the lord of all, the patriarchal structure of all families is undermined.
But from Penelope's viewpoint and that of her son, the suitors are threatening to usurp the place that rightly belongs to the missing Odysseus. As
his son and heir, Telemachus must defend both his mother's honor and
his own right of succession. He takes his grievance against the suitors before the assembly of the people, and unhappy teenager that he is, finds it
hard to control his emotions as he speaks:

"I would defend myself if I had the power. But what's been done to me is beyond enduring; my house has been ravaged. . . . I entreat you, by Olympian Zeus, and by that Justice which both convenes and dissolves the assemblies of men. Leave it be, my friends! Leave me to pine alone in bitter grief, unless my father, good Odysseus, in his anger really did wrong the strong-greaved Achaeans, in return for which you now, angry toward me, in revenge do me harm by urging these people on. It would be better for me if you yourselves devoured my stores and herds. If you devoured them, perhaps some day there might be recompense; for we would constantly pursue you through the town, demanding back our goods until everything was restored. As it is, now you are laying incurable woes upon my heart." In wrath he spoke, and dashed the sceptre to the ground, letting his tears burst forth, and pity fell on all the people.

As he embarks on his quest for his father, Telemachus is guided by Athena to visit some of the other legendary figures of the Trojan War, all long since returned to their homelands. Nestor, Menelaos, and Helen, all of whom knew and admired Odysseus, share with Telemachus the lessons of war and the legacy of the *Iliad,* lessons his absent father could not impart. In this way, their memories of the missing hero contribute to the upbringing of his son. Telemachus returns home having absorbed the full legacy of his father's life and example. Now all that remains is their long-sought reunion. On first beholding his father's return to Ithaca, Telemachus cannot believe his eyes. Father and son fall into each other's arms, overwhelmed with tears. Telemachus, counseled by the wise Athena and schooled by the trials of his search, embraces Odysseus knowing that he has finally become a son worthy of his honored father. After two decades—an entire lifetime for this boy who has only now become a man—Odysseus finally speaks to his son:

"It is I, I am as you see me, and after suffering much and wandering long, I have returned in the twentieth year to my native land. . . ." Saying this, he sat down again, but now Telemachus, throwing his arms round his great father, began to sob and pour forth his tears, and in them both arose a desire to lament. Loud were their cries and more unceasing than those of birds, ospreys or crook-clawed vultures, when farmers take away their young before the wings are grown: so pitifully fell the tears beneath their brows.

Odysseus and Telemachus are so overcome with sadness over the two decades they have lost that words temporarily fail them. In time, they will get to know each other. For now, they can only hold each other tightly, racked with sobs. But the words that fathers and sons speak to each other are usually even more important to the development of their mutual affections than feelings that cannot be verbally expressed. This is especially the case when fathers talk to their sons, for being the elder partners in the friendship, they are naturally more adept at putting their thoughts and emotions into words.

Throughout the Western tradition, we find expressions of tenderness by fathers toward their sons. Sometimes these moments are mixed with sterner words aimed more at correction than at love. In Wordsworth's poem "I Have a Boy of Five Years Old," we find an example of the tender approach:

I have a boy of five years old;
His face is fair and fresh to see;
His limbs are cast in beauty's mould,
And dearly he loves me.

O dearest, dearest boy! my heart
For better lore would seldom yearn,
Could I but teach the hundredth part
Of what from thee I learn.

By contrast, Plutarch's depiction of Cato the Elder offers a sterner model of the father-son relationship. Cato is the ultimate Roman paterfamilias, the king in his own household. He sets an example of unblemished probity, and his word is law. Yet even here, there's a tender dimension. In writing the lives of eminent Greeks and Romans, Plutarch provides a multitude of examples of the classical ideal of manliness. His account of the life of Cato is one of the most representative. Famous for his sense of honor and integrity, Cato was also, as Plutarch illustrates, a loving husband and dedicated father. Alternating between the stern moral rectitude he demonstrated in his dealings with everyone and the special tenderness a father reserves for his son, Cato encouraged his son to excel at everything he undertook, while at the same time accommodating the limitations placed on the boy by his fragile health:

> Such was Cato's approach to the noble task of forming and molding his son for the pursuit of virtue. The boy was an exemplary pupil in his readiness to learn, and his spirit was a match for his natural goodness of disposition. But since his body was not strong enough to endure extreme hardship, Cato was obliged to relax a little the extraordinary austerity and self-discipline of his own way of life.

In gratitude not only for the education that he received from his father but also for Cato's sympathy for his frail health, the boy went on to distinguish himself on the battlefield, going out of his way to prove that his frailty would not prevent him from behaving honorably; he thus contributed to the honorable legacy of the whole family. Plutarch recounts the battlefield exploit that brought the son of Cato a special commendation from his commander:

> His son, in spite of a delicate physique, became an excellent soldier, and fought with great distinction under Aemilius Paulus at the battle of Pydna, when the Romans defeated king Perseus. During the fighting his sword was either struck out of his hand or else slipped from his grasp when it became moist with sweat. The young man felt deeply ashamed at losing it, and so he turned to some of his companions and, rallying them to his side, charged the enemy again. The fighting was fierce, but at length he succeeded in clearing a space, and there he came upon the weapon amid the heaps of arms and corpses, where the bodies of friends and enemies lay piled high upon one another. Paulus, his commander, was greatly impressed by the young Cato's courage, and a letter has come down to us written by the father to his son, in which he praises him in the highest terms for his gallantry and for the sense of honor which he showed in recovering his sword. . . . In this way Cato was justly rewarded for the care which he had devoted to his son's education.

As the example of Cato illustrates, the education of children by fathers in the home can have major consequences for their future success as citizens and statesmen. This aspect of the father-son relationship is rendered in striking colors by Shakespeare's *Henry IV, Part I*. The age-old tension in private life between father and son—between the gravity of age and the impetuosity of youth—is compounded when the tension is also between a king and his heir. A brilliant exploration of a flawed relationship between a father and a son, and its grave consequences for the wider sphere of society and politics, the play moves back and forth between the political and familial with a speed and candor that point to their often unhappy connection. In the following scene, Henry takes his son, the irresponsible Hal, aside and severely chastises him for his life of sloth and dissipation. In the king's words we hear the echoes of countless generations of disappointed fathers confronted with idle and rebellious sons: What have I done to deserve this? Don't you have any feeling for me? God must be punishing me for my sins in giving me such a worthless son!

> King: *I know not whether God will have it so*
> *For some displeasing service I have done,*
> *That, in his secret doom, out of my blood*
> *He'll breed revengement and a scourge for me;*
> *But thou dost in thy passages of life*
> *Make me believe that thou art only marked*
> *For the hot vengeance and the rod of heaven*
> *To punish my mistreadings. Tell me else,*
> *Could such inordinate and low desires,*
> *Such poor, such bare, such lewd, such mean attempts,*
> *Such barren pleasures, rude society,*
> *As thou art matched withal and grafted to,*
> *Accompany the greatness of thy blood*
> *And hold their level with thy princely heart?*

The king concludes his devastating rebuke with a reminder that, despite Hal's many failings, his father still loves him. As with all relationships between fathers and sons, tenderness and affection alternate with high expectations and stern words when they are disappointed. Everyone is sick of the sight of you, Henry lectures his son, except for

your father, who—amazingly enough, given your bad behavior—actually
wants to see more of you, so blinded is he by affection:

> *For thou hast lost thy princely privilege*
> *With vile participation. Not an eye*
> *But is aweary of thy common sight,*
> *Save mine, which hath desired to see thee more;*
> *Which now doth that I would not have it do—*
> *Make blind itself with foolish tenderness.*

Prince Hal is suitably chastened by his father's merciless broadside.
But despite his somber promise to "hereafter, my thrice gracious lord, be
more myself," the king remains unsure of his son. His loss of confidence
in Hal is made all the graver by the political dimension of their relationship. Henry recalls the fact that he won his throne by overthrowing an
utterly weak and unworthy king, Richard II. Now he in turn is being
plotted against by another young man, Hal's cousin Hotspur, scion of the
powerful rival clan the Percys. Henry laments the fact that while
Hotspur reminds him of himself when he went against Richard, his own
son reminds him of the unworthy king he deposed, a frivolous nonentity
addicted to vanity. Henry's faith is so shaken that he wonders whether his
weak-willed and self-indulgent boy might be capable even of treason,
deserting his own father for Hotspur and the Percys if siding with them
meant he could continue his life of wanton pleasure:

> King: *For all the world,*
> *As thou art to this hour was Richard then*
> *When I from France set foot at Ravenspurgh;*
> *And even as I was then is Percy now.*
> *Now, by my scepter, and my soul to boot,*
> *He hath more worthy interest to the state*
> *Than thou the shadow of succession;*
> *For of no right, nor color like to right,*
> *He doth fill fields with harness in the realm,*
> *Turns head against the lion's armed jaws.*
> *Why, Harry, do I tell thee of my foes,*

Which art my nearest and dearest enemy?
Thou that art like enough, through vassal fear,
Base inclination, and the start of spleen,
To fight against me under Percy's pay.
To dog his heels and curtsy at his frowns,
To show how much thou art degenerate.

Stricken with shame and remorse that his father could have so low an opinion of him as to think he would desert to the other side, Hal implores Henry to give him another chance. Not only will he not desert his father for Hotspur but he will be his father's champion in defeating the usurper, the young man who is his opposite number in the rival Percy clan:

Prince: *Do not think so, you shall not find it so.*
And God forgive them that so much have swayed
Your Majesty's good thoughts away from me.
I will redeem all this on Percy's head
And, in the closing of some glorious day,
Be bold to tell you that I am your son.

As Shakespeare's play so clearly illustrates, the best writing about fathers and sons has the honesty to admit that everything isn't perfect. Sometimes fathers are disappointed in their sons, or have mixed feelings about fatherhood. In his essay "On the Affections of Fathers for Their Children," the Renaissance humanist Montaigne asks whether a man and his son can really be friends. He is frank about his belief that they cannot. A father can inspire respect and affection in a son, but he cannot be his son's friend in the way a peer can be a friend. There are secrets a father can share with a friend of his own age that he can't share with his son. And no father could permit a son to criticize his faults in the way that he would accept from a friend:

The relation of children to their fathers is one of respect. Friendship is kept alive by communication, which, by reason of too great disparity, cannot exist between them, and would haply conflict with natural duties.

For neither can all the secret thoughts of the father be communicated to his son, in order not to beget an unseemly familiarity, nor can the admonitions and corrections, which are among the first offices of friendship, be administered by the son to the father.

Precisely because a father should govern his son by living up to the same high standards he wants his son to absorb, there must be some distance between them. A father's influence over his children should not stem from their economic dependence on him, since that is a crass motive not compatible with sincere affection. And the children's respect for him should not be based on fear of punishment, for then their loyalty is enforced and not voluntary:

> A father is indeed miserable who holds the affection of his children only through the need they have of his assistance, if that may be called affection. He should make himself worthy of respect by his virtue and abilities, and worthy of love by his kindness and gentle manners. No old age can be so decrepit and musty in a person who has lived an honorable life, but it should be revered, especially by his children, whose minds he should have trained to their duty by reason, not by want and the need that they have of him, nor by harshness and compulsion.

If fathers sometimes have mixed feelings about their sons, the same goes for sons about their fathers. As we've already seen from Plutarch's account of the life of Cato the Elder, a father generally had much more control over his son's education in the classical world than has been the case for at least the last two centuries. The autobiography of John Stuart Mill, however, recalls a famous exception to this rule.

Mill's father, the distinguished utilitarian philosopher James Mill, prescribed every aspect of his son's studies: a rigorous immersion in the classics, history, and science to be learned in near total isolation from other children, and no holidays, sports, or frivolity of any kind. Furthermore, the elder Mill shielded his son from any contact with religion and designed his education so as to mold an atheistic comrade-in-arms for "the great and decisive contest against priestly tyranny for liberty of thought." In recalling his childhood, his home schooling, and his formidable father, Mill's autobiography has an undertone of bitterness toward a brilliant but emotionally distant parent, and a childhood utterly lacking in boyish highjinks or familial tenderness:

> It will be admitted, that a man of the opinions, and the character, above described, was likely to leave a strong moral impression on any mind principally formed by him, and that his moral teaching was not likely to err on the side of laxity or indulgence. The element which was chiefly deficient in his moral relation to his children, was that of tenderness.

The reader is touched by Mill's dutiful but not entirely convincing excuses for his father's coldness:

> I do not believe that this deficiency lay in his own nature. I believe him to have had much more feeling than he habitually shewed, and much greater capacities of feeling than were ever developed. He resembled most Englishmen in being ashamed of the signs of feeling, and, by the absence of demonstration, starving the feelings themselves. If we consider further that he was in the trying position of sole teacher, and add to this that his temper was constitutionally irritable, it is impossible not to feel true pity for a father who did, and strove to do so much for his children, who would have so valued their affection, yet who must have been constantly feeling that fear of him was drying it up at its source.

Finally, there is Mill's sad observation—so familiar among those whose fathers have more children late in life—that the father who was so distant with his first offspring lets his feelings blossom with his second family, showering on the new children open displays of affection that were rigidly withheld from the first family. How many grown men today are left with the bitter reflection that their fathers learned only late in life to express a love for their new children that the grown-up sons have never experienced?

> This was no longer the case, later in life and with his younger children. They loved him tenderly: and if I cannot say so much of myself, I was always loyally devoted to him. As regards my own education, I hesitate to pronounce whether I was more a loser or gainer by his severity.

HUSBANDS AND WIVES

Our next family tie to consider is that of husband and wife. The treatment of marriage in Western literature is complicated, often moving and sometimes ambivalent or troubling. An early example is Homer's touching depiction in the *Iliad* of Hektor and his wife, Andromache. Standing on the walls of Troy, they talk together as they play with their infant son and look out over the battlefield. In contrast to Achilles, the solitary and self-absorbed hero of the Greeks, the Trojan prince Hektor is as much attracted to the pleasures of family life as he is to the terrible glories of battle. Perhaps more so—which may explain why, when he actually encounters Achilles, his opposite number on the Greek side, he loses his nerve. The Western tradition overflows with examples of this dual allegiance—the private satisfactions of hearth and home pulling against our sense of duty to the common good.

Hektor listens with a heavy heart as Andromache describes in wrenching detail how important their marriage is to her and implores him not to imperil it on the battlefield. In words that bring tears to a reader's eyes some three thousand years after they were composed, Andromache says to her husband: *You are everything to me!* Because I have no family of my own, you are not only my husband but my entire family summed up in one man:

> Hektor smiled as he looked at his son, but Andromache, as she stood close beside him, wept and clung to his hand, calling him by name as she spoke to him: "My dearest one, your own bravery will be your undoing, and you have no pity for your baby boy, or for me who must soon be your widow. For very soon the Achaians will set upon you and kill you. It would be far better for me to sink into my grave if I lose you, for once you have met your fate, there will no consolation for me in this life— only sorrow. I have no father, no honored mother. Hektor, you are father to me, and mother, and brother, even as you are my young husband. Have pity on me then, stay here with us on the rampart; don't make your child an orphan and your wife a widow."

Duty wins out, as it must. Hektor understands the tragic tension between the pull of private love and the summons to public duty. But he also understands that, if men like him are not willing to risk their lives in combat, their families will suffer destruction at the hands of their country's enemies. If Hektor goes to war, he risks depriving his own family of a husband and father. But if men refuse to go to war, they ultimately imperil all families. As if foreseeing the victory of the Greeks and his own death at the hands of Achilles, Hektor is tormented by the vision of his wife becoming the slave of the Greeks after they capture Troy. Torn between the competing calls of family and country, "tall Hektor of the shining helm" bids farewell with heartrending words:

> "It is not so much the coming anguish of the Trojans that troubles me, not even King Priam's or my brethren's, the many and brave that shall fall in the dust before their foes, as does your anguish in the day when some bronze-armored Achaian leads you away weeping and robs you of the light of freedom. You must live in Argos and work the loom at another woman's bidding, and carry water from mount Messeies or Hypereia, and sore constraint shall be laid upon thee. And one day, seeing you weep, a man will say of you: This is the wife of Hector, who was bravest in battle among the Trojans, breakers of horses, in the days when men fought about the Ilion."

If this is to be his family's fate along with the other Trojans, Hektor doesn't want to live to see it:

> "So they will speak of you, and it will be a fresh grief for you to lack a husband as you once had, who could ward off the day of your slavery. But may I be dead and the heaped-up earth hide me before I ever have to hear you weeping and know from this that they are dragging you away into captivity."

In the *Iliad* Homer offers us the portrait of the doomed soldier, fated never to see his family again. In the *Odyssey* he depicts another perennial motif in the Western tradition, the soldier who returns home safely after many dangerous adventures. When Odysseus first appears to Penelope, she is unsure whether it is really her beloved husband, since twenty years have passed and both have visibly aged. To convince her that it's really him, Odysseus describes their bed, mentioning details of its construction that only he could know, since he made it himself out of a single piece of wood carved from an enormous tree that grows right into their bedroom, and that no other man (of course) has ever laid eyes on. Sparked into recognizing Odysseus at last, Penelope feels her knees and her soul grow wobbly. First Penelope, then Odysseus, succumbs to loud weeping, and they fall into each other's arms wailing with joy and relief, each awash with sorrow at what the other has suffered and over the years lost to them as a couple:

> As he spoke, her knees grew weak as did her very soul, when she recognized the clear proofs Odysseus had given. Then she burst into tears and ran straight towards him, threw her arms around Odysseus' neck and kissed his face. . . . She spoke, and roused even more his yearning to weep. Holding his beloved and faithful wife, he began to weep. As when the welcome land appears to swimmers, whose sturdy ship Poseidon wrecked at sea, confounded by the winds and solid waters, only a few escaping the foaming sea to climb ashore, and while thick salt and foam crusts their flesh they climb ashore the welcome land and are escaped from danger—so welcome was her husband to her gazing eyes. She never let her white arms go from around his neck.

Penelope and Odysseus fall into bed; there, after catching up on two decades' worth of lovemaking, they sit up until dawn telling each other the extraordinary tale of what has happened to each during Odysseus's long absence. They spend the night sharing their secrets and getting to know each other again:

> After their lovemaking, Penelope and Odysseus took further pleasure in talking, each one telling his tale. She, the royal lady, what she had endured at home, watching the ravening throng of suitors, who, using her as an excuse, slew many cattle and sturdy sheep, while shores of wine were drained from out the casks. He, highborn Odysseus, told of all the miseries he brought on other men and what he bore himself in anguish. She was glad to listen to all he told her. No sleep fell on her eyelids until he had told her all.

Not every great writer, of course, was a fan of marriage. In contrast with Homer's moving depictions of the love between a husband and wife, Sir Francis Bacon had a more jaundiced view. A wife and children,

Bacon warns, are "hostages to fortune" and "impediments to great enterprises, either of virtue or of mischief." One might say that a family is
to a man's peace of mind what exposure is to an arbitrageur: You may
start out thinking you know what you're getting into. But your spouse
may turn out not to be the person you imagined, and it will be too late
then to change your mind and withdraw your investment. Despite all the
joys of family life, many men choose to forgo the beauty of tall Hektor's
fair Andromache in favor of the solitary self-sufficiency of the glorious
Achilles. Doubtless there are many justifications for bachelorhood.
Bacon lists a few:

> There are some that account wife and children but as bills of charges.
> Nay more, there are some foolish, rich covetous, men that take pride in
> having no children, because they may be thought so much the richer.
> For perhaps they have heard some talk, Such a one is a great rich man,
> and another except to it, Yea, but he hath a great charge of children, as if
> it were an abatement to his riches. But the most ordinary cause of a sin-
> gle life is liberty, especially in certain self-pleasing and humorous minds,
> which are so sensible of every restraint, as they will go near to think their
> girdles and garters to be bonds and shackles.

For those more critical of the institution of marriage, this is what it
comes down to: A man fears to marry because he will lose his freedom.
Montaigne sums it up with deadpan wit: Marriage is "a bargain to which
only the entrance is free." What begins during courtship as "a lively affection," he goes on, is changed by marriage into "a bargain that is usually concluded to other ends" and involves "a thousand extraneous
entanglements." In other words, the love of a man and woman during
courtship is gradually worn down by the obligations of property, clan,
and child rearing, so that "its continuance [is] forced and constrained,
and depending on something other than our will." Friendship, by contrast, has no purpose beyond itself. Friends can enjoy each other's company for its own sake without any worries about money, mortgages,
in-laws, or kids. He concludes with a drollery so dry you could use it in a
martini: "I married at thirty-three, and concur in Aristotle's opinion,
which is said to have recommended thirty-five."

Well, we all know how urbane and witty the French are about these matters. For a more optimistic view, consider a letter written by Benjamin Franklin, that soul of sober American common sense, hard work, and decency, to a young friend who is contemplating an early marriage. It is full of kindness and encouragement about the solid, lasting contentment that marriage can bring both partners:

> Treat your wife always with respect; it will procure respect to you, not only from her, but from all that observe it. Never use a slighting expression to her, even in jest; for slights in jest, after frequent bandyings, are apt to end in angry earnest. Be studious in your profession and you will be learned. Be industrious and frugal, and you will be rich. Be sober and temperate, and you will be healthy. Be in general virtuous, and you will be happy. At least, you will, by such conduct, stand the best chance for such consequences.

We've already seen how the logician and utilitarian philosopher John Stuart Mill surprises us with the mixed feelings with which he recalls his father—forbearance tinged with regret, gratitude interwoven with sadness. He surprises us again with a remarkably generous and warm-hearted tribute to his wife. In Mill's recollections of his marriage to Harriet Taylor, a woman "eminently meditative and poetic," he describes an emotional and intellectual closeness in which his wife is partner and peer in all his endeavors. In both his autobiography and the introduction to what is perhaps his best-known work, *On Liberty,* Mill's tributes to his wife reveal a marital love founded on deep respect and shared labors, a marriage that was no less than "the fusion of two minds." There can be little doubt that this brilliant but shy and reclusive man found in marriage to this extraordinary woman an emotional release, passion, and tenderness that had been lacking in his all-too-English upbringing. Marriage to Harriet Taylor made up in good measure for the emotional distance of his father. What comes through more than anything else is Mill's gratitude:

> Alike in the highest regions of speculation and in the smallest practical concerns of daily life, her mind was the same perfect instrument, piercing to the very heart and marrow of the matter; always seizing the essential idea or principle. The same exactness and rapidity of operation,

pervading as it did her sensitive as well as her mental faculties, would with her gifts of feeling and imagination have fitted her to be a consummate artist, as her fiery and tender soul and her vigorous eloquence would certainly have made her a great orator, and her profound knowledge of human nature and discernment and sagacity in practical life, would in the times when such a career was open to women, have made her eminent among the rulers of mankind. Her intellectual gifts did but minister to a moral character at once the noblest and the best balanced which I have ever met with in life.

Surely this is one of the keys to a happy marriage—when a husband admires his wife for qualities that he feels she possesses in greater abundance than he does. To praise such a person is only sweet, never burdensome, because however much you admire the other's virtues, it only makes that person's affection for you all the more gratifying and flattering. To revere someone who loves you is the finest source of one's own self-esteem—because, after all, you're the one she chose. What comes through again and again in Mill's recollections of his wife is his gratitude to her for making up his own deficiencies, rounding out his own mind and emotions. He admires her so deeply because while he arrived at his commitment to compassion and justice through rigorous logic and deduction, she felt them as a spontaneous movement of the heart. While he had to teach himself what to think, her mind was guided by the generosity of her temperament:

> Her unselfishness was not that of a taught system of duties, but of a heart which thoroughly identified itself with the feeling of others, and often went to excess in consideration for them, by imaginatively investing their feelings with the intensity of its own. The passion of justice might have been thought to be her strongest feeling, but for her boundless generosity, and a lovingness ever ready to pour itself forth upon any or all human beings who were capable of giving the smallest feeling in return. The rest of her moral characteristics were such as naturally accompany these qualities of mind and heart: the most genuine modesty combined with the loftiest pride; a simplicity and sincerity which were absolute, towards all who were fit to receive them; the utmost scorn of whatever was mean

and cowardly, and a burning indignation at everything brutal or tyrannical, faithless or dishonorable in conduct and character.

AN ADULTEROUS INTERLUDE

As the preceding foray into the Western tradition shows, there is a good
deal of literature that conveys the complexity of married life. Still, that
literature tends to focus more frequently on courtship, the period preceding marriage, or on adultery, the period portending its breakdown,
than on married life itself.

Jane Austen, for example, is among the greatest of those who have explored the ironies, confusions, hope, and heartache of love between
young men and women. Yet all of her novels are chiefly about courtship
rather than the married life for which her characters long. We learn very
little about what happens to her couples after they've tied the knot. Mr.
Darcy and Elizabeth Bennet, Emma Woodhouse and Mr. Knightley—
Austen's couples tend to walk off into the sunset after the wedding, and
to be perfectly frank, they seem to shrink a little in size and interest. As
for the married couples we encounter in the novels from the outset, they
are portrayed less vividly than the courting couples; they look more like
walk-on parts and are often a little wearied by preoccupation with their
children, money problems, and other quiet dilemmas kept largely off-
stage. Their inner lives are generally hidden from view, either because
they are fairly uncomplicated and commonplace or because the obligations of marriage place an embargo on the open and honest expression of
passion, sentiment, and dissatisfaction that is permissible for those who
are merely contemplating the bond. There's no danger in Elizabeth and
Mr. Darcy having a heated spat. In fact, it's positively healthy, because it
helps them get to know each other thoroughly. But for Elizabeth's father,
Mr. Bennet, to confront his wife openly with his true opinion of her fool-
ishness and bad judgment in matchmaking would explode the compromise tacitly devised over many years of wedded life, whereby each
agrees not to invade the other's domain.

At the opposite extreme from Austen's tactful reticence on what happens after the marriage ceremony, when disappointment and disillusion-

ment of a kind never suspected during the sweet and heady days of courtship, may set in, Romantic novelists of the Rousseauian bent—of whom Austen disapproved—were far more excited by the creative literary possibilities furnished by adultery and illicit sexual passion outside of marriage than by a happy and tranquil family life. In the novels of Flaubert and Balzac, the happily married couples are rather dull, almost cloyingly content, and merely provide a foil against which the brilliant passions, intrigues, and excesses of the adulterer and jaded hedonist can shine more brightly and the bitterness of those whom marriage has failed can assume a more darkly brooding hue. In Flaubert's *Madame Bovary* we encounter the peak of disgust with bourgeois family life. Emma's fevered and fruitless fantasies of being whisked away by coach in the dead of night by a swashbuckling lover out of the pages of Sir Walter Scott contrast with the daytime reality of her dull-witted, plodding husband. Even her daughter is portrayed as disagreeably soiled, whining and stupid, an object of revulsion to her own mother.

Little wonder that, as the Palladian elegance of the courtship rituals so delicately traced by Austen hardened into the heavy brocade and gaslit funerary sumptuousness of the Victorian household, French novels became a byword in Little England for all that was scandalous. One of my favorite paintings in the Center for British Art at Yale University— containing a square mile or so of high-minded and mediocre Victoriana, including full-length portraits of dogs and horses rendered with the dignity of Van Dyck's portraits of kings—is an enormous painting entitled *Adultery*. A woman lies sprawled in voluptuous abandon across the divan in one of those gloomy, heavily curtained parlors. Though she is dressed respectably as a lady of means and position, her wanton prostration shows all too clearly that every vestige of propriety has been lost to some debauched mésalliance. The final proof? Lying on the Turkish rug, just beyond the lady's languorously outstretched fingertips, from which it has fallen as she has perhaps lapsed into an opium-induced transport, is a slim volume, bearing but a single word on its spine: BALZAC.

In contrast with those wicked French, Tolstoy tries his level best to give a balanced presentation of the joys of domesticity in contrast with the brilliant whirl of adultery and high society, where aristocratic women who have done their duty in providing an heir are expected to spice things up by taking a lover or two, as long as they are discreet and the outward appearances of respectable society and family status are preserved. Tolstoy would like his readers to join him in seeing the former as preferable, a more solid and lasting joy than the glittering emptiness of the court and opera. But—let's face it—his portraits of happy family life in the country are a bit boring. Take *War and Peace*. Natasha Rostov, a delightful girl who is full of the sap of life when she is still in Petersburg society and in love with the dashing Prince Andrei, does seem a bit frumpy and crushed in her eventual marriage to the decent but unexciting Pierre, as if she has settled for second best after losing the man who really thrilled her. As Tolstoy unforgettably puts it in *Anna Karenina,* all happy families are the same—only the unhappy ones are different.

Perhaps there's just something about a happy marriage that doesn't require much artistic embellishment. Many operas are about doomed passion, star-crossed lovers, infidelity, and mismatched partners. But it's hard to imagine an opera by Verdi or Puccini about a stable marriage. Whatever the reasons may be, we find in Western literature that the full complexity of the relationship between husband and wife is often best conveyed not by the details of their personal intimacy but by reflections on raising children. That's where the beauty and depth of feeling reside. In the Greek and Roman thinkers, the Renaissance and Enlightenment humanists, down to the Victorians, we find voluminous reflections on the art of raising children, and particularly boys. It seems as if the emotional richness of family life is best detailed through reflecting on this noble joint enterprise between husband and wife, their own work of art. To that we now turn.

EDUCATING BOYS

In *The Education of Cyrus,* Xenophon, the ancient Greek general and student of Socrates, details the classical model of manhood by giving an idealized account of the Persian monarch Cyrus the Great. The key to Cyrus's future greatness, according to Xenophon, was his education. In the Persian Republic, where Cyrus grew up, the boys are educated throughout childhood and adolescence to prefer the common good to their own selfish desires. Their path to manhood is a lifelong moral and intellectual training. They learn by doing, because in addition to their formal schooling, they must perform good deeds to help the community. Respect for elders receives heavy emphasis. Moreover, the boys have the older citizens to look up to as role models. The older men never ask the boys to carry out a task or perform a duty that they are not willing to shoulder themselves:

> They teach the boys self-control, and it greatly conduces to their learn-ing self-control that they see their elders also living temperately day by day. And they teach them likewise to obey the officers; and it greatly conduces to this also that they see their elders implicitly obeying their officers. And besides, they teach them self-restraint in eating and drink-ing; and it greatly conduces to this also that they see that their elders do not leave their posts to satisfy their hunger until the officers dismiss them; and the same end is promoted by the fact that the boys do not eat with their mothers but with their teachers, from the time the officers so direct.

Special care has to be taken in the schooling of adolescents by mak-ing sure that they have something to keep them busy all day long, both to occupy their minds and to drain their rambunctious energies from more troubling outlets:

> This, then, is what the boys do until they are sixteen or seventeen years of age, and after this they are promoted from the class of boys and en-rolled among the young men. Now the young men in their turn live as follows: for ten years after they are promoted from the class of boys they pass the nights, as we said before, about the government buildings. This they do for the sake of guarding the city and of developing their powers of self-control. For this time of life, it seems, demands the most watchful care.

There are many variations on this classical model of education for boys. Marcus Fabius Quintilianus—better known as Quintilian—also wrote extensively on this theme. A celebrated professor of rhetoric and an attorney under the Roman Empire, he was also the personal tutor of the emperor Domitian's grandnephews. His writings, much admired while he lived, remained influential during the Renaissance and the Enlightenment. What is most striking about Quintilian's ideas on education is their combination of levelheadedness and compassion. For Quintilian, the purpose of education is to shape a boy's character according to the highest Roman ideals of integrity, patriotism, piety, valor, service, and devotion to family and ancestors. But he reveals a surprisingly tender and sympathetic understanding of the temperaments of children, and none of the harsh militarism or worship of conquest and domination that one might expect of an education in Imperial Rome, particularly in the emperor's family. Boys must be allowed to romp and play, he says, because they can't be expected to study all day long cooped up in a classroom and because games teach them early lessons in fair play and decent conduct:

> True character, too, reveals, itself with less reserve in play: and let us remember that no child is so tender in years as not to learn at once the distinction between right and wrong, and that he requires to be molded with the greatest care at any age when he is still innocent of deceit and yields most readily to his instructors. For you would sooner break than bend straight those who have once become set in vicious habits.

Quintilian firmly opposes frequent and excessive corporal punishment on the grounds that it breaks a boy's spirit and makes him obey his elders only out of fear, concealing a surly resentment of authority behind a mask of cringing submissiveness:

> Remember too that, when children are beaten, many unseemly cries, of which they will afterwards be ashamed, often escape them in their grief or fear, and the shame of this breaks and humiliates the spirit and makes them, sick at heart, shun the very light of day.

Education becomes even more important when the pupil is born not merely to be a citizen but to rule. Desiderius Erasmus, the Renaissance humanist and theologian, offers in his *Education of a Christian Prince* a guide for the education of this very select set of pupils. Nothing is more

important for the education of boys destined to become rulers than providing them with models of noble conduct to admire at an age when
their minds are malleable and their feelings are open to suggestion:

> It is not enough just to hand out precepts to restrain the prince from vices
> or to incite him to a better course—they must be impressed, crammed in,
> inculcated, and in one way and another be kept before him, now by a
> suggestive thought, now by a fable, now by analogy, now by example, now
> by maxims, now by a proverb. They should be engraved on rings, painted
> on pictures, appended to the wreaths of honor, and, by using any other
> means by which that age can be interested, kept always before him.

According to Erasmus, we need make no apology for censoring the
opinions and ideas with which a boy comes into contact, for he is not yet
old enough to choose goodness over evil on an entirely voluntary basis.
It's up to the educator to provide the right environment for his pupil by
surrounding him with examples of honorable conduct and insulating him
from exposure to the charms of lewdness, depravity, and corruption, in
order to encourage the boy to identify good conduct with everything he
finds most admirable and pleasant. Especially if it is his destiny to rule
others, a boy must be insulated from corrupting contact with vice and
vulgarity, for otherwise we'll be breeding a monster to set over his unfortunate future subjects:

> The deeds of famous men fire the minds of noble youths, but the opin-
> ions with which they become imbued are a matter of far greater impor-
> tance, for from these sources the whole scheme of life is developed. In
> the case of a mere boy, we must immediately be on guard, to see that he
> gets only the virtuous and helpful ideas and that he be fortified as by cer-
> tain efficacious drugs against the poisoned opinions of the common
> people. But if the prince happens to be somewhat tinged with the
> thoughts of the common people, then the first effort must be to rid him
> of them little by little, to weed out the seeds of trouble and replace them
> by wholesome ones.

Erasmus chooses some of Aesop's fables as especially suitable reading material for a boy prince, and by reading those fables, we can see his
pedagogical method at work. "The Lion and the Mouse," to take one ex-

ample, will delight a boy because it features animals having conversations. But the charming tale conveys a lesson that a future ruler cannot learn too thoroughly or too soon: Do not look down on even the humblest of your subjects, just because Providence has placed you in the highest rank of men. Sometimes help can come from the lowliest of your fellow creatures:

> A Lion was awakened from sleep by a Mouse running over his face. Rising up in anger, he caught him and was about to kill him, when the Mouse piteously entreated, saying: "If you would only spare my life, I would be sure to repay your kindness." The Lion laughed and let him go. It happened shortly after this that the Lion was caught by some hunters, who bound him by strong ropes to the ground. The Mouse, recognizing his roar, came up, and gnawed the rope with his teeth, and setting him free, exclaimed: "You ridiculed the idea of my ever being able to help you, not expecting to receive from me any repayment of your favor; but now you know that it is possible for even a Mouse to confer benefits on a Lion."

A consistent theme in classical and Renaissance writings about child rearing is that external guidance and habituation, however carefully and lovingly applied, are not enough to make a boy grow up into a virtuous man. Providing the correct environment is a necessary first step; children are too malleable and too open to first impressions for us not to build a wall of decency around them to protect them from stumbling into depravity. But for a moral education to take hold in a boy, he must develop a conscience. He must possess, so to speak, an inner teacher in his own soul, who will prompt him to do good and avoid evil even when no one is there to watch over him, admonish him, or exhort him. According to Jacopo Sadoleto, writing in the sixteenth century, conscience will never develop in a boy unless he also has a capacity for shame. If a boy can't blush he's in trouble, because that means he does not have the capacity to feel ashamed of himself:

> The blush is the pledge of a good disposition and of the virtue we look for in a boy, so that there seems much fitness in the saying "He blushed—all's well." For shame itself is a habit of taking precaution against the occurrence of anything which may cause a blush: and while it

is appropriate to any time of life, it is the chief grace of youth: nor should we be wrong in describing it as the averter of crime and the bulwark of temperance and virtue. And I would urge upon any parents, with whom my influence is likely to have weight, that they delay not to cherish and increase in their children this root of shame which nature has planted in their fresh minds.

Sadoleto's praise for the therapeutic value of shame runs against all of our prevailing orthodoxies, which argue that shame distorts a child's character by burdening him with guilt. But Sadoleto asks: If a boy is not capable of feeling ashamed of himself for being bad, how will he ever develop that internal moral compass that will keep him on the right course even when his parents and teachers aren't watching? Aren't burning cheeks and a few hours of feeling guilty a form of behavior modification preferable for many boys to Ritalin, and likelier to produce a change in conduct than conflict mediation? And if a boy learns that he will be forgiven if his contrition is genuine—if his tears of shame and sorrow over letting his parents down are greeted with a rain of hugs and praise for being brave enough to admit his mistake—won't he come to associate being good with being lovable? Sadoleto believed parents who encourage the capacity for shame in their children are doing them a favor that will serve them well for their whole lives:

> They can rely upon reaping a rich harvest for their pains. For though a sense of shame may not actually be virtue itself, it is the chief support to virtue: since it is the dread of an evil name and of disgrace: and this is a stern and vigilant guardian of virtue. So those who call shame a kind of divine timidity seem to me to get nearer the right definition of this emotion. It alone dreads the loss of that one wellnigh divine possession, which we win from high honor and office—to wit, our credit and good repute.

According to another eminent Renaissance humanist, Leon Battista Alberti, one very concrete application of the value of shame is that a well-reared boy will never show disrespect toward his elders or refuse them his help and deference. Children owe courtesy and service to their elders for all their elders have done for them:

Let the young not be slow in helping all elders in their age and weakness; they should hope that in their own old age they will receive from youth the same respect and kindness they themselves have shown their elders. Let them, therefore, be diligent and prompt in giving them comfort, pleasure, and rest in their tired old age. Let them not think there is any greater pleasure or happiness for the old than seeing their young virtuous and deserving of love.

The other side of the coin here is that, if parents are diligent in educating their children to be good, they will have the sweet satisfaction of seeing their children grow into adults who deserve love and respect and who feel gratitude toward their parents, elders, and ancestors. That reciprocity improves the moral tone not only of the family but of society as a whole:

> And I tell you there is no greater comfort for the old than to see that those in whom they have placed all their hopes and expectations, those for whom they have been ever solicitous and full of care, are esteemed, loved, and honored for their customs and virtues. Those men are happy who in their old age see their children entering upon a peaceful and honorable life. A peaceful life shall be the reward of men of irreproachable customs; an honorable one, that of virtuous men. Nothing so much as vice disturbs the life of mortals.

Alberti's observations bring us to another important theme in the education of boys. If we have high expectations of our sons, we must also have high expectations of ourselves. We cannot ask them to aim for virtues that we ourselves do not possess, or at least strive to achieve. Ultimately, the chief responsibility for a boy's upbringing rests not with the boy but with the man who must guide him. As Xenophon observed, the education of boys warrants tremendous care and attention from the civic authorities. When a boy's education is provided at home by his father, even greater care is warranted, because the entire responsibility falls on the shoulders of that one man. As Alberti observes, he becomes the main model for the son:

> A father's duties do not consist solely in filling the granary and the cradle, as they say. The head of a family must be vigilant and observant above

all. He must know all the family's acquaintances, examine all customs both within and without the house, and correct and mend the evil ways of any member of the family with words of reason rather than anger.

The love of a father for his son can deepen their mutual understanding as he teaches the boy how to become a man. Yet the same qualities that make the father an ideal teacher may complicate the emotional bond between father and son. A father should not be overly familiar. He should be his son's first and best teacher, but he cannot be his schoolyard pal. By contrast, if he is too cold and distant a teacher, as we saw in John Stuart Mill's autobiography, he risks retaining pedagogic authority at the cost of filial affection, and possibly leaving his son emotionally stunted and ill-equipped for love and friendship when he grows older. A delicate balance indeed! As Alberti concludes:

> He must use a father's authority rather than despotism, and counsel where it is of more value than commanding. He must be severe, firm, and stern when necessary, and he must always keep in mind the well-being, peace, and tranquillity of his entire family as the ultimate purpose of all his efforts and counsels for the guidance of the family in virtue and honor. The head of the family must first of all be on the watch for the first sparks of vice to appear among his children's appetites and must put them out immediately if he does not wish to be compelled later to extinguish the flames of corrupt desire at greater cost, with sorrow and tears.

To these arguments about the importance of the father as a role model, Montaigne adds that a boy must have the feeling that education does not hamper his freedom but allows it to blossom by seeking the right outlets. Echoing Quintilian, the Renaissance humanist rejects the idea that education should be confined to rote learning. To do so turns a young mind into a tomb where the desiccated corpses of the great works are interred. On the contrary, Montaigne argues, a boy's education needs to speak to and through his experience. His education should be a journey undertaken with others as his experiences widen from family to society. The success of this journey is to be measured not in the quantity of passages memorized but in the quality of his character and the breadth of his moral experience:

Let the tutor demand of him an account not only of the words of his lesson, but of their meaning and substance, and let him estimate the profit he has gained, not by the testimony of his memory, but of his life. Let him show what he has from a hundred points of view, and adapt it to as many different subjects, to see if he has yet rightly taken it in and made it his own. Let his conscience and his virtue shine forth in his speech, and be guided solely by reason. Make him understand that to confess the error he discovers in his own reasoning, though he himself alone perceive it, is a mark of judgment and honesty, which are the chief qualities he aims at.

As we conclude this tour of the West's wisdom about fatherhood and family life, let's return to the personal interaction between a father and a son who is growing into manhood—the emotional context surrounding the formal instruction. Sometimes these encounters are best preserved in letters. Lord Chesterfield's letters to his son provide a good example. Chesterfield, who died in 1773, never intended these letters to be seen by others. But he achieved posthumous fame as an author upon their publication by his son's widow. These letters illustrate the fine balance a father needs to strike in reaching his son. Hearty praise and stern admonition may ring louder in a boy's ears when they come from a father rather than a schoolteacher. They must be employed very carefully in order to avoid puffing a boy up or crushing him. Lord Chesterfield shows how warmhearted affection, albeit tinged with severity, can encourage a son to live up to high standards of decency, learning, and manners. "Dear Boy," he always begins:

> Though I employ so much of my time in writing to you, I confess I have often my doubts whether it is to any purpose. I know how unwelcome advice generally is; I know that those who need it most, like it and follow it least; and I know, too, that the advice of parents, more particularly, is ascribed to the moroseness, the imperiousness, or the garrulity of old age. But then, on the other hand, I flatter myself, that as your own reason, though too young as yet to suggest much to you of itself, is however, strong enough to enable you, both to judge of, and receive plain truths: I flatter myself (I say) that your own reason, young as it is, must tell you, that I can have no interest but yours in the advice I give you; and that

consequently, you will at least weigh and consider it well: in which case, some of it will, I hope, have its effect.

Like fathers down through the ages, Lord Chesterfield doesn't want his son to think he is issuing orders. He only wants to help the boy avoid the pitfalls that he blundered into as a youth because he lacked a mentor of his own:

> Do not think that I mean to dictate as a parent; I only mean to advise as a friend, and an indulgent one too: and do not apprehend that I mean to check your pleasures; of which, on the contrary, I only desire to be the guide, not the censor. Let my experience supply your want of it, and clear your way, in the progress of your youth, of those thorns and briars which scratched and disfigured me in the course of mine.

Finally, a none too subtle reminder from father to son that Dad still controls the purse strings—though perish the thought that a son would try to please a father only because of an inheritance!

> I do not, therefore, so much as hint to you, how absolutely dependent you are upon me; that you neither have, nor can have a shilling in the world but from me. . . . I say, I do not hint these things to you, because I am convinced that you will act right, upon more noble and generous principles: I mean, for the sake of doing right, and out of affection and gratitude to me.

Having begun this chapter with one American president, let's end it with another—one who exceeded in every way the standards of virtuous family life beneath which the other fell so abysmally far. All fathers, it is wise to remember, were sons once themselves. The lucky ones are those who learn valuable lessons at their fathers' side. Theodore Roosevelt hoped to pass on to his son Ted the precepts he had received from his own beloved father. In a letter to a relative, TR recalls his efforts to impart to Ted the most important lesson of life—that a real man "loathes cruelty and injustice" and combines courage with tenderness. Sometimes it's acceptable for a boy to get into a fight, if he is fighting to protect those who cannot defend themselves:

Now, do you want to know the real underlying feeling which has made me fight myself and want Ted to fight? Well, I summed it up to Ted once or twice when I told him, apropos of lessons of virtue, that he could be just as virtuous as he wished if only he was prepared to fight. . . . I have wanted to pass on to my boys some of what I got from my own father. I loathe cruelty and injustice. To see a boy or man torture something helpless whether in the shape of a small boy or little girl or dumb animal makes me rage.

TR then makes a confession that might surprise those who know him only as the hero of the charge up San Juan Hill and the tireless explorer and big game hunter of the American interior:

I am not naturally at all a fighter. So far as any man is capable of analyzing his own impulses and desires, mine incline me to amicable domesticity and the avoidance of effort and struggle.

It was his father, TR continues, who taught him to supplement his natural leaning toward a peaceful home life and study with physical and moral courage when these were called for. It is possible to be both kinds of man:

I was fortunate enough in having a father whom I have always been able to regard as an ideal man. It sounds a little like cant to say what I am going to say, but he really did combine the strength and courage and will and energy of the strongest man with the tenderness, cleanness and purity of a woman.

What an appropriate capstone for our reflections on fatherhood and family life. For here we find an American hero praising his father in 1901 for possessing that correct balance of masculine and feminine traits that stretches back to the earliest origins of the West, in Homer, the Apollo of Delphi, and the image of the chariot of the soul. It is a teaching about the balance of love and daring in a man's soul that has woven like a jeweled filigree throughout three millennia of experience and insight, sometimes fading but never disappearing—a moral and erotic vocabulary of manliness that, as TR's letter reveals, was with us until just yesterday.

TR also reminds us a little of Plutarch's description of Cato as he goes on to say that his father struck just the right balance between sympathy for his frail health and a refusal to baby him if he thought his son could withstand a challenge:

> I was a sickly and timid boy. He not only took great and loving care of me—some of my earliest remembrances are of nights when he would walk up and down with me for an hour at a time in his arms when I was a wretched mite suffering acutely with asthma—but he also most wisely refused to coddle me, and made me feel that I must force myself to hold my own with other boys and prepare to do the rough work of the world. I cannot say that he ever put it into words, but he certainly gave me the feeling that I was always to be both decent and manly, and that if I were manly nobody would long laugh at my being decent.

And so it is that a man famed for his toughness tries to explain to a relative how he was a timid and sickly boy until his father taught him the correct balance of active and thoughtful virtues, so that he might better understand how TR was trying to educate his own son to be gentle when necessary and a fighter when necessary. Fathers and sons reading the letter can only sigh a little and quietly ponder whether they have ever experienced such a father or ever been one for others.

V.

COUNTRY

FOR MANY, THERE IS NO GREATER PROOF OF MANLINESS THAN LOY-alty to one's country, and no greater test of a man than the obligations he shoulders as a patriot. Indeed, patriotism might well be the one life experience where the other paths to manhood explored so far—love, courage, pride, and family—converge in a united whole of thought and deed, that balance of moral and reflective virtues that emerges time and again throughout the history of the West as the essence of true manliness.

For patriotism assuredly asks us to love. The patriot loves his country as a whole, with its dense weave of traditions and collective memories, and he sees his fellow citizens as friends united to serve the common good. Above all, he loves the principles of justice, honor, and faith, upheld by patriotism when it is at its best.

Because he loves his country, the patriot is capable of courage on its behalf. He is willing to fight—even die—to defend his country and its way of life. The patriot is also courageous in the more subtle sense we examined in Chapter 2: He has the civic courage to resist patriotic passion when it is not motivated by a healthy moral aim. Sometimes, the true patriot must have the courage of character to stand up for his country at its best, even if that stance runs counter to the fake patriotism of an unreflecting conformism to the fashion or prejudices of the day.

That ability to distinguish between enlightened patriotism and mere boosterism or mob psychology calls, in turn, for pride. A true patriot is loyal to his country only when that loyalty is compatible with honor. If it is real, patriotism can never ask us to undertake base, shameful, or unjust deeds on our country's behalf; if it does, a proud man knows it is a sham.

Finally, the keenest patriot is very often a devoted family man. For, as we saw in the last chapter, for most men, devotion to family is the strongest motive for wanting a better society—a place where his wife and children will be safe and happy, and one whose moral code reinforces the parents' efforts to guide their children along the right path to the future.

There are times, to be sure, when a man's moral and intellectual fulfillment are at odds with the demands of loyalty to country. If the country we live in is oppressive and corrupt, if it is ethically bankrupt, if cronyism has driven out merit, a man will be hard-pressed to reconcile his duty to his loved ones, or to his wider web of friendships, with patriotism in this narrow, fraudulent sense of mere obedience to authority, conformism rooted in fear, or getting ahead by currying favor with the powers that be.

There are times—unhappy times—when a man must reject his own country as it now is for the sake of his country as it once was or could be, and become a patriot on behalf of the broader ideal of justice for mankind. If patriotism means loyalty to a tyrant, then agonizing as it may feel, deserting one's country may be necessary for preserving one's loyalty to that country as it ought to be. The great novelist Thomas Mann, having fled Germany to live in the United States when Hitler came to power, was once asked if he wasn't sad at having to leave his country. His reply was that he *had* no country as long as the Nazis were in power. As long as Hitler ruled, there was no Germany, except in those like him and other émigrés who carried the true Germany in their hearts, in the hope that they might someday return the soul of the true Germany to its native soil.

For all these reasons, therefore, it is fitting that we conclude these reflections on manliness with the virtue of patriotism. For only when we have an understanding of the true meaning of patriotism will we see how the other paths to manhood might converge in serving it. Moreover, we need to bear in mind that patriotism does not mean precisely the same thing in all parts of the world and during all periods of history. American patriotism is a special case in point. For reasons I'll explore in the rest of this chapter, its mix of qualities is unique. In thinking about how American patriotism differs from other varieties, the difference between

the American model of manliness and those of other traditions, civilizations, and eras will be thrown into sharper relief. In the case both of
patriotism in particular and of manly virtue in general, some qualities
are common to all peoples; some are resoundingly and exclusively
American. As I will suggest momentarily, the specifically American ingredient can be summed up in one word: optimism.

When we think about how manliness in America expresses itself in
patriotism, it is, of course, impossible to divorce ourselves from the extraordinary and uncertain times we are now living through. Throughout
their history, Americans have never ceased displaying courage, both as
citizens and as warriors when called upon. Never has that been more
true than since September 11, 2001. In the days following the dastardly
attacks on New York and Washington, Americans from all walks of life
and religious and ethnic backgrounds—firefighters, doctors, office workers, airline passengers, Muslims, Jews, Christians, Hindus—displayed a
courage that makes us weep with sorrow for those who were lost but also
with gratitude that we have been privileged to witness such shining
deeds of valor by ordinary men and women, who found in themselves an
extraordinary measure of bravery and self-sacrifice. They are now immortal. We will speak of them generations hence in the same breath as
Thermopylae, Dunkirk, and Entebbe. The continuing war on behalf of
democracy against tyranny will confer on all of us—in ways large and
small, requiring strength of mind, character, and conduct—the privilege
of trying to live up to their example.

As America and the other democracies settle into the long haul of this
war against terrorism, we continue to wonder about the terrorists' motives. Is their lethal hatred of the West, although expressed in terms of
religious fanaticism, reducible to some concrete territorial or economic
grievance? Clearly not. The sincerity of their religious convictions is precisely what makes the terrorists so dangerous.

This is not to say that they interpret the content of their own faith
correctly. They don't, any more than John Brown, Torquemada, or the
Crusaders who slaughtered unarmed Jews and Muslims were exemplary
Christians. As we saw in Chapter 2, all of the world's major religions have
theological doctrines that limit the meaning of a just war to self-defense
and the defense of the oppressed against unprovoked aggression, and

strictly forbid the deliberate killing of unarmed civilians and noncombatants, particularly women and children. Al-Qaida and other such groups
represent neither the mainstream beliefs of their own religion nor the
nations and peoples for whom they claim to fight. They are the proxies of
tyrannies like Iraq (under Saddam Hussein) and Syria, and they use the
same methods such regimes employ on a daily basis to maintain their
own repressive power—the intimidation, torture, and slaughter of innocent men, women, and children. Our war against terrorism is fundamentally a war against the tyrannies who house and support them and share
their murderous values. In defending and protecting America, we are
also making a stand on behalf of the ideals of manhood explored in this
book.

Nevertheless, the terrorists are animated by an authentically pious
rage. It is a mistaken version of piety, but it has all the passion of a righteous zealot convinced he is killing people on the direct orders of God.
The terrorists' chief motivation is an irreducible and limitless hostility
toward America and liberal democratic civilization in general. They envy
its prosperity and fear its strength, but not primarily because they want
its prosperity for themselves. Although there are doubtless motives of
this kind among some of their comrades, who live in bleak penury and
who simply hate those who are more fortunate than themselves, al-
Qaida's leader is a millionaire, and the actual masterminds of the attacks
on New York and Washington already lived in the sunny uplands of suburban comfort. If barbecues, SUVs, and Kmart were enough to make
them satisfied, prosperity would already have dispelled their hatred. As
one of the Mujahideen in Afghanistan was quoted as saying in *The Daily
Telegraph,* "The Americans love Coca-Cola. We love death."

No, the main motive in their war against liberal democracy is that, as
they mistakenly see it, the West's prosperity and power threaten to corrode the piety of their world by introducing into it our values of individual liberty, tolerance, representative government, and entrepreneurial
self-advancement. At bottom, their rage is motivated by the fear that the
West has triumphed historically and irrevocably over their own premodern culture. As in a cornered animal, fear lashes out in a fury of self-
preservation. The desire to smash America's most visible symbols of
historical triumph—the glittering towers of Manhattan's financial dis-

trict and the geometrically modernist headquarters of American military might—is the deadly culmination of that rage. In a curious way, we have to recognize the terrorists' intrinsic motivation before we can accurately identify it, and thereby take steps to defeat it. From Hitler and Stalin to Saddam and bin Laden, we must continually relearn the lesson first taught by Aristotle: "No man becomes a tyrant to get in out of the cold." As we saw in Chapter 2 when considering the distorted versions of courage, people who commit mass murder don't do so because they want more economic development or a reasonable adjustment of their borders. They do it because they believe in an ideal.

This may be a hard lesson for the West to face again. Not because, as the terrorists vainly fancy, we are weak-willed and have no convictions but because, on the contrary, we are generous and optimistic as a matter of both temperament and conviction. One of the premises of our civilization is that human beings are not naturally warlike, and that there are no independent and irreducible sources of violent hatred in the human soul. We like to believe that if the blessings of democracy, the rule of law, our individual liberty to live pretty much as we please, and the material means to pursue those vocations were extended to our enemies, that soothing balm of freedom would melt away their hostility and aggression—as it has with earlier generations of peoples in the West, who gradually gave up their premodern religious and racial intolerance and invested their energies in advancing themselves and their families through education and peaceful economic enterprise. We are optimistic that an overriding preference for individual liberty and tolerance is natural to human beings everywhere, and that, once we are able to argue successfully on the basis of what Jefferson called "a decent respect to the opinions of mankind" and make those benefits clearly understood, the darkness of prejudice and aggression will be steadily dissipated by the light of reason. Uniquely among nations, American patriotism and love of country are inseparable from this spirit of optimism. When the American ideal of manhood engages with the rest of the world, this is the spirit it offers. Let's look at some of the reasons why.

FREEDOM IN ALL JUST PURSUITS

Why do I say that American patriotism is uniquely connected with a spirit of optimism? Patriotism has been experienced by all peoples, in all places, and at all periods of history, from the earliest annals of recorded history to the present. Indeed, patriotism is probably one of the most widespread and universally accepted virtues. But traditional patriotism differs significantly from the American variety. The very word *patriotism* is connected with the words for *father* and *fatherland*. Traditionally, love of country was very much connected with love of the ancestral clan and soil. As we saw in the last chapter, there was virtually no distinction in premodern societies between being loyal to your country and being loyal to your blood kin. Many ancient Greek city-states believed that their people had occupied those sacred patches of soil from time immemorial, often going back to the founding of the city by a god. Each Greek city-state was like a closed world, a tightly knit whole bound by ties of kinship and rooted in the land. Patriotism meant loyalty to your own people, your own kind, your own gods. It was often flagrantly xenophobic by to-day's standards. Outsiders could not fully belong; indeed, they were not really people at all. Even the more broad-minded of the city-states like Athens did not allow foreign residents to become full citizens, although it welcomed outsiders as traders and merchants. They were resident aliens, and entitled as such to the same protections under law as a citizen. They could bring suit against others in court. Their belongings and personal safety were protected by the state as they were for full citizens. But because their ancestors had not been Athenians, they could not become full citizens. They needed special permission to own houses and property, certain public offices were barred to them, and they were forbidden to intermarry with citizens. If they served in the military, it was usually in segregated units and not alongside native Athenians.

As the classical scholar Sir Ernest Barker has noted, citizenship in a Greek polis was more like membership in a church with a particularly close-knit congregation than it was like our modern notion of citizenship. Traditional patriotism could inspire citizens to spectacular acts of self-sacrifice for the common good. Generations of children have been thrilled to read about the Spartans holding off the Persians at Thermopylae, the Athenian fleet's stunning victory at Salamis that thwarted the Persian invasion, Horatius at the bridge holding off the Etruscans in order to preserve the freedom of his fellow Romans, or the stern Spartan mother who tells her son as he leaves for war that she would rather see him brought back on his shield as a corpse than to return alive having disgraced himself as a coward. When citizenship is almost literally like being the member of a family, a son of the soil, service and self-sacrifice need little prompting. They are as instinctive as eating and drinking. Citizens of such countries fight as wholeheartedly and as spontaneously on their behalf as a son would fight to protect his mother or a parent its child. Many ancient cultures compared dying a patriotic death in combat to returning to the womb of the earth, the common soil from which the citizens had sprung as a band of brothers.

From the very beginning, by contrast, American patriotism was connected to universal principles of justice, liberty, reason, and good government. Americans were loyal to their government because it derived its authority from the natural right of every individual to "life, liberty, and the pursuit of happiness," as Jefferson put it in the Declaration of Independence. Jefferson says these liberties are "self-evident" from a study of human nature and "nature's God." When Jefferson uses this phrase, he does *not* mean the Christian God, Jehovah, the Lord of Hosts. He does not make the old-fashioned patriotic identification of the righteousness of our country's cause with the will of God, so that a patriotic German or Spaniard could imagine that God or Christ was personally leading their troops against their godless foes.

No—Jefferson is going out of his way to say that a man's loyalty to the United States does *not* require this kind of patriotic attachment to the God of a specific denomination or, indeed, to any particular religious faith. "Nature's God" is reason itself. Her principles are universally valid. They are not a revelation but a philosophical truth. Jefferson's God is the God of Spinoza, Descartes, and Locke, what used to be called "the God of the Philosophers," the God of the Enlightenment, as opposed to the God of traditionally pious believers in divine revelation. Of course, Jefferson was not the only Founding Father, and there were traditional believers among the others who contributed an equally important dimension to Americans' love of country, as I will explore further in a moment.

The main point for now is that the principles of the American founding have universal validity, and are dependent on rational assent rather than on the mystique and fervor of the Old World patriotism of Europe and the ancients. This does not mean that American patriotism is weaker or less capable of fostering patriotic duty, bravery in combat, or self-sacrifice. On the contrary: At every period of their history, Americans have shown themselves capable of the kind of bravery, honor, and self-sacrifice that was inspired by the older kind of patriotism. Throughout the Civil War and the wars of the twentieth century fought on behalf of the ideal of democracy, and to thwart the aims of fascist and communist tyranny, American blood has been shed in an immortally honorable cause. And the tragedy of September 11, 2001, blazed a new trail of glory for citizens who found it in themselves to become heroes. Think of the citizens on Flight 93, who resolved to take action against the terrorists bent on crashing it into the Capitol building. In the best American tradition, and under the most harrowing of circumstances, they held a miniature town meeting, taking a vote and then saying a prayer before they stormed the cockpit. "Let's roll," one of them said, a phrase that has already entered history. Ordinary citizens, tourists, and businesspeople were suddenly transformed into citizen-soldiers fighting for democracy. And they reminded us again that, although courage and the other virtues may manifest themselves differently in men and women, both men and women can ascend their highest peaks. They now live forever in the sunlight of eternal honor.

When Americans have most successfully lived up to their nation's ideals, they have never identified love of country with a closed group. The American dream can be extended to people all over the world, because it is based on natural rights that people everywhere possess, whether their governments recognize those rights or not, and whether their authority is derived from the consent of the governed or not. That's why Lincoln called America "the last best hope of man on Earth." Its freedoms and benefits are for everyone, not just for us. On the level of the highest principle, Americans cannot be xenophobic and truly be

Americans. For the same reasons, American patriotism is inseparable from a belief in the benign progress of history. Americans believe that the blessings of freedom and democratically elected government should and must spread to all nations and peoples, because it is natural to want freedom and unnatural to want to live under tyranny.

This is what Jefferson means in the Declaration when he appeals to "the opinions of mankind" in setting forth the Americans' grievances against the British monarchy. Jefferson was well aware that the belief in individual liberty and the rights of man did not extend to all of mankind. Representative democracy was virtually unknown in Europe and the rest of the world, and in none of those countries would those who believed in Jefferson's democratic values—the values of the Enlightenment—have constituted more than a sliver of the population. The friends of liberty tended to come from the ranks of the best educated, which almost inevitably meant those from a privileged background. When Jefferson appeals to the enlightened opinion of mankind, he is not being naïve about what the actual majority of mankind would have thought of the Declaration. Instead, he is expressing his optimism about the *future*. When the message of the American Revolution spreads to Europe and the rest of the world, a majority of mankind must eventually come to embrace it. Why? Because—again—it is natural to prefer liberty to enslavement and to prefer enlightenment over ignorance and superstition. For its entire history, America has combined a heartfelt loyalty to its own homeland with a benevolent desire to share its blessings with other peoples. What other imperial power known to us from history, upon unleashing a just retaliation against a despotic government that had slaughtered over three thousand of its own citizens on American soil, would have taken care to drop food packages along with its bombs in order to distinguish innocent Afghanis from their tyrannical regime? Among the first acts of the Bush administration after September 11 was to dramatically increase humanitarian aid to Afghanistan, and the president made a personal appeal to schoolchildren to give a dollar for aid to Afghani children—resulting in millions of extra dollars for relief work. Once again, American patriotism in our own times continues to inspire acts of nobility that will enter the annals of virtuous deeds alongside those of the ancient republics.

So far, in discussing what makes American patriotism uniquely optimistic, I have stressed its secular side as embodied in Jefferson. But when we look at the full picture of the American founding, we see that two streams come together in a course we've already traced in this book—on the one hand, the classical tradition of civic virtue and liberal education and, on the other, a profound faith in the God of Mount Sinai and the New Testament. The American founding, in other words, is a particularly revealing case in practice of that age-old debate between pride and faith that we considered in connection with Aristotle, St. Augustine, the Renaissance humanists, and their successors down to the modern age.

Jefferson best illustrates the classical contribution to the American founding. His *Notes on the State of Virginia* show how American democracy and civilization brought a new complexity to the traditional meaning of manliness. From the outset, Americans drew upon the classical and Renaissance ideals of their European forebears as they developed a new code of manly honor for their experiences in the New World. Jefferson writes that liberal education is the key to happiness, because it equips us with the capacity for just pursuits. A devotee of the secular Enlightenment, educated in the classics and steeped in the views of Locke, Hume, and Rousseau, Jefferson explicitly rejects a reliance on the Bible for educating the youngest children "at an age when their judgments are not sufficiently matured for religious inquiries." Instead, they should be taught history and the classics:

> Instead, therefore, of putting the Bible and Testament into the hands of the children at an age when their judgments are not sufficiently matured for religious inquiries, their memories may here be stored with the most useful facts from Grecian, Roman, European and American history. The first elements of morality may too be instilled into their minds; such as, when further developed as their judgments advance in strength, may teach them how to work out their own greatest happiness, by showing them that it does not depend on the condition of life in which chance has placed them, but is always the result of a good conscience, good health, occupation and freedom in all just pursuits.

Several points are worth dwelling on here. It is sometimes pointed out that, in his famous claim that every individual has a right by nature to "life, liberty, and the pursuit of happiness," Jefferson makes no attempt to define the meaning of happiness—leaving it entirely a matter of spontaneous, unguided choice or even impulse. In this light Jefferson can be seen as a libertarian, even as a supporter of "doing your own thing," no matter how trivial or frivolous, as long as no one else is harmed. But a close reading of the lesser-known *Notes* reveals that Jefferson was anything but a moral relativist. He very clearly defines here what he means by *happiness*. The way we "work out" our "greatest happiness," he argues, is by pursuing an education that enables us to develop our highest capacities, and thereby to rise in life according to our natural abilities. Happiness doesn't just mean doing your own thing: rather, it amounts to having "freedom in all just pursuits," and "is always the result of a good conscience, good health [and] occupation."

Jefferson provides an especially noble statement about how modern democracy requires a traditional conception of liberal education, echoing all of the most articulate defenders of virtue stretching back through the Renaissance to Plato, Aristotle, and the Stoics. He shares the view that happiness is a balance of active and contemplative virtues that we have encountered many times previously in this book. Echoing the Stoic philosopher and emperor Marcus Aurelius, Jefferson says that happiness "does not depend on the condition of life" in which chance has placed us. As we recall from Chapter 3, the only true freedom, according to Marcus, came from devoting oneself to the virtues of the soul, not the pleasures of the body that enslave us. If we devote ourselves to the soul, we will be free even if chance places us in the situation of a slave in chains. By contrast, if chance should place us on the throne of the world, if we devote ourselves to bodily pleasures and ignore the soul, we will truly be slaves no matter how much worldly power, prestige, wealth, and pleasure we may sample. Some fifteen hundred years later, Jefferson, whose own education was steeped in the classics, preserves this Stoic maxim of manly integrity. But he also expands its meaning by harnessing the cultivation of the soul's virtues to the democratic ideal of meritocracy. If merit is based on the equal opportunity for individuals to rise in life through their talents, diligence, and good character, then the spread of educational equality of opportunity will allow young men of natural ability to rise above the accidental circumstances of their birth. Proposing a constitutional amendment to assist public education, Jefferson wrote:

> By that part of our plan which prescribes the selection of the youths of genius from among the classes of the poor, we hope to avail the State of those talents which nature has sewn as liberally among the poor as the rich, but which perish without use, if not sought for and cultivated.

Important as public education may be for promoting meritocracy and the rise of natural talent, it's even more important for nurturing the civic culture of a democracy. Jefferson maintains that an educated citizenry is essential to good and accountable government. By learning from the past, we will be on guard against threats to freedom in the present, recognizing potential tyrants and usurpers in our midst for what they are:

> Of the views of this law, none is more important, none more legitimate, than that of rendering the people the safe, as they are the ultimate, guardians of their own liberty. History, by apprizing them of the past, will enable them to judge of the future; it will avail them of the experience of other times and other nations; it will qualify them as judges of the actions and designs of men; it will enable them to know ambition under every disguise it may assume; and knowing it, to defeat its views. In every government on earth is some trace of human weakness, some germ of corruption and degeneracy, which cunning will discover, and wickedness insensibly open, cultivate and improve.

Potential enemies of freedom will come not only from abroad, Jefferson warns, or from the restless and ambitious among our fellow citizens, but perhaps from among our elected rulers themselves. The democratic form of government, although preferable to all systems based on arbitrary authority, such as the monarchies and aristocracies still predominant in the Old World, is not in itself a perfect safeguard against ambition. The men we elect, if not monitored carefully by the electorate, may dream of becoming dictators. Human nature doesn't change, and even when a government has been as carefully designed as the American system to forestall both majoritarian and minoritarian tyranny, there will still be men who dream of tyranny and plunder. A democratic citizenry must know enough about past history to unmask these wolves in sheep's clothing before they succeed in their designs. "Every government degenerates when trusted to the rulers of the people alone," Jefferson concludes. "The people themselves therefore are its only safe depositories. And to render even them safe, their minds must be improved to a certain degree."

But if Jefferson embodies the classical heritage with its appeal to liberal education and the nondenominational God of the philosophers, other Founders had a profoundly religious basis for their patriotism. Consider the immortal summons to revolution delivered in 1775 by Patrick Henry. He does not appeal to the God of nature or to the enlightened segment of mankind that can understand the rationality of individual freedom and rights. He appeals directly to the Lord of Hosts, to Jehovah, the God of the prophets, the Old Testament, and the New Testament. In his speech, we hear more of the voice of the old Christian patriotism than of the new rational patriotism of Jefferson and the Enlightenment. This is an appeal to men of faith to defend our way of life. As righteous men, we have God on our side:

> There is no longer any room for hope. If we wish to be free—if we mean to preserve inviolate those inestimable privileges for which we have been so long contending—if we mean not basely to abandon the noble struggle in which we have been so long engaged, and which we have pledged ourselves never to abandon, until the glorious object of our contest shall be obtained—we must fight! I repeat it, sir, we must fight! An appeal to arms and to the God of Hosts is all that is left us!

At the same time, Henry combines this appeal to the Christian God with a familiar theme from classical definitions of manliness going back to Seneca—that sometimes a death suffered in the struggle for liberty and human dignity is preferable to a life lived on one's knees:

> It is in vain, sir, to extenuate the matter. Gentlemen may cry, Peace, Peace—but there is no peace. The war is actually begun! The next gale that sweeps from the north will bring to our ears the clash of resounding

arms! Our brethren are already in the field! Why stand we here idle? Is life so dear, or peace so sweet, as to be purchased at the price of chains and slavery? Forbid it, Almighty God! I know not what course others may take; but as for me, give me liberty or give me death!

Time and again, we find the old debate between civic pride and religious faith that we examined in Chapter 3 running through the reflections and the speeches of the Founding Fathers and other eminent Americans. Consider, for example, a stirring Fourth of July speech given by Josiah Quincy to commemorate the American Revolution:

> When we speak of the glory of our fathers, we mean not that vulgar renown to be attained by physical strength, nor yet that higher fame to be acquired by intellectual power. Both often exist without lofty thought, or pure intent, or generous purpose. The glory which we celebrate was strictly of a moral and religious character; righteous as to its ends; just as to its means.

Here, too, we find more emphasis on America's righteousness as a nation devoted to God than on the more secular approach to American virtue characteristic of Jefferson or Hamilton—that it is the most reasonable regime in human history, and therefore deserving of rational assent to its authority. For Quincy, faith is higher than the intellect. The intellect has its place, but in the absence of faith any account of civic virtue that is merely worldly, or that counts on a man's capacity to behave worthily in strictly human terms, will very likely degenerate into mere vainglory and a lust for worldly status and possessions. As he tells us, "intellectual power" on its own, unsubordinated to God's will, has no moral compass. A man can have a huge IQ but be completely lacking in "lofty thought" or "pure intent." Quincy is very much closer to the Augustinian and the Christian view in general of civic pride, while Jefferson is closer to the Aristotelian and classical strain. For Quincy, there is no independent human capacity for pride in the morally worthy Aristotelian sense of a man who derives his honor from serving justice and the common good. In other words, there is no distinction such as the one Aristotle made between the virtue of pride and the vice of vainglory. In the absence of God's will and our obedience to Him, a man's pride inevitably collapses *into* vainglory. His aspirations to a merely worldly virtue cannot stand on their own. Unless guided by religious ends and righteousness, they remain on the level of "vulgar renown."

CAN THERE BE GREAT MEN IN A DEMOCRACY?

From its inception, the American Republic was blessed by a dazzling array of extraordinary statesmen like Madison and Jefferson, and statesmen-warriors like Washington. Sympathetic observers from abroad like Charles James Fox, the Whig leader in the British House of Commons, spoke admiringly of how the heroic leaders of classical antiquity, the citizen-statesmen of Athens and Rome, seemed to have been reborn on the soil of the New World and in such numbers as to put to shame more powerful, ancient, and wealthy nations like Britain. And yet, when the new republic was still in its infancy, a nagging doubt arose among its leading thinkers: Will a democratic society dedicated to the principle of equality be capable of continuing to produce great leaders in the future? Or will the egalitarian principle produce a leveling of talent and a resentment for extraordinary achievement? In other words, was the original spirit of American optimism justified in remaining optimistic that the republic would continue to produce men worthy of protecting and extending the task of the Founders? This debate was most famously joined not by an American but by a visiting foreigner. His reactions to America provide a fascinating comparison, not only between Old World and New but between the traditional European vision of manliness and the emerging American model.

For nine months during 1831 and 1832, America was visited by a young French aristocrat, Alexis de Tocqueville. From this brief tour of a still very young nation, the admiring nobleman wrote *Democracy in America*. It has been regarded ever since as the single most powerful and prescient account of the democratic civilization emerging in the New World. So much was it admired in the United States that the book became a part of the American canon of classics. But, although Tocqueville certainly wanted to be read by Americans, and was pleased as he grew older to find his work well received by his American audience, his original motive in writing it was to send a wake-up call to France and the aristocracies of Europe.

America was in many ways a primitive and untamed wilderness compared with the splendid old aristocracies of Europe. But Tocqueville saw in the new nation's manhood a vigor and an idealism that made the European gentleman seem a little tired and cynical by comparison. For Tocqueville, America was an entirely unprecedented experiment in human affairs, an attempt to join democratic self-government with the highest standards of civic, moral, and religious virtue. According to the old traditions of gentlemanly honor going back to Aristotle, democracy was the worst imaginable form of government because it placed authority in the hands of the lowest common denominator, with no regard for the superior claims of the virtuous few. Having never actually experienced a successful democratic government in practice, Tocqueville's brethren in the ruling classes of Europe tended to identify it with scenes of mob rule and demagoguery—the dreadful democracies of ancient Greece, in which the wretched majority vented their resentment against the wealthy and successful through murderous class warfare and the confiscation of property. These traditional nightmare scenarios about popular government had been reinforced by the Jacobin Terror of 1793–94 and the violent excesses of class warfare in the French Revolution, with its attempts to abolish private property and religion, and its project for the wholesale liquidation of the upper orders.

Tocqueville saw that America now made that old-fashioned European conservative dread of "mobocracy" irrelevant. Through its system of checks and balances, the American constitution prevented the concentration of power in the hands either of the privileged few or of the spontaneous majority. It was in fact much closer to the "mixed regime" praised by Aristotle and the Renaissance humanists as the best possible social order—a middle-class regime that avoided the extremes of mob violence and aristocratic haughtiness, and encouraged the decent majority to prosper through hard work and talent.

Not only did America compare favorably with Europe, the young nobleman believed, but it was in many ways superior to it. Although

Tocqueville found America fascinating completely on its own terms, what really fired his imagination and intellect was that America showed the way to the future for Europe and the entire world. As he confesses, "I saw in America more than America itself; I sought there the image of democracy itself." America had already charted the path that all nations must follow if they are to avoid the twin pitfalls of violent revolution or reactionary conservatism. He wanted other young aristocrats in Europe to abandon their purblind, unreasoning hostility to the forces of benign reform, progress, economic opportunity, and public education in their own countries. America proved that the aristocracies of Europe could share their privileges without running the risk of losing everything. Not only should they not oppose the democratic movement in their own countries—they should lead it. In this sense, the new democratic ideal of manhood emerging in America could provide the flower of European manhood with a worthy goal.

When Tocqueville looked at the lives of the American Founding Fathers—men like Washington, Jefferson, Adams, and Madison—he realized what most Europeans still did not. These were not wild-eyed radicals, country bumpkins, or barbarians. They were, in fact, the flower of the Enlightenment, the kind of well-educated, cultivated, and gracious gentlemen that the best elements of the European aristocracies already admired in their own countries. Their opposite numbers were not the blood-soaked demagogues Marat, Danton, or Robespierre but civilized progressives like Lafayette and Necker. While friends of the Enlightenment and of modern progress and democracy in Europe had as yet had few opportunities to govern, in America such men had been entrusted with founding an entire nation according to the ideals of individual liberty and equality of opportunity. That made them something quite extraordinary, endowing them with the mythical stature of those ancient Roman statesmen whose service to that ancient republic still commanded such admiration among liberally educated Europeans. Tocqueville, more than most Europeans of his class and era, realized that men like Cato, Cincinnatus, Marcus Brutus, and Cicero weren't just imaginary creatures trapped like a unicorn in crumbling old books. Only a few years before, men such as these had walked the earth and founded

a new republic, the true successor of the Roman Republic at its most virtuous. When another French admirer of America, the young Marquis de
Lafayette, had served with Washington during the Revolutionary War,
he too saw in this man the reincarnation of the statesmen of ancient
times.

To be sure, Tocqueville did not believe that American democracy was
the best of all worlds. He was firmly of the belief that no one social order
could achieve *all* good things. If you got one version of justice, another
would have to be sacrificed. If some virtues were encouraged, others
would get less attention. He admired America, but it was not a utopia.
Tocqueville believed that America was best at promoting a kind of widespread and sober egalitarian virtue, best revealed in American man's capacity for hard work, his entrepreneurial daring, his love of adventure in
opening up the continent, and his profound religiosity going back to the
simple and dignified austerity of the Puritans and other dissenters from
the established churches of Europe. A man like Benjamin Franklin
summed up all their virtues: he was thrifty, diligent, hardworking, self-
disciplined, fascinated by scientific and technical innovations, and animated by a rock-solid belief that virtue was its own reward.

But there were certain virtues peculiar to aristocracy that a democracy could not match: grandeur, refinement of taste, boldness and
breadth of vision, lavish patronage of the arts, and a love of heroic self-
sacrifice, particularly in war. These virtues required a privileged caste of
inherited wealth, liberal learning, and leisure, with a disdain for commerce and a love of the extraordinary and the magnificent. This is why,
when Tocqueville poses the question as to whether a democracy can produce great men, his answer is very mixed.

When historians write about aristocratic ages, he observes, they "generally attribute everything that happens to the will and character of particular men." Great generals, statesmen, heroes—these men make the
world. By contrast, historians living in democratic times "attribute hardly
any influence over the destinies of mankind to individuals, or over the
fate of a people to the citizens." Democratic historians view history in
terms of broad, anonymous social and economic forces. Individuals
count for next to nothing. "According to them, each nation is inexorably

bound by its position, origin, antecedents and nature to a fixed destiny which no efforts can change."

Writing in the 1830s and '40s, Tocqueville is already seeing the rise of socialist ideologies in Europe. When discussing the democratic view of history, he is not literally describing America so much as using it to express a concern about Europe. The democratic view of history tends to submerge the individual human capacity for moral and reasoned choice in vast class and economic forces. In Tocqueville's view, this collectivization of judgment is a source of emasculation: It corrupts civic culture, because it encourages a man to believe that he is ruled by fate, that he has no capacity to rise above conformity to his class or his place in the economic order. We all have the same basic materialistic drives.

The constant emphasis of socialist theories on the materialistic motives for human behavior and the resulting necessity of class conflict feeds what Tocqueville worriedly calls a "doctrine of fatality." Among its consequences is the belief that extraordinary men cannot make a difference in the world through their actions on behalf of good or evil. The liberty of the individual is swamped by the tidal wave of social and economic determinism. This is a peculiarly modern form of tyranny. In Tocqueville's view, the greatest danger for the future prospects of manly virtue within a healthy democratic civilization is this doctrine of fatality. We don't need to worry too much about Caligulas and Neros emerging in our midst because their day is past. The tyranny we need to guard against is a more corrosive, hidden, and subtle kind, a psychological tyranny within the soul of democratic man. The belief in economic and historical determinism threatens to tyrannize us internally and psychologically by robbing us of the capacity to act and choose freely; it will reduce everyone to such a level of gray and petty anonymity that, as midgets surrounded by midgets, we will no longer believe ourselves capable of producing extraordinary individuals like the Founding Fathers: "Perusing the histories written nowadays," Tocqueville concludes rather glumly, "one would suppose that man had no power, either over himself or over his surroundings. Classical historians taught how to command; those of our own time teach next to nothing but how to obey."

Surveying the European scene, where the conflict between Left and

Right is intensifying, Tocqueville warns his European readers that they must be on guard against losing their capacity for individual freedom of choice to one or the other of these opposed fanaticisms:

> I would add that such a doctrine is especially dangerous at the present time. Our contemporaries are all too prone to doubts about free will, because each of them feels himself confined on every side by his own weakness. But they will freely acknowledge the strength and independence of men united in a social body. It is important not to let this principle be lost sight of, for the great aim of our time is to raise the souls of men, not to complete their prostration.

To be sure, when turning more concretely to the American experience, Tocqueville does not deny that manly honor exists in the new republic. The Americans, however, do not share the old European elevation of martial honor above the arts of peace as being most worthy of admiration. Their heroes are not Alexander the Great or Julius Caesar but Daniel Boone, Lewis and Clark, and the other men who opened up the frontier to spread the arts of agriculture and commerce:

> In the United States, martial valor is prized very little. The courage which is best known and most esteemed is that which emboldens a man to brave the dangers of the ocean in order to reach port more quickly, and bear the privations of the wilderness without complaint, and a solitude more cruel than those privations, the courage which makes a man almost insensible to the loss of a fortune laboriously acquired, and instantly prompts him to fresh exertions to make another. Courage of this kind is peculiarly necessary to maintain the American community and make it prosper, and it is held by them in peculiar esteem and honor. To betray a lack of it is to incur certain disgrace.

American men, according to Tocqueville, are more inclined to honor the kind of bravery needed to explore the wilderness or expand trade routes, because they value commerce and success in business much more highly than they do the old aristocratic love of courage in war and noble self-sacrifice on the field of battle:

> The Americans are constantly driven to engage in commerce and industry. Their origin, their social condition, their political institutions, and

even the land they inhabit, urge them irresistibly in this direction. Hence their present condition is that of an almost exclusively manufacturing and commercial association, placed in the midst of a new and boundless country whose exploitation for profit is their principal object. This is the characteristic which most particularly distinguishes the American people from all other nations at the present time.

They are not so much princes as princes of commerce. Although "one still finds some scattered notions detached from the old European aristocratic conception of honor" among the Americans, "they have no deep roots or strong influence. It is like a religion whose temples are allowed to remain but in which one no longer believes."

Tocqueville sums up his reflections on manly honor in America with a chapter candidly entitled "Why there are so many men of ambition in the United States but so few lofty ambitions." It is among the bleaker of his reflections on the New World. In it, he returns to the old debate that we examined in Chapter 3 over the meaning of pride and its relationship to both arrogance and humility—the view of pride as a mean between two extremes first formulated by Aristotle. Because America promotes equality of opportunity for individual advancement, success in commerce is the ticket for most men to improve their lot in life. Success in commerce requires the bourgeois virtues of patience, diligence, sobriety, hard work, and the postponement of gratification—not the daring, subtlety, splendor, and brilliance required of a great conqueror, statesman, or artist. Commerce is a down-to-earth goal, where success is open to most if not all men if they apply themselves. For Tocqueville, because the bourgeois virtues are so widespread and because material prosperity is the surest proof that a man possesses them, a life devoted to success in commerce suffers from a narrowness of vision and a rather cramped understanding of the soul:

> Thus among democratic nations ambition is both eager and constant, but in general its aim is not lofty. Life is generally spent in eagerly coveting small prizes that are within reach. . . . They strain their faculties to the utmost to achieve paltry results, and this speedily and inevitably narrows their range of vision and circumscribes their powers.

The danger is that these modest democratic ambitions will sap our capacity for a broader, higher vision and for boldness of spirit. Writes Tocqueville, "I confess that I believe democratic society to have much less to fear from boldness than from paltriness of aim." There is always the danger that a young man who begins by working hard and saving for tomorrow, having ended up a millionaire, will at an older age give up his earlier self-discipline and lose himself in material pleasures: "Very vulgar tastes often go with the enjoyment of extraordinary prosperity, and it would seem that their only object in rising to supreme power was to gratify trivial and coarse appetites more easily." To counteract this emasculating tendency to plutocracy and hedonism, democracy more than other political systems needs an external challenge from time to time: "The leaders [of a democracy] would do wrong if they tried to send the citizens to sleep in a state of happiness too uniform and peaceful." Indeed, its leaders should deliberately seek out such challenges, perhaps in the form of a just war. In this respect, the current war against terrorism and its state sponsors is justified not only as self-defense and as a struggle against tyranny but because of its invigorating effects on American civic culture. Democratic leaders should "sometimes give [citizens] difficult and dangerous problems, to rouse ambition and give it a field of action.

"Moralists are always complaining," Tocqueville concludes, "that pride is the pet vice of our age." Yes, he concedes, pride is bad when it is synonymous with arrogance. But isn't the danger that democracy suffers from too little pride rather than too much? The drawback of democracy is that its emphasis on material prosperity can make a man think he is fit only for the basest pleasures and the most paltry pursuits—such a man "thinks he is born for nothing but the enjoyment of vulgar pleasures . . . and dares not face any lofty enterprise; indeed, he can scarcely face such a possibility." Given that democracy already promotes humility in spades, Tocqueville asks, couldn't we do with a little more pride?

> Far from thinking that we ought to preach humility to our contemporaries, I wish men would endeavor to give them a higher idea of themselves and of humanity. Humility is unwholesome for them; what they most lack, in my opinion, is pride. I would willingly exchange several of our small virtues for this one vice.

How justified is Tocqueville's worry that democracy does not give enough scope for grand ambition and honor in a man? One hesitates to take issue with so brilliant and sympathetic an observer. And yet, perhaps more than Tocqueville realized, the Americans of his own time were well aware of this potential defect in the democratic character and desired both to praise the nobility of the Founders and encourage the rising generation to aspire to their lofty heights.

During the years that Tocqueville visited and wrote about America, its homegrown statesmen and opinion makers had already seen the need for a public rhetoric that would commemorate the great deeds of the Founders and preserve their examples as an inspiration for the present and future generations. John Quincy Adams, who became president in 1825, paid tribute to the Founders in a stirring blend of classical and Christian themes, and by making their achievements of a generation before sound as if they had occurred centuries ago, he invested their fame with an ancient venerability. In praising Washington and Franklin, he alludes to the doctrine of the just war in describing Washington as a peace-loving man who drew his sword only when his fellow Americans were endangered by tyranny. Franklin is presented as the peacetime counterpart to the military leadership of Washington, the repository of those middle-class virtues of applied science, the spread of learning and informed opinion, and the arts of commerce:

> The Sword of Washington! The Staff of Franklin! O, sir, what associations are linked in adamant with these names. Washington, whose sword was never drawn but in the cause of his country, and never sheathed when wielded in his country's cause. Franklin, the philosopher of the thunder-bolt, the printing-press, and the ploughshare! What names are these in the scanty dialogue of the benefactors of human kind! Washington and Franklin! What other two men whose lives belong to the eighteenth century of Christendom have left a deeper impression of themselves upon the age in which they lived, and upon all after time?

Adams offers a further praise of Washington that duplicates exactly the idea of manliness as the correct balance of active and contemplative

virtues—and of the superiority of statesmanship to battlefield courage—
that we have encountered so often in this book:

> Washington, the warrior and the legislator! In war, contending, by the
> wager of the battle, for the independence of his country, and for the
> freedom of the human race—ever manifesting, amid its horrors, by pre-
> cept and by example, his reverence for the laws of peace, and for the
> tenderest sympathies of humanity; in peace, soothing the ferocious
> spirit of discord, among his own countrymen, into harmony and union,
> and giving to that very sword, now presented to his country, a charm
> more potent than that attributed, in ancient times, to the lyre of
> Orpheus.

Finally, in accordance with that other strain in the heritage of the
founding—the understanding of America as a nation whose merits are
based primarily on its piety—Adams links the destiny of America to the
will of God:

> And may every American who shall hereafter behold them, ejaculate a
> mingled offering of praise to that Supreme Ruler of the Universe, by
> whose tender mercies our Union had been hitherto preserved, through all
> the vicissitudes and revolutions of this turbulent world; and of prayer for
> the continuation of these blessings, by the dispensations of Providence.

So, while Tocqueville may have been justified in part by his worry
that America would fail to honor great men and inspire new ones to
emerge, we see here that an American civic rhetoric was developing that
tried to graft the American experience onto the praise of manly virtues
stretching back to antiquity and the Bible.

Moreover, sometimes eminent Europeans saw in Americans examples of manliness superior to what their own much older civilization was
producing. For Charles James Fox, the English Whig leader and ardent
champion of the rights of man, George Washington served to remind
Europeans of the purity of an ideal of which Europe had too often lost
sight:

> How infinitely superior must appear the spirit of principles of General
> Washington in his late address to Congress compared with the policy of

modern European courts! Illustrious man! Deriving honor less from the splendor of his situation than for the dignity of his mind. It must, indeed, create astonishment that, placed in circumstances so critical, and filling a station so conspicuous, the character of Washington should never once have been called in question.

Fox observes that America's enormous physical distance from the Old World had preserved its morals from the taint of European grandeur, arrogance, power seeking, and hypocrisy. Now, however, it is America herself who will teach Europe the meaning of a virile virtue and an honorable manliness:

> Separated from Europe by an immense ocean, you feel not the effect of those prejudices and passions which convert the boasted seats of civilization into scenes of horror and bloodshed. You profit by the folly and madness of the contending nations, and afford, in your more congenial clime, an asylum to those blessings and virtues which they wantonly condemn or wickedly exclude from their bosom! Cultivating the arts of peace, under the influence of freedom, you advance by rapid strides to opulence and distinction.

Some decades later, Ralph Waldo Emerson wrote in praise of great men from all eras of civilization, framed in the broadest possible terms, making us wonder again whether Tocqueville might have been a bit too worried that Americans would not preserve an appreciation for extraordinary achievement. "It is natural to believe in great men," Emerson proclaims. "Nature seems to exist for the excellent. The world is upheld by the veracity of good men: they make the earth wholesome." Emerson goes on to argue that the search for great men is one of the chief means by which lesser men can improve their own characters by paying tribute to a superior measure of excellence: "The search for the great man is the dream of youth and the most serious occupation of manhood. We travel into foreign parts to find his works—if possible, to get a glimpse of him." Finally, he says, although true greatness is to be preferred to mediocrity, a decent mediocrity is preferable to vain and ill-founded claims to greatness: "Let us have the quality pure. A little genius let us leave alone."

These are just a few examples of eminent Americans who believed that an appreciation for great men would contribute to an education in democratic citizenship, and help forestall excessive materialism or a flight into private pastimes. There's an even more striking example of an American who shared Tocqueville's respect for lofty ambition and his concern over the threat to it posed by the leveling trend in American culture. His identity may come as a surprise. But if any American lives up to Emerson's praise of genius, it is he.

TOWERING GENIUS DISDAINS A BEATEN PATH

Around the same time that Tocqueville wrote his somewhat despairing reflections, an ambitious young man from the wilds of the frontier delivered a speech in Springfield, Illinois, that uncannily echoes many of Tocqueville's worries about the decline of grand ambition but also suggests a solution. That young man summed up many of the American traits that Tocqueville found both fascinating and admirable; he represented a new kind of man not yet known or understood in the Old World. He could not have been more different in his background from the privileged young count. He was a man of origins so humble that they would likely have precluded him from playing any great role in the affairs of a European state. He had little formal education and certainly nothing resembling the gentlemanly immersion in history and the classics that Tocqueville and the more genteel Founders had received. Yet he was ambitious, had an extraordinarily roving and fertile mind, and seemed to draw from the very air he breathed the lessons that college students from more privileged backgrounds had to read Cicero and Plutarch to discover. His speech to the Young Men's Lyceum in Springfield is one of the most unusual orations in American history, one that in every way responds to the French aristocrat's anxieties about the America he so much admired. The speaker's name was Abraham Lincoln.

Lincoln's theme is how a young man's ambition might find satisfaction in a democracy. He asks: Can democracy find room for "an Alexander, a Caesar or a Napoleon"? His resounding answer is: "Never! Towering genius disdains a beaten path." Right away, we see that the young Lincoln views the issue somewhat differently than did

Tocqueville. The French observer's worry had been that democracy, with its creed of egalitarianism and its reduction of ambition to success in business, would sap the energies of the soul that give a man the dream of becoming an Alexander or a Caesar—the daring, the boldness, the pride and love of glory. Lincoln's concern, by contrast, is that such men *will* arise but ordinary democratic politics, with its emphasis on the peaceful arts of business and commercial prosperity, will disgust them because of its inability to satisfy their grand ambitions. In that case, he worries, these men will turn against the democracy and attempt to tear it down.

In voicing this concern, Lincoln is reviving a theme that we have encountered many times throughout this book, going back to our earlier discussions of courage and pride. The problem is how to harness those aggressive energies that, left untended, might drive a man to become a usurper and tyrant, and redirect them toward the service of the common good. Because ambition is reduced to such a paltry level in a democracy, Tocqueville is convinced that this danger is no longer even present. The concern is not that young men will use their ambition for tyrannical and base ends rather than just and noble ones but that the wellsprings of *any* kind of grand ambition will dry up and die in their flat American bourgeois souls. Accordingly, Tocqueville prefers to err on the side of encouraging an excessive pride as opposed to what he sees as the excessively sheeplike humility that is coming increasingly to predominate.

For Lincoln, however, the old Aristotelian problem—the problem of how to promote courage as a mean between extremes of rashness and passivity, and how to harness manly pride in the service of the common good—has not fundamentally changed at all. In fact, the Aristotelian problem is more relevant than ever, precisely because Tocqueville is correct that ordinary democratic politics quashes the ambitions of the proud. Whereas earlier, more aristocratic societies provided an outlet for such ambition by offering these men the chance to win honor from a small circle of the privileged, democracy offers far fewer such outlets. The danger, though, is not—as Tocqueville feared—that grand ambition will vanish but that it will be more strongly tempted to the path of tyranny and domination than ever before.

Tocqueville is worried that democracy will be defined by the likes of

Bill Gates. But Lincoln already foresees the danger of a Hitler and the possibility that tyrants far worse than Nero and Caligula will emerge in the very midst of that one regime which is most opposed to tyranny because it believes in the equality of every human being. Tocqueville is worried about the passive nihilism of soft morals, luxury, conformism, and apathy. Lincoln is worried about the contempt of the ambitious for a world that offers them no place. It should go without saying that Lincoln, who will become president twenty-two years after giving this speech, is not merely being hypothetical or talking about people other than himself. The speech clearly has an autobiographical overtone. He is speaking not only to the young men in the audience but to himself when he asks: Is there room in America for *my* ambitions? Can I find a way of serving the republic that will satisfy my longing for distinction? Might I succumb to the temptation of destroying the democracy if it cannot provide me with a project in its service sufficiently challenging to demonstrate my abilities?

Lincoln begins by surveying the remarkable successes of the young republic to date: "In the great journal of things happening under the sun, we, the American people, find . . . ourselves in peaceful possession of the fairest portion of the earth. . . . We find ourselves under the government and . . . political institutions conducing more essentially to the ends of civil and religious liberty than any of which the history of former times tells us." An older Lincoln will more pithily and memorably sum up these achievements as "the last best hope of man on Earth."

The danger to America, he continues, does not come from any foreign foe because of America's huge geographic extent and physical distance from potential aggressors: "All the armies of Europe, Asia, and Africa combined . . . could not by force take a drink from the Ohio, or make a track on the Blue Ridge, in a trial of a thousand years." Like Tocqueville, he believes the danger comes from within—an inner corrosion of the spirit. Ironically, it is America's very success to date that poses this danger. New Founding Fathers, says Lincoln, will not be needed. The experiment was a brilliant success, and its fundamentals need not be repeated or redesigned. So the young men of today cannot look forward to being future Washingtons. "The field of glory is harvested, and the crop is already appropriated. But new reapers will arise, and they, too, will seek a field." What will these new reapers of glory do? Here is where Lincoln shows himself at his most original and farsighted. He firmly rejects that excessively optimistic strain of the Enlightenment, going back to Hobbes, Locke, and Voltaire, that argued that tyrannical ambition would melt away as men came to understand that their natural needs were satisfied by economic prosperity and tolerance of one another's private beliefs. Some of the Founders, notably James Madison, had echoed this view, arguing that, once men's ambitions were directed to the peaceful competition for success in commerce, the more dangerous ambition for glory would fade away. According to Lincoln, the theory may be fine, but the evidence of history is overwhelmingly in the other direction: "It is to deny what the history of the world tells us is true to suppose that men of ambition and talents will not continue to spring up against us. And when they do, they will as naturally seek the gratification of their ruling passion, as others have so done before them." The chance to become Jay Gould or J. P. Morgan will not deter some young men from dreaming of becoming Caesar or Napoleon. Human nature does not change.

And that brings us to the central problem. Men such as these, who belong to "the family of the lion" and "the tribe of the eagle," are not going to be satisfied with "a seat in Congress" (and that includes Illinois) or even—Lincoln is quite sure about this in 1838—the presidency. If we cannot find a way of channeling tyrannical ambition into civic virtue and pride on behalf of the common good, the ambitious man will have only one alternative. If he cannot gratify his passion for honor by serving the republic, he will win his fame by overthrowing it:

> Distinction will be his paramount object, and although he would as willingly, and perhaps more so, acquire it by doing good as harm; yet, that opportunity being past, and nothing left to be done in the way of building up, he would set boldly to the task of pulling down. Here, then, is a probable case, highly dangerous, and such a one as could not have well existed heretofore.

Lincoln's solution to this scary scenario is not as surefooted or as compelling as his diagnosis. The kind of decent patriotism Lincoln hopes the proud man will embrace is harder to maintain in the present, he concedes, than it was during the era of the Revolution and the Founders. That was an age of passion and glory in a just cause which electrified an entire people. The impact of its inspiration is fading, Lincoln says, with every passing year. We no longer feel we live in an age of giants like Washington. Moreover, while passion is required by a just revolution against tyranny such as the American revolution against George III, for American leaders to encourage an excessively passionate attachment to country today, when no such external oppressor looms, would be to feed the forces of lawlessness and mob rule. "Passion has helped us, but it can do so no more. It will in future be our enemy. Reason, cold, calculating, unimpassioned reason, must furnish all the materials for our future support and defense." Above all, we need to encourage "sound morality and . . . a reverence for the constitution and the laws."

Although this is an eminently prudent conclusion, it cannot help but feel anticlimactic compared with the heady dangers of Caesarean ambition Lincoln stirs so skillfully in his listeners in the first part of the speech. Fortunately, Lincoln's own life eventually provided him with a more satisfying solution to the problem of democratic ambition than the one he gives here so many years before assuming the helm of his country's affairs. In this speech, the young Lincoln dismisses even the presidency as an insufficiently alluring ambition for "the tribe of the lion." But as president Lincoln found a vocation that enabled him to draw upon every ounce of his character, his formidable trove of moral, spiritual, and intellectual energies, to save his country from dismemberment and to begin righting its most heinous wrong, the curse of slavery. Like Churchill in the next century, Lincoln was neither happy nor terribly impressive when his political career was confined to the quotidian affairs of the economy and other peacetime concerns. In effect, the unfolding history of America presented him with the very choice he prophesies in his speech: the great man who must choose between investing his "ruling passion" in serving the republic or in destroying it. Challenged by those who would destroy it, he emerged as that very savior. He is living proof of Aristotle's teaching about the great-souled man—he will only rise to the occasion, will only rouse himself and give his full efforts, when his country is faced with the gravest calamity. Only then can he justify his ambition and win honor from the citizenry. The Civil War enabled

Lincoln to display his full greatness of soul. He seems particularly deserving of Emerson's praise of the great man: "Let us have the quality pure. A little genius let us leave alone."

MEN WHO GREATLY DARED

In suggesting that Lincoln was the living embodiment of Aristotle's great-souled man, we must not forget for a moment that his sense of public mission was saturated with that profound piety that is inseparable from the American character. Both before and after Lincoln, as we have already seen, civic virtue and faith weave around each other in the speeches and deeds of the greatest statesmen and writers. One of the most moving and beautiful of the many tributes paid to Lincoln after his assassination came in 1865 from Henry Ward Beecher, the famous abolitionist and Congregational minister. Beecher's tribute sums up with perfect eloquence the way Lincoln's life provided an answer to Tocqueville's justified worries about the absence of great men in a democracy, and vindicated America's capacity to match if not surpass the high-water marks of past civic greatness by producing, from the humblest ranks of the egalitarian society, a man equal to the noblest heroes of antiquity, both biblical and secular.

Harry Jaffa, one of the preeminent Lincoln scholars, has aptly suggested that Lincoln's career, culminating in the defeat of the Confederacy and the Emancipation Proclamation, was in effect a second founding of the United States, a second American Revolution in which the last and most glaring contradiction between the republic's ideals of liberty and equality and the reality of its social life—slavery—was removed. Beecher's speech is a blend of religious and civic fervor in honoring this second founder.

There is no historic figure more noble than that of Moses the Jewish lawgiver. There is scarcely another event in history more touching than his death. He had borne the great burdens of state for forty years, shaped the Jews to a nation, filled out their civil and religious polity, administered their laws, guided their steps, or dwelt with them in all their journeyings in the wilderness; had mourned in their punishment, kept step with their march, and led them in wars, until the end of their labors drew nigh. The last stage was reached, Jordan only lay between them and the promised land. Then came the word of the Lord unto him, "Thou may not goest over. Get thee up into the mountain, look upon it, and die."

Beecher prophesies that Lincoln, as America's Moses, will enjoy immortality in the company of American Founders such as Washington and biblical kings such as David:

Again, a great leader of the people has passed through toil, sorrow, battle, and war, and come near to the promised land of peace, into which he might not pass over. . . . And now the martyr is moving in triumphal march, mightier than when alive. The nation rises up at every stage of his coming. Cities and states are his pall-bearers, and the cannon beats the hours with solemn progression. Dead, dead, dead, he yet speaketh! Is Washington dead? Is David dead? Is any man that ever was fit to live dead? Disenthralled of flesh, and risen in the unobstructed sphere where passion never comes, he begins his illimitable work. His life is now grafted upon the infinite, and will be fruitful as no earthly life can be.

Lincoln is perhaps the supreme American example of the age-old teachings about the manly virtues that we looked at in our earlier discussions of courage and pride. Although he was not experienced in actual battlefield combat, his moral courage during the Civil War imposed on him tests of a severity that easily equaled or even surpassed the terrors of combat, draining him of every ounce of energy, leaving him often depressed and on the brink of collapse, despairing of eventual success and racked by doubts about his own fitness for the task. Indeed, as the burdens of his presidency mounted, Lincoln's youthful worship of ancient heroes ("the tribe of the lion," as he'd put it in his Springfield speech) was transmuted into a finer and more transcendental quality, an almost saintly purity and modesty combined with an unflagging perseverance utterly lacking in bombast or vanity. Beginning as an aspiring Brutus, he ended as a Solomon.

Beecher compares Lincoln's death with Moses bringing his people to the edge of the promised land and glimpsing it before dying. Lincoln preserved the Union and abolished the evil of slavery, thus showing his people the way into the land of milk and honey. But the completion of the journey was left to subsequent generations, and was not as fast in coming as our honor for Lincoln should have required of us. It cannot be an accident that the greatest leader of the modern civil rights movement, Dr. Martin Luther King, Jr., also compared the struggle for civil rights with Moses glimpsing the promised land. Since he, too, was cut down in his prime by an enemy of liberty, the parallel with Beecher's praise of Lincoln as Moses is especially touching. In keeping with his theological convictions, King believed that a man's inner spiritual strength to do good came from renouncing violence, and that no American could be free as long as any Americans were oppressed—whether black or white. There could hardly be a better example of Emerson's maxim that moral force gives a man both fearlessness and tranquility. King, too, was a new American founder and a model of American manhood. Just as Lincoln wanted to complete the Founders' work by abolishing slavery, King wanted his fellow Americans to live up to Lincoln's promise and complete the extension of rights to the disadvantaged.

America has been blessed with many men who displayed moral courage and who achieved that traditional balance of the active and re-flective virtues. I have already mentioned John McCain. It comes as no surprise that McCain's own hero is Theodore Roosevelt—a warrior who placed the honor of public service above the honor of combat; a conser-vative who believed in using the power of government to discourage ex-cessive inequalities of wealth and spread equality of opportunity; a man of religious conviction who believed that the truest proof of one's piety was to avoid sectarian cant or religious intolerance and place one's spiri-tual energies at the service of one's country.

Roosevelt was also one of the most eloquent speakers and writers among American statesmen, with a beautifully cadenced prose style that combines American straightforwardness with more subtle echoes of jux-taposition and lyricism reminiscent of Gibbon. If Emerson could be de-scribed as the poet of the American mind, TR is, among statesmen, the poet of its historical odyssey. In his many public lectures, particularly to colleges and schools, he often begins—as had Lincoln—by invoking the greatness of America's past achievements as a standard we must live up to in the present and future:

> There was scant room for the coward and weakling in the ranks of the adventurous frontiersmen—the pioneer settlers who first broke up the wild prairie soil, who first hewed their way into the primeval forest. . . . Behind them came the men who completed the work they had roughly begun; who drove the great railroad system over plain and desert and mountain pass; who stocked the teeming ranches, and under irrigation saw the bright green of the alfalfa and the yellow of the golden stubble supplant the gray of the sagebrush desert. . . . Such is the record of which we are so proud. It is a record of men who greatly dared and greatly did.

TR shared Lincoln's concern that, with such a glorious past to look back on, we will conclude that nothing great remains to be done. Spiritually, America will be the victim of its own success if that success lulls us into complacency:

> It would be a sad and evil thing for this country if ever the day came when we considered the great deeds of our forefathers as an excuse for our resting slothfully satisfied with what has already been done.

America's most precious resource is not its wealth, or its intellectual and artistic culture, impressive though they are. Underlying them, and most necessary of all, is American virtue:

> It is character that counts in a nation as in a man. It is a good thing to have a keen, fine intellectual development in a nation, to produce orators, artists, successful business men; but it is an infinitely greater thing to have those solid qualities which we group together under the name of character—sobriety, steadfastness, the sense of obligation toward one's neighbor and one's God, hard common sense, and, combined with it, the lift of generous enthusiasm toward whatever is right. These are the qualities which go to make up true national greatness.

Now that the epic phase of American history is over—the Revolution, the Civil War, the opening of the frontier—Americans must dedicate themselves to a new ideal, the ideal of service: "Unless democracy is based on the principle of service by everybody who claims the enjoyment of any right, it is not true democracy at all."

The ideal of service replaces the outward conquest of the frontier with a new frontier of the spirit—an inner struggle to purify and ennoble the American character through a dedication to the common good. Like so many of his forebears, TR regarded faith as indispensable to the democratic character. But his Christianity was very much a civil religion, not a private search for salvation or a turning of one's back on society at large as corrupt and tainted:

> The religious man who is most useful is not he whose sole care is to save his own soul, but the man whose religion bids him to strive to advance decency and clean living and to make the world a better place for his fellows to live in.

Roosevelt was not a leveler or a radical egalitarian. He firmly believed in the equality of opportunity for an earned inequality of result. The glory of America was not that it reduced everyone to the same condition but that it liberated a man to rise as high as his talent and hard work would take him, as long as government provided a safety net of basic humanitarian and educational services meant to give everyone a level playing field. TR was born to privilege, and he was not ashamed of the fact that he could pass those privileges along to his children. But he staunchly believed that those who inherit wealth and status in a democratic society have a special responsibility to contribute to the advancement of those less fortunate, and to pay their country back for the privileges and head start in life they have received. This is what gives a young man "the right stuff." As he told the students at the Harvard Union in 1907:

> Remember always that this Republic of ours is a very real democracy, and that you can only win success by showing that you have the right stuff in you. The college man, the man of intellect and training, should take the lead in every fight for civic and social righteousness. He can take that lead only if in a spirit of thoroughgoing democracy he takes his place among his fellows, not standing aloof from them, but mixing with them,

so that he may know, may feel, may sympathize with their hopes, their ambitions, their principles—and even their prejudices—as an American among Americans, as a man among men.

In my view, the president in recent times whose creed of service most closely resembled TR's was John F. Kennedy. In his 1952 inaugural speech as senator-elect from Massachusetts, he framed his theme with the question Were we truly men? In this brief, eloquent address, he picks up many of TR's characteristic themes, including the theme of service and the debt owed by the privileged to the rest of the democracy:

> For those to whom much is given, much is required. And when at some future date the high court of history sits in judgment of each of us, recording whether in our brief span of service we fulfilled our responsibilities to the state, our success or failure, in whatever office we hold, will be measured by the answers to [these] questions. Were we truly men of courage, with the courage to stand up to one's enemies, and the courage to stand up, when necessary, to one's associates, the courage to resist public pressure as well as private greed?

Central to Kennedy's definition of manliness is the Emersonian theme of moral courage. Like TR before him and McCain later, Kennedy was a genuine war hero. But like those men, he, too, valued public service far more highly than battlefield courage, and moral courage more highly than physical bravery. And he, too, believed in a new frontier—a spiritual frontier of service. In terms of his accomplishments as president, he was not on a level with Lincoln, TR, FDR, or Reagan. It was left to his successor, the tormented and undervalued Lyndon Johnson, to legislate successfully the civil rights for which Kennedy had felt an instinctive sympathy. But Kennedy began the effort at a time when many in his own party and administration thought the political risk was too great and the gain too meager. When Lincoln's true successor, the Reverend Martin Luther King, gave his "I Have a Dream" speech to 250,000 people in front of the Lincoln Memorial, his triumph was possible in no small part because of Kennedy's support for civil rights, including sending federal troops to Alabama to enforce court-ordered integration and intervening personally to secure good treatment for King in the Birmingham jail. Those were noble acts. In his aspirations to public service, in the way he served his country in war and peace, and in the way he died, John F. Kennedy was a man who greatly dared.

WHERE WE STAND

We've seen in this chapter how an enlightened patriotism provides a field of action where all the paths to the manly heart converge—a field of action where the balance of active and reflective virtues that is the essence of manhood can flourish. We've also seen why the American brand of patriotism is inseparable from its optimism.

As this exploration of the five paths to the manly heart comes to an end, we inevitably return from the traditional teachings to the extraordinary challenges of the present—challenges that galvanize those teachings with new potential. In the aftermath of 9/11, as we begin the new century with another just war on behalf of democracy and against tyranny, we urgently need to reengage the American tradition of patriotism. We need to reexamine the words and deeds of past American heroes in order to draw on their power to inspire as we face the perils yet to come. But we also need to reexamine the patriotic tradition in order to remind ourselves that, while our optimism is mostly a source of moral strength, it can sometimes be a source of moral lassitude.

When optimism slips the bounds of the American nation-state, with its well-founded institutions and traditions of character, it can drift into a fuzzy realm of unrealistic expectations for world peace, or utopian projects for the abolition of property and other modern liberties—projects whose actualization always requires a tyrant. When American optimism loses its rootedness in the history and experiences of the greatest living success story of a viable democratic civilization, floating into a baseless fantasy world of pacifism and good but muddleheaded intentions, we need to remember that our most admirable American heroes have always combined optimism about the progress of liberty with a healthy awareness of the existence of tyrants and recognized the need, if freedom is imperiled at home or among our fellow democracies abroad, to raise the sword of justice on behalf of "the last best hope of man on Earth."

In recent years, other democracies—above all, Israel—have not been permitted the luxury of our optimism. If one takes the population of Israel as a factor of the population of America, the three thousand casualties of the attack on the World Trade Center and Pentagon shrinks to a relatively small number—about a hundred. For Israel, a democracy the size of Delaware surrounded by a host of grimly repressive tyrannies, juntas, and oligarchies, carnage on that scale from terrorist attacks is a reality with which they have lived for decades.

I realize that such a comparison is not the whole story. Sorrow over the murder of innocents has its own ghastly economy of scale, and there is something more morally devastating about three thousand victims than there is about a hundred. Nevertheless, it is a salutary reminder that Israel is still, as Daniel Patrick Moynihan so memorably put it years ago, the "miner's canary" for liberal democracy and Western civilization as a whole. Those of us in the other liberal democracies have grown a bit inattentive in recent years to the canary's alarm about the darkness ahead, and the explosions have now roared out of the pit all the way back to scorch us.

We must never abandon our compassion and our optimism about human nature and the universal benefits of spreading liberal democracy to the world. For Americans to become cynical about those ideals would be a more lasting and terrible victory for the terrorists. But we do need to be a little more tough-minded. Too often, we have had a tendency to dismiss the actual claims of terrorists as rhetoric stemming from a confused state of mind. They may say that they are fighting for the honor and dignity of their people and faith, and that they want to destroy their enemies and the interlopers who occupy their sacred soil. We knew—or thought we knew—that what they really want is "the peace process" leading to a Western standard of living, and that once this was in sight, religious and ideological hostilities would evaporate. The time has come to start listening to the terrorists' own explanations of their conduct and to take them seriously. Oddly enough, to fight terrorists effectively, we need to stop patronizing them. For this reason—to return to a theme I first advanced in the introduction—we need more than ever to consider the dark side of masculine aggressiveness, fanaticism, resentment, and misplaced idealism, as a foil for decent aspirations to an honorable and civilized code of conduct.

This means, unavoidably, taking a more pessimistic view of the prospects for peace in international conflicts between democracies and tyrannies with which America is involved. Some degree of security can be achieved. Opposing sides can agree to lay down their arms, or at least limit their attacks on each other. They can find economic issues on which limited cooperation is possible, and aid from the West can contribute to that cooperation. But these palliatives, however useful and well-intentioned, will never on their own erase the stronger collective desire of a warlike minority for revenge, honor, and the glory of finally triumphing over a hated and feared enemy. What Lincoln called "the tribe of the lion" is still with us.

In such circumstances, where innocent lives and not merely academic doctrines are at risk, there may be little if any prospect for "conflict resolution." It may be that the best we can hope to achieve is to support the side that shares our own liberal democratic institutions and values—most notably Israel, the miner's canary. We should side with the liberal democracies against the tyrannies and their terrorist proxies not only for our own strategic security and that of our allies but in order to defend liberal democracy around the world, and to increase whatever chance there may be that the tyrannies themselves, cowed and impressed against their wills by its splendor, confidence, intellectual vigor, and might, may eventually come to embrace its blessings and free their own peoples from the grip of repression—or be toppled by them. The ultimate beneficiaries of the West's war against the tyrannies will be the millions who live in fear and needless poverty under their yoke. In this most important of ways, the war against terrorism will be a war on behalf of optimism.

CONCLUSION

Books reflect their times as you write them. As I was writing this one, a number of other books appeared lamenting the decline of manhood and the lack of understanding for boys. Opinion was shifting. Then our world was shattered and transformed by the events of 9/11 and the ongoing war against terrorism. Sometimes history will not allow us the luxury of a debate. From the firefighters who gave their lives to save others to the inspiring leadership of Mayor Giuliani, American men suddenly knew exactly how to act. And, in the comparative calm of the aftermath, as people began to come out of their shock and reflect on the madness, they also began asking: Has manliness come back? Is the crisis of manliness over?

On the level of immediate events, the answer was a resounding *yes*. As the firefighters and rescue workers achieved daily feats of heroism, as young soldiers hunted down the Islamo-fascists of al-Qaida (brave only in murdering children and beating up women) in the treacherous barrens of Afghanistan, there was no longer any silliness about finding "gender-neutral" ways of describing them. They weren't "persons." They were *men*. They were not superior to women. But they did things that women simply could not do—not only because women lack the physical strength but because their temperaments generally do not prepare them for combat to the same degree as does a man's. This has always been obvious to anyone with common sense, but it had been obscured by decades of vain blather and grandstanding by the professional class of the perpetually offended. Now it shone forth once more in all its self-evident clarity. Men and women aspire to the same heights of excellence, but along different paths of psychology and experience. And it's good that this is so.

Throughout this book, I've looked at popular culture as a source of clues for changes in the Zeitgeist that are often still subconscious. Popular culture often runs ahead of the opinion elites in charting shifts in values. Sometimes the clues emerge from the silliest of entertainment confections, sometimes from grotesque and nihilistic excesses in music or personal style. But the clues point the way to an emerging new consensus about manliness; even as I was writing this book, I could feel it in the air.

I've talked about the balkanization of the sexes, first undertaken by the more radical versions of feminism on behalf of women, later imitated by elements of the men's consciousness movement on behalf of men. That trend is still going strong. We're still frequently trapped between the Mother Goddess and Iron John, polarized opposites that lead with equal certainty to a dead end in the search for mutual understanding between men and women. At the same time, however, there has been a loosening of the language code formerly thought necessary to preserve the two sexes as irreconcilable "gendered identities." Suddenly you can use the forbidden words again, the everyday casual talk by which men and women relate to each other, often in the guise of jokes, as they search for a common ground for understanding one another's differences. Guys and chicks. Guy talk. Chick flick. Be a man. Be a guy. He acted like a man. She was a great broad. The expanding guy-talk industry celebrates all the cherished old male props—sports cars, golf clubs, humidors. The Rat Pack style of Frank, Dino, and Sammy is suddenly glamorous again. When Bill Maher greeted his female guests on *Politically Incorrect* with a grinning "Hey Gorgeous!" he showed how acute his Zeitgeist antennas were. No one was offended. His women guests were powerful, beautiful, and successful people. They already knew they were gorgeous. And maybe without his knowing it, his ability to speak this way signaled the demise of his own show's theme. Maybe the reign of political correctness was over.

But—not so fast! As a conservative, I do have a self-appointed duty to act as the Grinch who stole Christmas on a variety of fronts. So I'm compelled to look for the cloud that envelops the silver lining. Some of my journalistic colleagues have already rushed into print to declare that manliness is back, that everything's fine now, that radical feminism is as dead as a dodo, and so on. But a cultural crisis that took a generation to emerge isn't going to vanish in a week or a year or even a decade. Celebrating the fact that we can use certain politically incorrect words again in casual conversation or in the entertainment world suggests that we are evading the deeper cultural divide by keeping things on the level of fashion. The self-conscious lingo of chicks and broads and guys and man talk remains no more than fashionably and superficially contrarian, and often a little infantile. It's a bit of daring that doesn't cost anyone very much, and it can lull us into thinking that the deeper sources of alienation and frustration felt by boys and men have vanished overnight.

In some ways, the frankness that we now flatter ourselves we can enjoy in discussing the sexes has led to even worse levels of vulgarity and debasement in popular culture. Take the slew of television shows with the "survivor" theme, which basically select people from the suburbs and treat them like lab rats. The creepy monitors who hover nearby encourage these losers in an unrestrained flow of verbal garbage, all drawn from the psychobabble of talk-television uplift. There's lots of emoting about guys and chicks and how they differ. There are altogether too many bared midriffs and too much bad hair, on the contestants' unfortunate attempt to imitate their favorite celebrities from *Dawson's Creek* or *Friends* on a Kmart budget. It's a real-time version of Jerry Springer, a wholesale attempt to give everyone his or her long-promised fifteen minutes of fame. Andy Warhol, our Raphael of the vapid, meant his remark ironically. The entertainment industry is methodically carrying it out with the kind of Protestant rigor formally reserved for building libraries and orphanages.

So we need to ask ourselves: How much has the underlying moral and spiritual crisis of manliness genuinely subsided? I believe that, unfortunately, all its major features are still firmly in place. To take the most obvious example, the devastating effects of the divorce culture and what David Blankenhorn calls "fatherless America" on boys and young men, who often carry their sense of betrayal, pain, and distrust from their parents' breakup far into their adult lives, where they find their own attempts to build solid marriages undermined by a nagging fear that they will be betrayed again.

But the full dimensions of this moral crisis extend far beyond family life. Throughout the lifetime of my generation of Baby Boomers, America has displayed a peculiarly divided state of mind. On the one hand, we've witnessed extraordinary exertions of valor and heroism again and again, from the unsuccessful but justified attempt to save Vietnam from communist tyranny to winning the Cold War to the current war on terrorism. If you look along this road from past to future, the way ahead seems to be ever brighter. On the other hand, during the period of this same steady progress against tyranny abroad, America became one of the most violent societies in the world—and one in which, with depressing regularity, from Timothy McVeigh to John Muhammad, men periodically became terrorists against their own fellow citizens.

The huge prison population of young males remains a daily source of shame in the wealthiest and freest country on earth. Whole generations of boys and youths whose aggressiveness requires a better outlet than robbery, rape, and murder are being spiritually destroyed. A recent study claims that the drop in the homicide rate thought to have taken place in the past decade is an illusion. The murder rate would be five times higher, these researchers claim, if not for medical advances during the same period that saved many crime victims who otherwise would have died. But, as the study goes on to point out, these nearly murdered victims face decades of physical and emotional trauma, and staggering costs for physical and psychological therapy that may last for the rest of their lives. There is something chilling about a society that can use medical technology unprecedented in human history and unmatched anywhere else in the world to "improve" violent crime by converting murders into maimings and lifelong trauma. And it's young men who carry out the vast majority of those crimes.

What is the connection between these two Americas? Can we find a way of connecting that bright road of progress and the advancement of the cause of liberty at home and around the world with that darker, sadder road that leads to devastation and despair, the misbegotten warfare of the sniper's bullet? As I've argued throughout this book, I believe it is the loss of an adequate moral, spiritual, and psychological vocabulary about manliness that keeps those two roads from coming together in a constructive and optimistic harmony. Men still have noble impulses. Faced with extraordinary challenges, they act as they should. America still has many strong traditions of religious faith, civic-spiritedness, military honor, charity, and community service. They are not always visible at the national level, but they feed the wellsprings of character. Everywhere you go in the United States—in neighborhoods, places of worship, schools, and service clubs— you see these forces at work.

But at the national level of the educational elites and the media, we witness a continuing culture of narcissism and the erosion of civic life and public dialogue. Politics has degenerated into an ever more insufferable caricature of battling viewpoints. Many of our educational elites still deride the need for children to learn history as a moral narrative in which good struggles to triumph over evil. The traditional role of liberal education as a character-forming experience is still, all too often, derided or treated with active hostility as an ideological camouflage for the domination of white males.

As an educator, I have a sense of what's superficial in the behavior of young people and what isn't. I don't much care how my students dress, but I do care what they think. I prefer a kid with a ring through his nose and ripped jeans who loves Plato to a well-dressed aspiring yuppie who disdains any form of learning not related to a future career and money-making. In the long run there should be no contradiction between the two—but a young person in college needs time to be excited more by ideas than by career goals. The same subtlety that parents and educators learn through their experiences in dealing with the young needs to be brought to wider public reflection on where America should be headed. Sometimes values are absolute; sometimes they are relative. Having principles and convictions doesn't mean embracing some ham-fisted set of prejudices, and bashing those who disagree. The art of thinking is precisely about knowing when the truth is absolute and when it is not. These nuances are lost in a lot of our public chatter, especially in the news and opinion media, where talented journalists disgrace themselves and their profession by screaming two-minute sound bites and boiler-plate talking points at each other while a crowd of kids looks on cheering like they were at a wrestling match.

What is most lacking in manliness today is this mature middle ground, where you can take your time to arrive at a view, and make an argument tinged with respect, not rancor, and have it treated with similar respect in turn, not just batted aside because it doesn't fit into the existing battle lines between Left and Right. But today moderation is often mistaken for weakness. We admire "attitude," the in-your-face style of the raptor-executive, the pop-star Nero, the talk-show bully. The five virtues examined in this book represent one attempt to find an antidote to this culture of jaded and cynical showboating. As in the image of the chariot of the soul with which we began, the proper ordering of these five virtues can lead a man to an integrated character—thoughtful, reflective, forceful when he needs to be, unafraid to state a coherent, well-considered view, and expecting a vigorous but civil debate.

This is what I mean by a moral vocabulary. I'm not just stressing the need for exact descriptions or eloquence in public speaking. Speech itself is a *deed*. When a man speaks reasonably and maturely, it's a matter of more than just correct vocabulary and sentence structure. To speak maturely engages a man's entire moral and psychological energies, drawing together his mind and his soul, and crystallizing them in words. And those words move others, not only on the level of rational persuasion but deep in our guts. Words can move us to tears, to laughter, and to zeal on behalf of a just cause. That's the vocabulary we need to recover.

PO-MO MAN

We hear a lot these days about "postmodernism." A term once known only to a minority of academics, in the last decade or so it has entered the popular lingo, showing up in *Vanity Fair,* strewn around to discuss "po-mo" television shows like *Buffy the Vampire Slayer* or *The Simpsons.* Conservative commentators now often use the term to sum up the forces of moral relativism in American culture, in the same way they use the terms *liberal* or *leftist.* Even the tendency—exemplified by Noam Chomsky or *The Nation*—to blame America for bringing 9/11 on itself is often dismissed as the fruit of "postmodernist" thinking.

This is not the place for a full-blown philosophical discussion of postmodernism. But its main features are directly relevant to these reflections on the continuing crisis of manliness. In the vulgar and simplified form in which it has spread throughout American universities, postmodernism has come to stand for the argument that the search for truth is really no more than a struggle for power based on gender and race. Indeed, the argument goes, there's no such thing as "truth" at all—which is why the word itself is usually set off in sneer quotes. If one were to argue, for instance, that the principles of American liberal democracy possessed universal validity as an ideal toward which all free peoples can strive, that would be dismissed as either hopelessly naïve or a deliberate attempt to dress up corporate greed and American materialism in the garb of a universal truth. The ideal of American democracy is seen as nothing more than candy coating for the power complex of interlocking corporate and political elites, the affluent white majority, and the dominant male gender.

In reaction to this concentration of power, the postmodernists teach, a slew of "new social movements" have grown up, an emerging "global civil society" of the dispossessed and marginalized—women, minorities, the poor, environmentalists, professors, and graduate students. And yet, of course, they too are motivated by that same pursuit of power. The central absurdity of postmodernism is that it contends that the existing power structure is unjust and oppressive—even as it pushes its own, alternative power structure. But, in encouraging the new social movements, postmodernists are not claiming that they would replace unjust power with a superior ideal, or with authority exercised justly and reasonably. Postmodernists are uncomfortable with such claims, for they profess not to believe in universally or eternally valid standards for justice, truth, and reason. So postmodernists argue instead that the coming victory of the oppressed will usher in a global nirvana, in which every source of human suffering, alienation, and unhappiness will vanish forever—a world without property or class distinctions, laws, political authority, sexual restraints, or intrinsic natural distinctions between men and women.

The incoherence of postmodernism's core claims is precisely what gives it a vague and amorphous appeal to young people in the universities, and it is directly connected to the crisis of manliness and the decline of mature argument. You begin by seeing the present predominance of

American democracy as unremittingly oppressive, the source of all evil, poverty, violence, and emotional dissatisfaction everywhere on earth, and the main impediment to happiness for everyone. When the Empire's power is finally shattered, we will live in a world without competition, merit, success, honor, reverence, or achievement—all mere tools for repressing "the new International" (to quote the leading postmodernist Jacques Derrida) of the marginalized. At bottom, it does no more than offer the perennial delusions of Marxism in a hipper, more up-to-date garb. The failure of life to be perfect in every way is America's fault. If American power were shattered, everyone in the world would be happy.

The incoherence of postmodernism is feeding the rapid decline of intelligent civic discourse in the universities, and this decline has a direct effect on the infantilization of young men. This incoherence lies at the core of radical feminism, which maintains that men are the oppressors, that they are "systemically" or collectively incapable of being just to women, but then goes on to demand that they be just. The same line of argument lies behind many criticisms of American foreign policy. On the one hand, it is maintained that America is the unmitigated and relentless oppressor of non-Western peoples, incapable of treating them justly, and incapable of understanding their unique worldview—because, remember, there are no such things as universally valid truth or justice, these being mere camouflage for imperialism. The critics then go on to demand that America nevertheless be just toward them and understand them, while simultaneously denying that this appeal to conscience, empathy, or reasoned insight about non-Western cultures is possible. As manifested both in radical feminism and in the critique of American foreign policy, postmodernism condemns its exponents to perpetual self-undermining immaturity. By maintaining that all claims about truth and justice are reducible to power, you do nothing more than convert the alleged oppressor into a foe who can never be won over, a foe who is impervious to an appeal to conscience and incapable of self-reform. In this way, the male gender and the American Empire become entirely and irrevocably what the postmodernist claims to want to reform.

MAKING OURSELVES MORE STUPID

What are the wider effects on manhood of this dismal view of life as a struggle for power? The postmodernist believes we must see the current reality in this harsh light, in order to spark a transition to the new global millennium of happiness for all. But since there is no prospect of such a utopia ever emerging, the reduction of all thought and idealism to a crude struggle for power has the predictable and deplorable consequence of feeding the worst currents in American culture, and provides an excuse for the most callow, smarmy, and belligerent traits of young men. Since there is no truth, only power, all that counts is *what I want.* There is no point in trying to make a reasoned argument to persuade someone because no one is capable of agreeing or disagreeing on rational grounds. People may claim to believe in the truth or in an ideal, but only a fool doesn't realize that they're just out for themselves.

Although postmodernism begins by exposing the power struggles of the present in the vain and silly hope that the violence and injustice of power seeking will disappear forever, it has the practical effect of bringing maturity into disrepute. Moderation is widely derided by young people as a laughably old-fashioned notion, maintained either insincerely to camouflage selfishness or because a person who appeals to fairness and decency must be weak, lame, uncool—a loser. Like the philosophy of the ancient Greek Sophists, postmodernism—however benign its intentions when confined to literary interpretation—has a coarsening effect on the wider culture. There's no need to make arguments, they hold, because there's no such thing as "truth." Moderation is sneered at as weakness or as a self-serving pose. This disdain for the possibility of the truth is exacerbated by the lack of a historical narrative in modern schooling, and derision for any kind of traditional moral restraint or reverence for the past. What's the point in honoring traditional virtues of gratitude and obligation, since all people are out for themselves?

In the universities, as the study of history declines, the curriculum is filled with each victim group's unique "story." Oddly enough, the reduction of higher learning to a series of self-absorbed victim groups goes together in perfect harmony with an increased reliance on quantitative methods. It's easier to quantify relations across or beneath national boundaries because you begin by setting aside the distinct histories of a peoples or nation-states, and the extent to which they are not compatible because of fundamental differences in religious faith, culture, political institutions, and ideals. Environmentalist groups in Buenos Aires, London, and Tokyo can sound superficially similar even though their national cultures may differ profoundly, and because of this superficial resemblance, their relationships can be mapped mathematically. Sometimes these social movements consist of no more than a thin upper crust of the Western-educated with a few fax machines and a modem. But pretending that they have more in common than they really do makes it easy to believe that a new "global civil society" is emerging.

Everywhere in the social sciences, formal modeling and other high-level quantitative skills are replacing the old-fashioned study of deep and complex differences between national cultures. Skills of advanced calculus comparable to those used in the hard sciences are deployed in the social sciences to "prove" such earth-shattering insights as: "Everyone tends to acts out of self-interest." The older generation of giants in comparative politics and international affairs at Harvard, Yale, and other illustrious schools—people like Daniel Patrick Moynihan, Daniel Pipes, Adam Ulam, Stanley Hoffman, and Harvey Mansfield—are not being replaced with younger people who share their historical, cultural, and linguistic abilities. One suspects that their deep knowledge of history, comparative religion, the history of ideas and of other languages makes the new number crunchers feel ashamed. In the nation's most prestigious universities, the study of political culture is being eaten away by an ever more barren behaviorism.

A friend of mine—a very canny psychologist and a mother very sensitive to how her boys differ from girls—recently observed that the criterion for professionalism now seems to be hatred of your own tradition: lawyers who hate the law and yearn to be social activists, academics who despise the classics, librarians who deride books as elitist. The social sciences increasingly amount to a marriage between formal modeling and victimology, the legitimization of self-willed ignorance in what are supposed to be America's finest schools. One thinks of Sonny Corleone's hilarious line when he slaps Michael upside the head at the end of *The Godfather: Part II*: "What? Didja go to college to get more stupid?" As the great American philosopher Leo Strauss once wrote, something is very wrong with the social sciences when they make us more stupid than we were in the first place.

THE VIEW FROM THE STREET

A sober and detailed knowledge of history, culture, religious faith, political institutions, and foreign languages—the only route for young men to gradually arrive at mature insights about the issues of the day—has over the last three decades increasingly been replaced by vacuous moralizing. Since students encounter an increasingly tedious emphasis on quantitative skills and methodology in the classroom, they look for some existential excitement in the tribal protests on the street. Predictably, the vast majority of those taunting the police or tearing down a fence at antiglobalization protests are young men searching for excitement and glory, Achilles in ripped jeans and ear studs butting heads with the Agamemnons of the G-8 or the International Monetary Fund.

The litany of moral abstractions can be instantly memorized—a world without violence or greed, equality for all, a world where we all live as one. These bromides substitute for a lack of substantive historical knowledge, so that a nineteen-year-old undergraduate from Oak Park or Scarsdale who knows little of the world, or even his own country, feels perfectly confident in asserting his opinions against prize-winning economists or presidents of other nations, and regards them as possessing every bit as much weight as those of lifelong scholars on the topic in question. He knows what's best for the people of Mexico because of "globalization"—a buzzword that usually means nothing more complicated than "selfishness." Behind many of the protests is a sophomoric maundering of the most doe-eyed, fatuous variety: Why must people hurt each other? Why can't we all live in peace?

The answers to these questions can be found in the dusty recesses of unused library collections all over the United States. Because of our disdain for the lessons of the past, we are doomed to reinvent the wheel over and over again. Telling many undergraduates today about Hitler, Stalin, or Pol Pot might as well be telling them about Genghis Khan. The story of these tyrannies, their dreadful rise and their justly accomplished destruction, has disappeared from classrooms, lest it make students too "judgmental" and not "sensitive" enough to people who have no views. Taking pride in America's defeat of Soviet tyranny might, heaven forbid, stimulate "jingoism."

As a consequence, many of the kids protesting globalization actually believe that no one before them has ever realized that people are greedy, and that capitalism can be rapacious, or imagined a world in which mankind was united and did not compete for possessions or status. Moreover, they know disturbingly little about the fact that the worst tyrannies of history—the totalitarian regimes of the Nazis and the Bolsheviks—were founded precisely on the desire for world peace, unity, human harmony, an end to capitalistic greed, and submerging one's individual will in the collective will of the people.

Utopias based on the accomplishment of world peace, brotherhood, equality, and love *always* end in tyranny. They must, because to set about actually implementing such ideals in the here and now inevitably requires crushing human nature and ridding it of its selfish impulses— by terror, by indoctrination, and by extermination. That is the irrefutable lesson of history, from the Jacobin Terror of 1793–94 to the Bolsheviks, Nazis, Mao Tse-tung, and Pol Pot. If the antiglobalizers' dreams of a "global civil society" ever had a chance of coming into existence, it could be achieved only by a Stalin to end all Stalins, for it would require the obliteration of everything that distinguishes human beings from one another—talent, faith, property, success, family, custom, and national loyalties—in an ongoing planetary tyranny. As Edmund Burke remarked of the French revolutionaries, at the end of every shining vista stands a gallows. It's not likely to happen. But because the history of previous projects for a utopian society and their disastrous consequences isn't being taught, young men today will have a very rough and painful passage ahead of them as life teaches them the contradictions between such vain and baseless longings and the complexities of the human soul—a lesson that could be softened if they were reading Gibbon, Macaulay, and Emerson, or (to come closer to our own times) Churchill, Acheson, and Kissinger, right now.

HONORABLE MOTIVES?

Like most observers, I have mixed feelings about globalization and those who protest it. Many of my brightest students do, and it's commendable in a young man to want to have a say about important issues. It's also ambitious. Young men still crave public distinction, as they always have. In any class of students, the women are likely to do at least as well as the men. But by and large, the women are content to work hard to reap the reward of a good grade. This is almost never enough for the young men. They want to compete with the other youths for the professor's attention. They want to be leaders. They want their own take on things to be recognized and honored. These are perfectly natural and ordinary longings, and a skilled teacher knows how to use them to motivate a young man to learn. But in the current culture, this honorable ambition for distinction has to be hidden under sententious moralizing, and the moralizing in turn enables the student to hide from his own lack of substantive knowledge. At its worst, this oblivion to his own ignorance makes a young man incapable of being shamed. No one's opinion counts more than his, and no one can teach him anything.

That's why, although there are genuine idealists who protest globalization, all too often such protests are an excuse for nihilism. There are too many Tyler Durdens from *Fight Club,* pretending to care about the oppressed but in truth just thrilled at an excuse to do drugs and smash things. Privileged kids have a blast trashing a fast-food outlet, little realizing that these hardscrabble businesses are often the only way people from backgrounds less privileged than their own can make their way in the world through hard work and talent. The American dream often begins in a Starbucks or a clothing outlet. After the fun is over, the protest kids go home and the maid washes their jeans and their "Fuck War" T-shirts.

I don't deny that one encounters genuine idealism among the protesters. Sometimes what's really bothering them is their instinct that the distinctive culture and character of their own country is being eroded by international economic trends. Although it seems more permissible to protest on behalf of the alleged victims in non-Western countries, at least some of the protesters in the West are experiencing the stirring of patriotism. And they're right to feel that way. The results of globalization, like every important policy alternative, are *mixed*. It *does* undermine the nation-state, and if conservatives were more consistent-minded, they would be forced to connect their defense of patriotism to the recognition that capitalism usually prefers profit to national sovereignty. The same global dynamic that breaks down barriers between nations to promote free trade and economic efficiency also serves those who want to infringe American national sovereignty in the name of international tribunals whose members include professional minions of the world's worst despotisms. You can't have it both ways. If you want the one-worldism of the multinational corporations, you're going to have a hard time resisting the one-worldism of the UN and the World Court. With a few exceptions, such as Roger Scruton, conservatives have not even begun to think through this problem, so busy are they bashing liberals and one another.

By the same token, young people who live off their parents' investments are not in much of a position to decry "corporate greed" or ruin the livelihood of poor immigrants working at McDonald's. Again, the problem in these debates is our lack of an adequate moral vocabulary and a mature middle ground. Men seek honor through public debate. It's better to recognize it and even encourage it, because if someone admits he seeks legitimate honor, he can be shamed by his lack of knowledge or his impetuosity. By contrast, the tendency to vacuous moralizing about a World Without Violence is an excuse for mental laziness.

"NOTHING TO KILL OR DIE FOR"

One of the great cultural tragedies only now dawning on us is the stigmatization of patriotism by the forces of globalization on *both* the Left and the Right. Economic globalization on the Right and global issues like environmentalism on the Left corrode the nation-state as the forum for a manly expression of civic pride, national honor, and reasoned debate. That process of corrosion goes hand in hand with the caricature of all forms of national honor as male "hegemony." The decline of narrative history and the weakening of the nation-state contribute to the intellectual emasculation of young males, prolonging their adolescence into their late twenties or even thirties.

When "all you need is love"—the right gut feeling for a moral abstraction—there's no need to learn how to stand up for yourself and make a coherent, strong, and civil argument. Young men are too often trapped in a state of perpetual boyhood, mushy sentimentality about "the planet" alternating with sulkiness and tantrums. Today, vast participatory rites of shared feeling and spontaneous sentiments are believed to be more authentic than old-fashioned policy debates or received wisdom. A global satellite feed showing celebrities singing "We Are the World" is more real to a young person, more in tune with the quicksilver impulses of youth itself, than a statesman's lengthy memoirs.

Celebrities are the role models for this amorphous and infantile character. The Proletariat of Marxist theory has given way to the Celebritariat of the stylishly disaffected, hip, and hedonistic. Rock musicians promoting "peace" or revolutionary causes of whose history they know little (like the Clash's *Sandinista!* album or Billy Bragg singing a rock version of the "Internationale") illustrate this mixture of adolescent posturing and vapid moralizing. "Child-centered learning," a favorite doctrine among curriculum planners for schools, undermines manly self-confidence by removing moral and historical reflections from education and replacing them with spontaneous emotional reactions to snippets from the newspaper and to the kitsch and consumerism of the surrounding entertainment culture. When schools fail to provide a moral and historical ballast for the male psyche, boys become slaves to pop culture, which mirrors back to them all of their own most childish urges. My male students still instinctively want to shine and be the center of attention. But too often they crumple easily in debate, because they have never learned to make an argument based on a strong, nonrancorous, and principled difference of opinion. When pressed to justify a point, their eyes often mist up, and they lapse into angry expletives.

The decline in manly debate is connected to the rise of the Celebritariat as America's new cultural ruling class, an aristocracy of alienation and expensive style that, for many boys and young men, provides role models for the way they would like to be. Many of the baleful trends I've explored here are summed up in John Lennon's song "Imagine," after thirty years still one of the world's best-selling songs, and one that has more recently become a kind of secular hymn for the forces of antiglobalization.

I am rarely at a loss for words, and like most political junkies I enjoy a good rant, especially after a dose of the television and newspaper opinion makers who can be counted on to make my blood boil—and stir my appetite for more reasoned polemics. But I must confess my stupefaction at how, in the painful months after 9/11, in schools, church basements, and community centers across the land, children's sweet voices swelled in repeated performances of John Lennon's 1970s ballad. That decent people truly believe this song is an appropriate tribute to the victims, that it contains some profound lesson for these trying times, sums up more completely than any other single example how much we desperately need some better guides for manly reflection.

"Imagine" has become the po-mo "Internationale." The sentiments the song arouses are genuine, but the message is their complete betrayal. Lennon was one of a handful of truly great artists of rock and roll, and a role model for male youths of my generation. His tormented voice, his command of the entire style book of pop music, and his sizzling attack on a song placed him in a class of immortals including Elvis and Jerry Lee Lewis. But Lennon's essential ignorance about politics betrayed him in this song, revealing that he lacked the education, patience, or experience to season his gut instincts into a proper argument. The failure of "Imagine" is not simply that it is sophomoric; it is that its message actually amounts to a celebration of totalitarianism. Not because Lennon intended such a thing. Quite the contrary: His idealism in the song is authentic and keenly felt. Yet its words exemplify the pitfall of substituting sentimentality for knowledge—a handicap that hobbled his generation, and continues today among their children.

Lennon didn't recognize the link between the message of "Imagine" and the principles of totalitarianism, because—like many antiglobalization protesters now—he knew little about what tyranny really is. He truly but naïvely believed that his was the first generation to realize that people should not be greedy and should give up war. You can have peace right now, he said, "if you want it." What of the lessons of history and the past? They don't count; we weren't alive then. "Imagine" paints a world utopia in which people have been stripped of every source of moral and spiritual satisfaction: no religion, no patriotism, no honorable struggle, no stimulating controversy, no property, no gratitude, obligation, or reverence. It is a world where there's "nothing to kill or die for"—two distinct pacifist images linked in what for Lennon was a single inspiring vision. But this vision is closer to what Nietzsche termed "the last man," the herd man of consumer mass society at its most degrading, a society of listless pleasures and minds empty of thoughts either disturbing or ennobling. It's a painful irony—the song has taken on enormous emotional meaning for a large proportion of the Western public—but at its core John Lennon's "Imagine" is an unwitting manifesto for the kind of monolithic global culture that only a Stalinist dictatorship could support. For only an apparatus of unprecedented and methodical terror, indoctrination, and extermination could bring about a world where people were systematically stripped of every defining trait that makes life rich and worthwhile.

WHERE DID THINGS GO WRONG?

John Lennon ended up as a peace activist, but he began as a pop star. His influence as a guru for world peace flowed from his earlier, more innocent fame as a joyous rock and roller. As in many trends in the crisis of manliness, the darker and more worrisome consequences originated in the freshness and exuberance of the 1960s. When we ask ourselves how things went wrong, we're inevitably drawn back to the sunnier beginnings of the thirty-year project to eradicate the traditional teachings about manliness.

People writing about manliness today often try to earmark exactly when the big change took place. When did manliness turn its back on tradition, whether for good or for bad? There are lots of enticing clues and defining moments from popular culture, art, and literature. Some would point to Marlon Brando's famous scene in the film version of Tennessee Williams's play *A Streetcar Named Desire* where, dressed in an undershirt, he shouts his wife's name up the fire escape like an enraged infant bellowing for his mother. His primal and uncouth behavior is taken to signify a break with more gentlemanly standards of the past, the kind of tuxedoed smoothie with the cigarette case and the Newport accent played by Melvyn Douglas in *Ninotchka*.

Not coincidentally, Brando's portrayal of an unvarnished working-class slob in *Streetcar* was grounded in his training in the Stanislavsky Method—where high culture took low culture as its new idol. For the Method school, reliance on instinct and spontaneity were thought to be more authentic than the self-conscious perfection of craft one associates with Laurence Olivier or John Gielgud. And for that reason, in the popular culture of the times, people sensed a connection between the Method school and the emerging rock culture spearheaded by Elvis Presley, who, although a country bumpkin by contrast with the hipsters at the Actors Studio, also stood for a loosening and blurring of the traditional male character.

Elvis was an originator of what trendy cultural criticism now calls "transgression." His music was an unearthly mix of black R & B, gut-bucket roadhouse rockabilly, and country, delivered in a ghostly vocal style straight from the swamp with a stage presence that was unabashedly androgynous—boogying hips combined with facial makeup, those weird zoot suit jackets with their plunging lines, and a high pile of swirling whiplash hair. The synthesis of New York Method acting and the new teenage culture spearheaded by Elvis was James Dean, who prefigured Elvis's sexually ambivalent beauty—the juvenile delinquent with the soulful eyes—and blended it with the urban hipness of the Beats.

This seismic shift in the meaning of manhood reached its classic expression in the Beatles. It's no accident that their meteoric rise in the United States took place within months of the assassination of John F. Kennedy. In Britain, the band's popularity had already been deliberately cultivated by the Labour government of Harold Wilson to give people something optimistic and fun to distract them from the dreariness of the stalled British economy, and to give them something to be proud of as Britain's status as a world power rapidly faded away.

I believe the Beatles played a similarly important role in the United States at a time of agonizing cultural disturbance, filling a psychological and aesthetic vacuum left by the unexpected death of the brave and handsome young president. JFK had combined the pragmatism of the old politics with the vigor and freedom from convention of the rising generation. He was hardheaded, dedicated to prosecuting the Cold War, and knew all about the dirty side of American party politics, willing to do what was necessary to win. But he was also stylish and casual, optimistic and idealistic. He had a young man's head of hair and a closetful of suits that had more in common with Savile Row and James Bond than with the baggy pants and suspenders of LBJ's generation. In him, the torch of leadership passed to the generation who had fought in World War II. His death shattered that link, disrupted the succession of power from old to young, and in the form of his hapless successor, the mentality of the older generation returned to the White House.

Had JFK lived, the generation of the 1960s might have followed him in remaining hopeful about mainstream politics. With his death, much of that generation collectively turned its back on ordinary civic life and hurled itself into the dream of the counterculture. The Beatles' style was in many ways a condensation and crystallization of those aspects of JFK that were most youthful and most non-conformist—the hair, the elegant suits and narrow ties, the cheeky and ironic humor. If you view one of JFK's press conferences alongside the famous Beatles press performances a year or so later, the similarities are striking: the same playfulness and self-deprecation, the informality masking a degree of contempt for the reporters, the emotional distance concealed by an air of breezy affability. In Kennedy, if only for a brief few years, the old politics of logrolling and compromise were united with a newer, fresher style, free from the ponderous morality and grim public manner of Eisenhower and Nixon. With his death, politics returned to normal—and the idealism was shifted to pop culture.

As musicians, the Beatles brought together all the preliminary versions of the counterculture, going back to Elvis and the Beats. For, although skillfully packaged in their early years as nice boys with clean hair and suits, the Beatles were a far cry from the fantasy that their young girl fans had of them as adorable teddy bears who had pillow fights in their hotel room. The Beatles were genuine bohemians. When they first played on a regular professional basis in the red-light district of Hamburg, they quickly became a favorite of German art students. The German kids learned that John Lennon and Stuart Sutcliffe, the Beatle who died before they hit the big time, were art students, who shared their own Dadaesque and Expressionist tastes. Indeed, for John, the Beatles as a whole were an act of Dadaesque artistic expression—a kind of ongoing experiment to find out *what it would be like* to be in a rock band. The famous "Beatle haircut" was a fashion the band members first adopted from their German art student fans, who had the traditional long bohemian locks, again radicalizing the androgyny and gender bending that Elvis had pioneered.

The originality of the Beatles' early music remains shattering to this day, in its summons to a new model of young manhood. When you play one of their first albums, it roars out of the speakers sounding like nothing else that had preceded it. Their originality was the gift of their ignorance. Because the Beatles learned American rock and pop music from abroad, they had no sure sense of the actual context of those musical idioms on their American soil. To them, it was a delightful toy box full of styles. Hence, their music combines styles that no American would ever have imagined could be combined. In the course of two or three minutes in a single song from those early albums, they switch happily back and forth between rock and country, R & B and rockabilly, as well as girl groups like the Shirelles.

The androgyny of their music is striking on many levels. Like Bob Dylan with "It Ain't Me Babe," the Beatles reject the old greaser macho pose struck by Jerry Lee Lewis or Dion and the Belmonts, the leather-jacketed bird dog. They don't want to be predators, any more than they want to be upstanding young men, ideal future husbands, or authority figures; they just want to be friends. The Beatles often side with the female characters in their songs, a remarkable departure for rockers in that era. One of their favorite poses is to play the part of the third party, the boy who is looking on at a relationship that is on the skids, and who gently upbraids his friend for not treating the girl more decently (as in "She Loves You" or "You're Gonna Lose That Girl"). Much of the Beatles' original charisma stems from the gutsiness of taking a gallant and sympathetic stance toward women that would have gotten them beaten up in many high schools of the era. They made sensitivity sexy, because they were in other respects so contemptuous of authority and so unquestionably cool in their looks, style, and powers of seduction.

Where Do We Go from Here?

I've suggested that the death of JFK created a rift in the continuity of American manliness. Sometimes they are referred to as the two cultures. Although I've been pretty hard on the counterculture of the 1960s and its influence down to the present in this book, my comments on the early Beatles are meant to remind the reader that I don't think its influence was all bad. The male culture of the 1950s was in many ways philistine and insensitive. The early and more innocent phase of the counterculture fostered a genuine openness to better understanding between men and women, and love based on friendship and equality.

In the years to come, though, the differences between the two cultures hardened into a much sharper conflict. Throughout this book, I've tried to steer a middle course between a closed-minded endorsement of one of these two cultures to the exclusion of the other and an ostrichlike wish to act as if all the hard differences have been resolved, that we've reached the end of history. We have to make sober judgments about what is better and what is worse for the development of a manly character, while recognizing that elements of manly virtue will be found both among the defenders of the status quo and among those who see themselves as its adversaries.

What matters most is where we go from here. I've suggested throughout this book that we are suffering from a temporary amnesia about the positive meaning of manliness. What seems to be far away is really only a little distance away, given the centuries of time over which the traditional teachings developed. Other writers have suggested practical solutions for some of the cultural crises I have discussed. Critics of the educational establishment are hard at work devising alternative curricular materials that try to address the decline of history as a moral narrative, and to restore some sense of the distinction between good and evil in the education of the young. Advocates of family stability are also energetically publicizing the sad story of fatherless families and their devastating effect on the social fabric, and particularly on the upbringing of boys.

My own approach has been broader and less pragmatic. I believe that the recovery of a healthy view of manliness and the manly virtues must above all else be a moral revolution, a revolution within the soul of the individual. The practical critiques of contemporary education, the statistical evidence of the family's decline—these exist in abundance. Moreover, the accumulated treasures of three thousand years of experience and reflection on manliness are still with us, right at our fingertips, old friends we have temporarily neglected. The five virtues of love, courage, pride, family, and country are still all around us. We grope inwardly for some kind of compass for putting them into practice, and the people who love us need us to strive for them. The five virtues are not only in books, although that is the first and best place to look for a coherent portrait of them. They are woven into the fabric of our characters, and our everyday dilemmas of family life, love, faith, and citizenship constantly stimulate those virtues in our association with others. All we need to do is—Remember!

A closing thought: I have described some disturbing trends in contemporary manhood. Some readers might wonder whether I find any cause for optimism at all. That's why I want to stress that I am very optimistic about the future of manhood in America. Indeed, the very reason for the urgency I have brought to my discussion of the negative trends is that I am so firmly convinced that it can all get better.

Why do I say this? Because, in my twenty years as an educator, I have never been so optimistic about my students as I am today. To the extent that the future is in the hands of these young people, I believe we have little to fear and everything to hope for. I know I have gone on at length about the defects in their education—their lack of historical depth, their addiction to the entertainment fashions of the present, their rush to judgment over issues that require time and maturity. But they are not to blame for those faults. We who are responsible for educating them bear the blame and the responsibility for making things better.

If I were not a university teacher, and read the things about the university that I and others who share my gloomy view of the current state of higher learning have written, I'd be tempted to give up on universities altogether. And that may happen. It's conceivable that universities as we know them today are doomed. If they continue distancing themselves from the larger society they inhabit and its full range of views, if they continue to decline into a Jurassic Park of politically correct dinosaurs, they may slide into oblivion. One of the really striking trends of the last decade or so is the emergence of the public intellectual—people like Allan Bloom, Camille Paglia, and Christopher Lasch who decided they wanted to break free from the confines of academia and reach a much wider audience of the educated reading public. These readers have no interest in the self-referential jargon and tiresome turf battles of professional academia; they yearn for professors to act like *real* professors and talk about the great affairs of the human mind and heart, like the teachers who inspired them when they were younger.

Academics who broke the mold were joined by others who had always operated outside the academy, independent scholars and historians who preferred the larger audience of the liberally educated to the narrow factionalism of the academy. During the same period, people all over America fell in love with the Great Books, as reading groups proliferated in living rooms and church basements. The brightest future for higher learning in America may well lie outside the university among these readers and writers. The true spirit of the university may actually be reborn among them. After all, universities that retain the most illustrious names today often began as modest groups of pious farmers and merchants reading books together. We may be witnessing a new beginning for the purity of that spiritual enterprise.

But that's a long way off, if it happens at all. For now and the foreseeable future, the vast majority of gifted and spirited young people will go to the established colleges and universities. Only there do we find any realistic hope of restoring the positive tradition of manliness as a source of moral and spiritual energy for men and women to draw upon as they face the dilemmas of the new century.

And that's why I am optimistic. I've given up on a lot of my colleagues. The reason we don't hear as much about political correctness in universities as we did a few years back is not because it's in decline but because, on the contrary, in contrast with that last rear-guard action to forestall it in the 1990s, its victory is even closer to being total. But the great thing is the *students,* and as long as even a small handful of people who respect liberal education make it into academia, great things can still be done. I've already discussed the students' failings. But alongside these failings, they also combine all of the best qualities of the two Americas and the two cultures—the energy, the passion, the flexibility, and the desire for something new and better. And, best of all, more and more of these students crave the traditional teachings. When they arrive at university, they have already spent years being spoon-fed and encouraged to form their own reactions to little snippets of information whose wider context they know nothing about. They've been told always to be original, always to be a nonconformist, while being given no rich intellectual and spiritual content to be original *about* or to *resist*.

Hence, when they arrive as freshmen, they are generally sick and tired of the pussyfooting around. They want to be told the truth, the way it is. They want something solid in exchange for their often exorbitant tuition fees. They don't want a pal who will "rap" with them about their "issues" and "concerns," a "guide from the side" (as the educational psychologists' lingo has it) instead of "a sage on the stage." They want that sage. They want to know about the whole wonderful, mysterious, frightening, and inspiring world of the past. They want to know about greatness because they aspire to be great, and so need a benchmark against which to measure their striving.

If anything, as an old friend of mine and a superb teacher recently remarked, the danger with these students is not that they will resist authority but that they will drink it in uncritically. They are so eager to stop wasting time and learn how things are that they may veer to the opposite extreme of too much reverence for a teacher. So a good teacher has to maintain a delicate balance between giving his students a satisfying meal of this wonderful new diet and making them get sick.

But the qualities the students bring to this new experience are immensely promising. They have the same heartfelt yearnings for love, honor, and spiritual fulfillment as previous generations. Among the best of them, these yearnings may be keener and deeper precisely because they have been denied any constructive outlets in their education so far. They are mercifully free from the rigid ideological divisions so often characteristic of my generation. They realize instinctively what Emerson wrote: "A foolish consistency is the hobgoblin of little minds."

They grasp intuitively that everything truly interesting in life—love, faith, learning, and honor—is shot through with paradox. It doesn't bother them to be conservative on one issue and liberal on another. They can be cultural conservatives and political leftists, or the reverse. They can be tolerant of sexual minorities while believing firmly in the family. When the Great Books are set before them, they are charmed and thrilled, and gobble them up with an astonishing vigor. Like Aristotle's portrait of the great-souled man, they finally have a challenge worthy of their talents.

As with every generation, their virtues are the flip side of their faults. The easy disdain for tradition, the impatience with reasoned argument, the impetuosity that have all been flattered and exacerbated by their education can, properly cultivated, bring forth already germinating qualities of open-mindedness, intellectual ferment, and boldness of thought. I see a lot of the nihilistic side they conceal from their parents. Yes, a lot of them do recreational drugs. They have too much casual sex. They sometimes look like they slept on a park bench. Unfortunately for simpleminded moralists, exactly these same kids can be A+ students while holding down a bartending job, starting a small on-line business, and playing in a band; they are capable of writing with astonishing brilliance, and they are strong-minded and original in their judgments.

And, most important of all, no matter how much casual sex they have, few lack the longing for a meaningful and lasting love. They don't always know where to look for the model. More often than not, they are distant from one or both of their parents, who are frequently divorced or separated. This gives many of the young men, in particular, a wounded air and an aura of incompleteness. They seem young for their age, despite all their superficial sophistication about sex and drugs, because they are yearning for the steadying influence of a father. If they're lucky, they will find it. Sometimes, to their surprise, they reunite with their own fathers, men who have finally overcome the bitterness of a broken marriage and realized that their sons are growing further from them every day. Some will find the right influence in surrogate fathers—teachers, grandparents, family friends. Like Telemachus, they may have to raise themselves by trial and error, but their instinct is sound and sure. They will make it. They will become men.

As dark as some of the present trends in American manhood may seem, then, I am convinced that we are poised at the brink of a tremendous Renaissance. History smiles on it. All the knowledge is at our fingertips. The world requires nothing less of us. Manhood is coming back.

PERMISSIONS

For permission to reprint copyrighted material, grateful acknowledgment is made to the following:

New English Bible. Copyright © Oxford University Press and Cambridge University Press 1961, 1970.

The Art of Courtly Love by Andreas Capellanus. Copyright © 1989 by The Continuum Publishing Company. Reprinted by permission of The Continuum Publishing Company.

Moral Essays by Seneca. Reprinted by permission of the publishers and the Trustees of the Loeb Classical Library from *Seneca: Volume III—De Beneficiis*, Loeb Classical Library Volume L 310, translated by John W. Basore, Cambridge, Mass.: Harvard University Press, 1935. The Loeb Classical Library® is a registered trademark of the President and Fellows of Harvard College.

The Education of a Christian Prince by Erasmus. Published by Octagon Books, a Division of Hippocrene Books, Inc.

"Television's Virus of Violence and the Jonesboro Schoolyard Shootings" by Dave Grossman, Lt. Col., U.S. Army (Ret.), Director, Killology Research Group, and the author of *On Killing* and *Stop Training Our Kids to Kill* (Random House, 1999).

Autobiography of John Stuart Mill. Jack Stillinger, editor. Copyright © 1969 by Houghton Mifflin Company. Used with permission.

Excerpts from *The Gathering Storm* by Winston S. Churchill. Copyright © 1948 by Houghton Mifflin Company, copyright renewed 1976 by Lady Spencer Churchill, the Honourable Lady Sarah Audley, and the Honourable Lady Soames. Reprinted by permission of Houghton Mifflin Company. All rights reserved.

"Brief Interviews with Hideous Men" by David Foster Wallace. Copyright ©
1998 by *Harper's Magazine.* All rights reserved. Reproduced from the October
issue by special permission.

Submitted excerpt from *Profiles in Courage* by John F. Kennedy. Copyright
renewed © 1983, 1984, 1989 by Jacqueline Kennedy Onassis. Foreword copyright © by Robert F. Kennedy. Reprinted by permission of HarperCollins
Publishers, Inc.

Submitted excerpts from *The Edge of the Sword* by Charles de Gaulle.
Copyright © 1960 by Criterion Books, Inc. and Faber and Faber, Ltd. Reprinted by permission of HarperCollins Publishers, Inc.

The Character Sketches by Theophrastus. Translated by Warren D.
Anderson.

Excerpt from *The Letters of Theodore Roosevelt: Volume II,* selected and
edited by Elting E. Morison, Cambridge, Mass.: Harvard University Press,
Copyright © 1951 by the President and Fellows of Harvard College.

INDEX